D1718206

Peace in the Ancient World

The Ancient World: Comparative Histories

Series Editor: Kurt A. Raaflaub

Published

Peace in the Ancient World

Concepts and Theories

Edited by
Kurt A. Raaflaub

WILEY Blackwell

Library of Congress Cataloging-in-Publication data applied for

Hardback ISBN: 9781118645123

A catalogue record for this book is available from the British Library.

Cover image: 1st Image: Eirene image: © age fotostock / Alamy Stock Photo
2nd Image: The Maat image: © age fotostock / Alamy Stock Photo
3rd Image: Buddha image: © Creative Commons / Mario Biondi CC BY-SA 3.0

Set in 10.5/13.5pt Galliard by SPi Global, Pondicherry, India
Printed and bound in Malaysia by Vivar Printing Sdn Bhd

1   2016

Contents

Notes on Contributors

Susanne Bickel is Professor of Egyptology at the University of Basel, Switzerland, and director of the University's King's Valley Project. Her research focuses on Egyptian religion and culture (especially the funerary texts of the 3rd and 2nd millennium), temple iconography and epigraphy, and archaeology. Her book publications include *La cosmogonie égyptienne avant le Nouvel Empire* (1994); *D'un monde à l'autre, Textes des Pyramides et Textes des Sarcophages* (co-ed., 2004); *Images as Sources* (co-ed., 2007); *Vergangenheit und Zukunft. Studien zum historischen Bewusstsein in der Thutmosidenzeit* (ed., 2013).

Johannes Bronkhorst is Emeritus Professor of Sanskrit and Indian studies at the University of Lausanne, Switzerland. His main area of interest is the history of Indian thought in the broadest sense: religious, philosophical, and scientific. Among his most recent books are *Aux origines de la philosophie indienne* (2008); *Buddhist Teaching in India* (2009); *Buddhism in the Shadow of Brahmanism* (2011); *Absorption: Human Nature and Buddhist Liberation* (2012).

Kurt A. Raaflaub is David Herlihy University Professor and Professor of Classics and History Emeritus at Brown University in Providence, R.I. His research focuses on the social, political, and intellectual history of archaic and classical Greece and of the Roman republic, on the social dimension of ancient warfare, and on the comparative history of the ancient world. Publications that are relevant in the present context include *War and Society in the Ancient World* (co-ed., 1999); *The Discovery of Freedom in Ancient Greece* (2004); *Origins of Democracy in Ancient Greece* (co-author, 2007); *War and Peace in the Ancient World* (ed., 2007).

Hans Van Wees is Grote Professor of Ancient History at University College London. His main areas of interest are the social and economic history of early Greece, archaic and classical Greek warfare, and the use of iconographical and comparative evidence in the study of the ancient Greek world. Book publications relevant in the present context include *Status Warriors: War, Violence, and Society in Homer and History* (1992); *War and Violence in Ancient Greece* (ed., 2000); *Greek Warfare: Myths and Realities* (2004); *A Companion to Archaic Greece* (co-ed., 2009).

Robin D. S. Yates is James McGill Professor of East Asian Studies and History and Classical Studies at McGill University in Montréal, Canada. His research interests include early and traditional Chinese history, historical theory, archaeology of culture, Chinese science and technology, and all aspects of Chinese warfare. His book publications include *Five Lost Classics: Tao, Huang-Lao, and Yin-Yang in Han China* (1997); *Women in China from Earliest Times to the Present: A Bibliography of Studies in Western Languages* (2009); *Birth of an Empire: The State of Qin Revisited* (co-ed., 2013).

Series Editor's Preface

The Ancient World: Comparative Histories

The purpose of this series is to pursue important social, political, religious, economic, and intellectual issues through a wide range of ancient or early societies, while occasionally covering an even broader diachronic scope. By engaging in comparative studies of the ancient world on a truly global scale, this series hopes not only to throw light on common patterns and marked differences, but also to illustrate the remarkable variety of responses humankind developed to meet common challenges. Focusing as it does on periods that are far removed from our own time, and in which modern identities are less immediately engaged, the series contributes to enhancing our understanding and appreciation of differences among cultures of various traditions and backgrounds. Not least, it thus illuminates the continuing relevance of the study of the ancient world in helping us to cope with problems of our own multicultural world.

In the present case, the problem of peace, an issue of crucial importance for all human societies (discussed in a comprehensive survey in an earlier volume of this series), is reexamined selectively and from a specific angle: what concepts and theories of peace ancient or early societies developed, what role these played and what impact they had, and why certain societies developed such concepts and theories and others did not. The comparative approach helps us understand successes and failures in humankind's path toward peace, and sharpens our awareness of the problems our own troubled time has with this issue.

Earlier volumes in the series are listed at the very beginning of this volume. Volumes in preparation include *The Adventure of the Human Intellect: Self, Society, and the Divine in Ancient World Cultures* (ed. Kurt A. Raaflaub); *After Slavery and Social Death* (eds. John Bodel and Walter Scheidel).

Introduction

KURT A. RAAFLAUB

For the first time ever, our age has developed a discipline of "peace studies" (even if much that runs under this label should more properly be called "war studies"). Think tanks and academic, as well as political, organizations try to find ways and draw up blueprints to secure peace, and in international relations and political science the issue of "peace" has become highly prominent. All too often, though, even highly competent specialists pronounce as a simple fact that "peace" is a modern invention, that only the recent past has produced practical and viable proposals to establish a solid foundation for peace, and that all earlier civilizations advanced but naive ideals and impractical dreams on the subject. This volume refutes such assumptions, offers an opportunity to track the ancient origins of at least some modern ideas on peace, and looks specifically at ancient efforts to identify, explain, and resolve the relevant problems on a conceptual and theoretical level.

In 2007, I published in the same series a volume on *War and Peace in the Ancient World*. That volume's contributions covered many ancient or early societies around the globe, and examined the question of how these societies dealt with one of the central and most urgent challenges posed to all of humankind: war and peace. The variety of responses to these challenges, which were revealed in those chapters, was illuminating.

Peace in the Ancient World: Concepts and Theories, First Edition. Edited by Kurt A. Raaflaub.
© 2016 John Wiley & Sons, Inc. Published 2016 by John Wiley & Sons, Inc.

As is often the case in endeavors of this kind, the collection of the evidence and assemblage of broad surveys is only the first step. Having gone this far, those involved consider it desirable and promising to add a second step (or more), to dig deeper, and to use the insights gained on this first step to explore specific issues and questions either across the board or in individual case studies. Usually, such follow-ups remain unfulfilled plans. In the case of war and peace, one particular question kept haunting us: why was it that among many highly accomplished ancient civilizations with a rich cultural, intellectual, and written record only a very small group—in fact, only two (China and Greece)—seemed to have developed an explicit discourse on peace and even specific concepts and theories of peace? What was it that kept others from doing so, even though at first sight they would have seemed perfectly capable of taking this step as well? This is the single question the present volume tries to answer.

In 2008, I convened a panel at the European Social Science and History Conference (ESSHC) in Lisbon. The contributors to the present volume joined me there to search for answers to these and related questions. Susanne Bickel (Basel) and Johannes Bronkhorst (Lausanne) explored the reasons of why Egypt and India did not develop a substantive and theoretical peace discourse, while Robin Yates (McGill) and I tried to explain why and how early China and Greece did. Hans Van Wees (UC London) served as a respondent. Our discussions were productive and we decided to aim at publication.

Given the success of the *War and Peace* volume, the Classics Editor of Blackwell Publishing (later Wiley-Blackwell and now Wiley), Haze Humbert, reacted very positively to the suggestion but worried about publishing a follow-up too soon. We decided to wait a few years. When we revived the project about three years ago, health problems, professional overextension, and urgent prior commitments on the part of various contributors caused a series of further long delays. All authors, though, had an opportunity to revise and update their chapters before submission. I am most grateful to them for their commitment, patience, and excellent contributions. I also thank Haze Humbert and her staff most sincerely for their trust and support.

I add here somewhat detailed summaries of the chapters' contents.

Chapter 1: Abhorring War, Yearning for Peace: The Quest for Peace in the Ancient World

This chapter establishes a framework for the more detailed investigations of the subsequent chapters by offering a broad survey over the quest for peace in ancient or early societies. It begins with five brief case studies that range from the "Iroquois

League" with its "Great Law of Peace" and early China to classical Athens, the late Roman republic, and the single extant discussion of peace in Greco-Roman literature preserved in Augustine's *City of God*. These case studies support the thesis that it took war experiences of extraordinary intensity to prompt ancient or early societies to think more consistently and intensely about peace than they normally did, to challenge traditional concepts and norms, and to formulate new ones. Even such experiences, though, may not have been sufficient to trigger the development of concepts and theories of peace. It is the purpose of this volume to find out what concepts and theories did emerge in this area, what factors made them possible and why such factors seem to have had an impact only in some societies and not in others, despite the ubiquity of intense war.

For in all parts of the ancient world wars were frequent and brutal, firmly supported by ideology and, often, religion. Those in power depended on wars to legitimate their position and demonstrate their superiority. Constant warfare molded and conditioned entire societies. Victories were celebrated in poetry, historical records, and art. In contrast, concern for peace is less pervasive in the extant record: in some form, most religions advocated it, and imperial ideologies celebrated it. Although critics did not fail to point out the price to be paid for it, the benefits of long-lasting imperial peace were real enough.

Cults and monuments offer valuable insights. Overall, cults of peace were rare. In both Greece (especially Athens) and Rome, peace (*eirēnē, pax*), although widely desired, was recognized and celebrated by cult and monuments only late and primarily for political and ideological reasons, even in hegemonic and imperial contexts. The concept of concord (*homonoia, concordia*) emerged in reaction to severe civil strife and was soon supported by a cult, but it was eventually instrumentalized to emphasize unity in the context of the Macedonian kings' and Augustus's consolidation of imperial power. Moreover, all this pales in comparison to the ubiquity of war and victory cults in these same cities. Shrines and statues of war deities, vowed in wars, and monuments celebrating victories made of the center of Rome a vast "memorial space" that continually reinforced Roman identity and conditioned every new generation to emulate its ancestors. The same was true for Athens where public spaces were crowded with monuments celebrating martial exploits and with statues and temples of Victory (Nikē) and Athena as the ultimate warrior goddess. In democratic Athens and oligarchic Rome, collective governments fostered the celebration of martial values through communal cults and monuments. In imperial monarchies, by contrast, the commemoration of victories was integrated into monuments that focused on the person of the monarch and his tutelary deities. Overall, imperial reassertion and aspirations left little space for monumental expressions of peace.

The chapter's final section deals with intellectual concerns with peace. The greatly interesting Indian and Chinese evidence will be discussed in separate chapters. In Rome, poets called for peace and praised Augustus for having achieved it. Historians were much more reluctant to do so, and politically engaged intellectuals had little to say on peace. Explanations include the charged topic of civil war—on which not even the victors liked to dwell—and the perspective of the leading class, to which peace was but a consequence of a well-functioning state; especially in the crisis of the late republic, debate therefore focused on the latter. Greek thinkers found it easier to deal with *stasis* that played out in a sphere over which the citizen communities had control; external war proved much more intractable. Still, in both areas the Greeks came up with remarkable, even theoretical, solutions that will be the subject of a separate chapter as well.

In sum, in most societies numerous obstacles prevented the emergence of a substantive discourse on peace, let alone of concepts and theories of peace. The chapter ends by formulating, as a thesis, three conditions that enabled societies to develop such concepts and theories: exceptionally harsh war experiences, which made peace an urgent need; a capacity for abstract and philosophical thinking; and the political and critical independence of the thinkers.

Chapter 2: Concepts of Peace in Ancient Egypt

"Peace," Susanne Bickel emphasizes, is not naturally given but a cultural product and, as such, varies greatly in the understanding of societies and periods. It needs to be examined in a conceptual context—considering world view, cosmology, theology, and moral values—and in a social-political context, looking at specific constellations, outside stimuli, and necessities to which society reacts. The Egyptian world view is dominated by a concept of antagonism that drives the universe and society: disruptive forces and deities oppose the forces and gods representing order, justice, and harmony. The equilibrium in the universe and society needs to be maintained by constantly overcoming (even violently) the tensions created by an intrinsic antagonism of opposing forces.

In the social and moral value system, the ideals of non-violence, self-control, and respect for social status are described with terms related to the semantic field of peace. "Peace" here designates both a personal attitude (non-aggressiveness) and condition (safety from attack). Such emphasis on "peacefulness," however, has no place in the sphere of politics and foreign relations. The Pharaoh's obligation is to fight to keep the universe in balance and his country safe. Accordingly, in foreign relations "peace" means subjection and a condition imposed by the victorious pharaoh on others. Bravery and victory are his prime qualities. The need to fight wars is never questioned, world view and economics foster domination and imperialism, and no discourse on peace can develop in these conditions. Nor is there space for concepts such as internal opposition or civil war.

The Egyptians aimed at controlling (directly or indirectly) neighboring regions to the south and east. In their ideological construct, supported by economic needs, the peaceful and orderly Egyptian interior was opposed to a wicked and criminal outside world that constantly aimed at attacking the Egyptian order. For the longest time, ideology, not real threats, thus justified wars that kept reaffirming the pharaoh's divinely sanctioned mission. Hence, there was no need to develop a concept of peace in opposition to warfare. Eventually, new powers arose in West Asia and forced the Egyptians to maintain a large army and to engage in frequent warfare to defend their dominant position. Even so, the pharaohs "imposed peace" from a position of superiority upon those who surrendered. The conquered and crushed enemy symbolized peace. War was fought outside of Egypt's borders and only marginally affected the country's population itself. Even when this, too, changed and Egypt lost its independence, conditions never favored the development of a concept of peace as an alternative value.

A unique exception is the peace treaty concluded between Ramesses II and the Hittite king Hattusili III in the aftermath of the battle of Kadesh (c. 1275 BCE). The well-documented treaty establishes peace as an equitable agreement on the basis of parity between the partners and defines peace as a state of non-violence, non-aggression, and mutual respect and aid. Yet, in a spectacular clash between ideology and the reality of politics, Egyptian self-presentation still embeds this treaty in the traditional framework depicting the pharaoh as the universal victor and Egypt's total control over the outside world.

Overall, then, both conceptual and ideological dispositions and the reality of Egyptian politics and history failed to offer an opportunity to reflect about peace as a political value. As Bickel concludes, "there was no *necessity* to create such a concept, nor even an *interest* in doing so, because (during the third and second millennium) Egypt was much more powerful than its neighbors and potential opponents, and later (in the first millennium) there was no *possibility* because the opposing forces overpowered Egypt and integrated the country into their political entities."

Chapter 3: Thinking about Peace in Ancient India

Johannes Bronkhorst begins with the famous rock inscriptions of the Mauryan emperor Aśoka. Turned Buddhist, he regretted the violence caused by his conquests and promoted righteous rule (dharma). Yet Aśoka himself did not renounce violence, and his successors did not follow his precepts. His empire turned out to be one of many attempts to unite "the world" (the Indian subcontinent) in a single state and thus to create peace through universal rule. Paradoxically, the "ultimate aim of permanent and universal peace led in practice to ceaseless and relentless war."

Two major and very different intellectual currents (the Brahmins and Buddhists) dealt with the Mauryan legacy. The Brahmins used a pragmatic approach, exemplified by the oldest extant treatise on statecraft (*Arthaśāstra*) that explicitly claims to advise rulers. The goal of any ruler is to conquer the world, and the treatise discusses ways to achieve this goal and, as a basic condition, to establish and secure the ruler's power. Permanent and universal peace is only achievable in this way, even if it is a distant goal or dream. More limited peace between or within kingdoms is not to be despised but a means to an end, to be abandoned when an opportunity emerges to gain power over others. Brahmanism was no religion but an ideology, a vision of a highly stratified society, with Brahmins occupying the highest positions and kings creating and expanding kingdoms. Other texts, too, confirm that Brahmanical teaching promoted the use of force and war to expand one's realm whenever the gains were likely to be larger than the risks. Hence, overall, Bronkhorst emphasizes, the "Brahmanical political tradition... was not actively in search of peace." Rather, the "victory of Brahmanism in the realm of religious, social, and political ideas expressed itself in what might be called a celebration of war, both in reality and in rhetorical contexts." Brahmins certainly wanted to live in peace but only in conditions that were favorable to them, and this concretely meant, under rulers who were powerful and successful, and whose aspirations were supported by the Brahmins' acceptance of war.

In sharp contrast, Buddhism was not pragmatic but idealistic, teaching a path, open to all (high and low), to avoid rebirth, which required followers to abandon society, refrain from violence, and survive by begging. The Buddhist theoreticians' main problem eventually was how to reconcile their nonviolent ways with the needs of the world. Their ideal was a righteous ruler who conquered the world in an unobjectionable manner. The solutions they proposed were initially impractical and unrealistic, and in the early centuries Buddhism was not able to produce constructive thoughts concerning political peace—although in the real world in which they lived peace was greatly important to them. Apparently, they had early on yielded certain areas of intellectual activity, including matters of statecraft, to the Brahmins as specialists with useful advice to offer and impressive manuals to back it up. This changed only with the emergence of a tradition that the most recent Buddha had in his earlier lives led a normal life, and even been a competent king. The stories told about this showed that one could be a committed Buddhist, even aspire to become a future Buddha, and still occupy a role in society. Logically, then, a Buddhist could also be involved in killing and war—if he did so for righteous reasons. This in turn opened the way for Buddhists to serve as royal advisors, profiting from the expertise of the Brahmins, even adapting some of their manuals, and borrowing the use of magic and spells to protect their kings. However successful the Buddhists were, though, "their competition with the Brahmins offered no opportunity to develop ideas about political peace. Quite on the contrary, where Indian Buddhism had originally looked with disapproval upon all forms of violence, including political violence, in the course of time they found ways to justify and contribute to it."

"Indian antiquity," Bronkhorst concludes, "has produced no credible ideas about *political* peace," despite the importance of *mental* peace in its culture. As a result, "war was endemic in India for all but the few periods in which one kingdom succeeded in uniting a major part of the subcontinent under a single ruler. Thinking about political peace did not play a credible role in ancient India and never exerted a noticeable influence."

Chapter 4: Searching for Peace in the Warring States: Philosophical Debates and the Management of Violence in Early China

Robin Yates takes issue with the long-dominant opinion that, beginning with Confucius, all thinkers in China's "Warring State" period (476–221 BCE: a period tormented by ceaseless war) agreed that peace could be established only by a unitary empire, and that this opinion prevailed throughout Chinese history virtually into the present. In fact, there were wide-ranging debates with many competing opinions about political and philosophical issues that were relevant in this context. Nor is the search for a system to overcome war and establish lasting peace to be confused with a "pacifist" attitude. In its early history, Yates emphasizes, China "was among the most inventive cultures in the arts of war;" it was "never a pacifist culture and Confucianism was never a pacifist ideology."

In the "Spring and Autumn" period (770–476), the state system disintegrated and competition among numerous polities increased. Such competition made administrative reorganization and centralization necessary, which was not possible without new types of experts who were able to offer advice and leadership, apply innovative solutions to the practical challenges of government, execute the rulers' policies, and integrate increasing numbers of commoners into the state structure. Members of lesser lineages embarked on such careers, supported by an education that was provided by professional teachers. Confucius was the first teacher of such experts, and soon many more schools were founded that specialized in such teaching. They all were confronted with the challenge of solving the anarchy of incessant warfare and social dislocation, of finding a way to establish lasting order and peace, and of defining the qualities and methods by which a ruler might achieve this.

Although it is difficult to determine to what extent the experience of intense and incessant war directly prompted a discourse on war and peace, philosophical debates about crucial political issues (including war and peace) thus began in the sixth century and intensified with the increase of competition among states. Apparently, though, the ideas of the philosophers had little immediate impact. Rather, the administrators of the various states sought their own solutions. Investing great resources into coercing the population to serve their rulers' needs, both economically and militarily, the states were increasingly able to establish order within their boundaries. This made it possible for philosophers and theoreticians to think about peace abstractly and to engage in a debate about the nature and realization of an ideal peace. Conceptually, many early Chinese thinkers saw "peace" not as the absence of war but as a condition with positive connotations. Yet of more immediate concern were the notions of order and disorder. Other political developments prompted a vigorous debate about the value of hereditary succession vs. merit-based rulership and of the qualities of a "true ruler." In some of these debates, the issue of war and peace was confronted head on, including discussion of detailed policies and institutions that a ruler could enact to achieve "perfect peace."

Against the majority's view that war could be ended only through the methods of peace (though what these methods were to be was vigorously contested), a group of "militarists" argued that unity could be created only by force; hence they focused on developing military, legal, and economic methods to strengthen their states and overcome the others by military might alone. Those who prevailed in the end (thinkers at the court of Qin) promoted a simple and pragmatic solution: peace "was to be created by the subordination of the weaker to the stronger, by military means if necessary, with only a thin veneer of morality or justification." Under the Qin and Han dynasties, internal unity and peace were indeed established, even if at great cost in lives and property.

Still, Chinese philosophers "endorsed the importance of the ruler ensuring peace and harmony with the cosmos." They as much as the rulers and statesmen themselves realized, however, that the maintenance of peace required the maintenance of a strong army and readiness to go to war. War and peace alternated with the rhythms of the cosmos. Perpetual peace was impossible and even unnatural.

Chapter 5: Greek Concepts and Theories of Peace

A strong concern for peace and just war connects Homer and Thucydides. The *Iliad* stands at the beginning of a long, intense, and public discourse on war and peace that can be traced through archaic poetry and philosophy to the dramatists and historians of the fifth century. The pervasiveness and public nature of this discourse seems to distinguish the Greeks from other ancient societies. Moreover, from early on, it included conceptualizations of war and peace as central communal issues, and attempts at theoretical categorization and analysis. Thucydides marks both a rapid intensification and increasing theorization of this discourse.

Three examples in and after the time of Thucydides illustrate innovative Greek efforts to establish peace by containing endemic inter-communal war and overcoming destructive intra-communal conflict (*stasis*): large-scale organizations to secure "international peace," a blueprint for peace requiring profound changes in thinking and attitudes, and the use of amnesty and geographical separation to eliminate *stasis* from the community.

Such efforts profited from the emergence of politically oriented philosophers (sophists) who enhanced the ongoing discourse on war and peace by adding theoretical sophistication. Thucydides' "pathology of civil war" thus incorporates a theoretical analysis of the causes and characteristics of *stasis*. Among various proposals offered to resolve this problem, those applying constitutional theory and aiming at a "mixed constitution" seemed especially promising. Containing endemic war proved more difficult, but new initiatives were built on theoretical foundations as well: thus, attempts were made to improve interpolis collaboration in "common peace" treaties and create an improved alliance system by limiting hegemonic power and strengthening the allies' influence. Other debates focused on mentalities by changing deeply ingrained attitudes toward war and empire, and on economic and social conditions by supporting trade to enhance interdependence among poleis and by supporting the lower classes to make them less dependent on and eager for war. By focusing on possibilities to overcome war and conflict, all these initiatives contributed to theoretical debates about peace, and hints survive in the evidence that peace was thematized directly in such debates as well.

In conclusion, it cannot be accidental that precisely in the period when warfare became much more pervasive and brutal, and when philosophy and political theory focused increasingly on political issues, the Greeks began to think in new ways about war and peace and to seek innovative and at least partly theoretical solutions to create peace by overcoming war and *stasis*.

Chapter 6: Broadening the Scope: Thinking about Peace in the Pre-Modern World

Prominent modern views consider peace a recent invention and dismiss earlier discussions of peace as idealistic or pious dreams, failing to yield practical results. On the contrary, Hans Van Wees points out, the chapters in the present volume demonstrate that the ancient world was not only deeply concerned with the issue of peace but produced, on the conceptual and theoretical levels, complex and sophisticated ideas about causes of war and possibilities to attain political peace. In some cases, these ideas were pragmatic enough to yield practical results.

In the ancient Near East, we find a concept that seems common in Bronze and Iron Age empires throughout the ancient world: a ruler is charged by the gods to maintain order (and in this sense peace) within his realm and harmonious relations between the human and divine worlds. By contrast, the Romans believed, like the builders of the ancient Chinese empires and modern imperialists, that peace could be established only by imperial conquest. Both these views assumed that maintaining peace necessitated force and that coercive power was legitimated by the desire for peace.

In stark contrast, in pre-imperial China, India, and Greece a range of ideas emerged that essentially rejected the use of force and cultivated inner balance and virtue as conditions for peace on the individual, state, and international levels. These ideas were often impractical and politically unsuccessful, but they were important because they assumed that endemic war and violence were the result of problems internal to human society and not due to external forces or a cosmic order: if people, officials, and kings pursued selfish goals and used violent means to achieve them, these attitudes needed to be changed to overcome war and violence. Methods to achieve peace thus relied on self-control and consent rather than coercion. Even small changes along those lines could reduce the likelihood of violence and war.

Another approach thought of peace as being the result of negotiations between individuals or collectives with competing self-interests. This approach underlies modern thinking about peace, concepts such as "balance of power," or the expectation that institutionally supported international trade will reduce threats of war. Far from being modern inventions, Van Wees argues, such ideas developed in ancient Greece on very similar lines. He traces this development from early Greece to Thucydides' analysis of the causes of wars that is based on a rational calculation of expected gains, costs, and risks.

Such ideas, known today as "Realism," broke fully through in the fourth century. They underlie "Common Peace" treaties, in which responsibility for maintaining peace was imposed on both the hegemonic power and the collective of signees, and are expressed powerfully by Plato, Isocrates, and Xenophon, who considered lasting peace desirable not least because peace was more profitable than war. The theories and practical solutions offered by Greek intellectuals anticipated nineteenth-century Liberal peace theories. Since, moreover, in Greece commoners economically often depended on war, some thinkers recognized that peace required the elimination of structural social and economic problems plaguing Greek communities. Their solutions included nonviolent ways to increase public revenues that could be spent on a welfare program supporting the lower-class citizens.

In conclusion, Van Wees proposes to add two structural factors to the list of conditions for the development of a substantive and even theoretical peace discourse in antiquity: the need to legitimate and consolidate certain forms of power (most obviously, empire) and the need for an intellectual response to the development of increasingly centralized and competitive states. Fourth-century Greeks went furthest in their intellectual and political efforts to create remarkably "modern" ideas about peace; this fact may be due to a strong sense of common ethnic and cultural identity and economic interdependence. All this requires further research and corroboration, especially on the levels of a broad "intellectual history" that "places ideas in their contemporary context," and of a broadly comparative approach as it is offered in this volume.

1

Abhorring War, Yearning for Peace: The Quest for Peace in the Ancient World[1]

KURT A. RAAFLAUB

Prologue

The dramatic date of the Chinese film *Hero* (*Ying xiong*) is the end of the Warring State Period (403–221 BCE), in which seven kingdoms fought ruthlessly for supremacy, causing massive slaughter and suffering for the population.[2] In the film, the king of Qin, determined to conquer all of China, has defeated most of his enemies. Over the years, however, he has been the target of many assassins. Three of these are still alive, Broken Sword, Flying Snow, and Sky. To anyone who defeats these three, the king promises great rewards: power, riches, and a private audience with himself. For ten years no one comes close to claiming the prize. Then an enigmatic person, Nameless, appears in the palace, bearing the legendary weapons of the slain assassins. His story is extraordinary: for ten years he has studied the arts of the sword, before defeating the mighty Sky in a furious fight and destroying the famed duo of Snow and Broken Sword, using a weapon far more devastating than his sword—their love for each other.

The king, however, replies with a different story: of a conspiracy between the four, in which Nameless' victories were faked to enable him to come close to

Peace in the Ancient World: Concepts and Theories, First Edition. Edited by Kurt A. Raaflaub.
© 2016 John Wiley & Sons, Inc. Published 2016 by John Wiley & Sons, Inc.

the king and kill him. Nameless indeed has a chance to achieve his goal. The king, exposed to his sword, tells him of his true aspiration: to conquer the warring states in order to overcome war and violence once and for all, to create a unified empire, and to establish lasting peace. Overcome by this vision, Nameless draws back his sword and walks out of the great hall—to die willingly under the arrows of the king's bowmen.

This is a powerful and beautiful film. Its message is exciting. It raises both hope and doubts: was there really an ancient ruler who pursued a true vision of peace—even if it could be realized only at the price of war and violence? Not unexpectedly, hopes prove illusionary. The film is based on a historical episode: the attempt of Jing Ke to assassinate the king of Qin in 227 BCE. But the film clearly does not intend merely to reconstruct history. The question of how to interpret it has raised intense debates; one interpretation sees it as an allegory for Mao Zedong and communism's unification of the world through global conquest, another, fueled by the Chinese government's approval, as advocating stability and security over human rights and liberty—although the film's director, Zhang Yimou, insisted that he did not pursue any political purpose. An any rate, the first emperor—he who displayed his army in a now world-famous terracotta replica near his necropolis—was no visionary of peace. Later Chinese historians did not even celebrate him as one of the greatest conquerors of all time, but rather castigated him as a cruel, arbitrary, impetuous, suspicious, and superstitious megalomaniac.[3]

Experts on war in the ancient world are numerous, those on peace harder to find; the bibliographies differ accordingly.[4] The topic this chapter addresses is huge. My purpose is twofold: on the one hand, to offer a broad survey over the quest for peace in the ancient world and to stimulate discussion;[5] on the other hand, to argue, at least in a preliminary way, for a thesis that will be tested in the subsequent chapters of this volume. To lay the ground for this thesis, I begin by presenting five brief case studies.

Five Cases and a Thesis

The first case is perhaps unexpected in this volume. It concerns a society that is not usually considered "ancient," although it is certainly "early" and has roots that go back to ancient times. What I have in mind is the "Iroquois League," founded by five (later six) Native American Nations in the north-east of today's United States. It is usually dated to around 1450 CE but strong arguments have been presented for the early twelfth century. The foundation of this League was marked by the acceptance of the "Great Law of Peace."[6] Its purpose, achieved to a remarkable degree, was to restore and maintain general peace, unity, and order among its member nations and beyond.[7] Depending on what founding date we accept, it lasted for three hundred or even six hundred years. Nothing like this ever came about in the ancient world, despite numerous attempts.

What interests here is the reason for the League's foundation. According to oral traditions preserved among the nations involved, it emerged in reaction to strife and warfare that had become excessive, uncontrollable, and fratricidal:

> Everywhere there was peril and everywhere mourning. Men were ragged with sacri-fice and the women scarred with flints, so everywhere there was misery. Feuds with outer nations, feuds with brother nations, feuds of sister towns and feuds of families and of clans made every warrior a stealthy man who liked to kill... A man's life was valued as nothing. For any slight offence a man or woman was killed by his enemy and in this manner feuds started between families and clans. At night none dared leave their doorways lest they be struck down by an enemy's war club. Such was the condi-tion when there was no Great Law.[8]

Dekanawidah, "the Great Peacemaker," a figure raised to superhuman status in some legends, was able to convince the warriors and their chiefs to "bury the hatchet," conclude peace, accept a "code of law" (the Great Law of Peace), and set up an organization that would guarantee its maintenance. Symbolically, a large tree (the "Tree of the Great Peace") was uprooted, weapons were bur-ied in the hole, and the tree planted again.[9] The politicial system adopted by the League, involving representation and equal vote (and thus elements char-acteristic of democracy), as well as a reassessment of the Law and the League's rationale in regular intervals, was known to the American Founders; whether and to what extent it influenced the constitution of the United States remains debated.[10]

The second case leads us to China in the Warring State Period (475–221 BCE, mentioned above). It received its name because of the endless wars for power and primacy that were based on two interrelated developments, among others: advances in technology made it much cheaper to produce individual weapons and equip large armies, thus encouraging the transition from aristocracy-dominated contests to mass fighting. States with larger resources were thus at an advantage, and this was crucial in propelling the ongoing consolidation of power among a shrinking number of an initial multitude of rivaling petty states, down to only seven among which the kingdom of Qin emerged victorious, cre-ating the First Empire. Wars in this period were brutal and relentless, causing profound and widespread misery that was increasingly resented and could not easily be overlooked. Not least for this reason, this was also a period of great intellectual ferment and social as well as political innovation, one of the most productive in Chinese history: it laid the foundations of thought patterns, structures, and developments for centuries to come. Among other intellectual advances, political thought and philosophy, represented most conspicuously by Confucius and his disciples and successors reached unprecedented heights, and their thoughts focused, typically, on two major issues, among others: how to help their patrons among the kings of the contending states to gain and secure victory and power, and how to overcome the chaos and misery caused by constant war and establish lasting peace. Substantive thinking about peace thus grew at least indirectly out of intolerable experiences of war.[11]

The third case takes us to Athens. Its history in the first half of the fifth century BCE was marked by its decisive contributions to victories over invading Persian armies in 490 and 480/79, its swift rise to power at the head of a widespread alliance system that was soon turned into a centralized naval empire, and, in close interaction with war and empire, its development of the most advanced democracy that was imaginable under the conditions of the ancient world. Although for different reasons than Sparta, Athens too became a somewhat militarized society. Between the Persian and Peloponnesian Wars (431–404 BCE between Athens and Sparta) Athens was involved in some kind of war in two out of three years, and its collective or "national" character was defined by "aggressive activism," a propensity for expansionist and interventionist policies. This tendency got Athens involved twice in serious conflicts with Sparta; the long and bitter Peloponnesian War ended with total defeat, the loss of empire, fleet, and fortifications, and almost with the city's annihilation.

The emergence of naval warfare and imperialism completely changed the face of war in the Greek world: it became permanent, ubiquitous, destructive, and total, involving most of Greece and affecting every sphere of life. In particular, as Thucydides demonstrates in memorable chapters, external war often went hand in hand with civil strife or even war (*stasis*) that prompted unprecedented excesses of cruelty and moral depravation.[12] Yet, at the same time, and again not accidentally, Athens in the fifth century was the center of an unparalleled cultural upswing in all spheres of intellectual and artistic achievement.[13] And it was especially in the last third of the century, under the experience of excessive war and *stasis*, that a long-standing discourse on war and peace was massively intensified: leading thinkers (especially philosophers, historians, and dramatic poets) turned their attention to analyzing issues of war and peace; they focused, in theory and practice, on finding ways to control war and civil strife and to secure peace. Moreover, as we shall see, the experience of *stasis* prompted the creation of a new term and concept denoting concord (*homonoia*).[14]

The fourth case concerns Rome in the period of transition from Republic to monarchy. Unlike the meteoric rise and fall of the Athenian empire, the Roman Empire was the result of a long development, stretching over many centuries, and of the efforts of many generations of leaders and citizens.[15] For centuries, the Romans were at war almost every year; in important ways, both elite and commoners were conditioned by war. By the middle of the second century BCE, Rome directly or indirectly controlled the entire Mediterranean, and its political system under the leadership of the senate and a powerful aristocracy had proved supremely successful.[16] But below the surface internal problems had been brewing, long neglected because all attention was directed toward the outside. These problems were caused largely by the opportunities and demands of a wide-flung empire that overwhelmed traditional structures and attitudes, and demanded broad and profound reforms. These in turn could not be realized without substantial changes in the power and privileges of the senatorial class and in the way politics were done, and for such changes the ruling class was not ready. The accumulated problems suddenly burst into the open in the last third of the second century and produced a long-lasting crisis that prompted violence in politics, increasingly vehement power struggles, and eventually a series of destructive civil wars.[17]

The last foreign enemy the Romans had seen in Italy was Hannibal in the Second Punic War (218–202 BCE). Although the civil wars were fought all over the empire, Italy was hit especially hard. In the first century—in the war between Romans and allies (91–88 BCE) that was a virtual civil war, in the civil wars involving Sulla, Marius, and Cinna in the 80s, in those between Caesar, Pompey, and his successors in the 40s, and in those among the triumvirs and eventually Antonius and Octavian (the future Augustus) in the 30s—the Romans repeatedly experienced a particularly vicious and brutal form of war at or near home that affected everybody and changed politics forever. Yet, again, this period also witnessed great cultural and intellectual achievements, with poetry, rhetoric, philosophy, historiography, and the arts reaching unprecedented heights.[18] It was in this period and under those particular circumstances, too, that the Romans for the first time engaged in an intensive discourse on peace that found its most conspicuous expression in poetry and monumental architecture.[19]

Finally, for the fifth case we stay in Rome but move to Late Antiquity. In late August 410 CE, the troops of Alaric, king of the Goths, stormed and plundered the city—an atrocity committed by an outside enemy that Rome had last suffered eight hundred years earlier and that made a profound impression throughout the empire.[20] It prompted pagans to blame the Christians, and this in turn provoked Augustine to write the books about *The City of God*.[21]

In the second part of this work, Augustine analyzes the divine and worldly states, their development and end, and here he includes a discussion of the highest good, which pagan philosophy tries to find in this world, while those familiar with the divine world find it only there and in eternal peace. Although every living being yearns for peace in this world, too, this kind of peace is precarious and limited. These thoughts form the background for an extensive discussion of peace, the most detailed that survives from all antiquity. Whether or not Augustine exploited an essay *On Peace* by the late republican scholar Marcus Terentius Varro, it is clear that many of the ideas Augustine put together in his work had a long prehistory, ultimately originating with late fifth-century Greek thinkers.[22] What matters especially for our discussion is that Augustine's discussion of peace again was motivated by an especially intense experience of war that devastated all certainties and challenged all traditional expectations and values.

The five case studies I have presented all converge to support one thesis: ancient or early societies began to think seriously and intensely about peace primarily—perhaps even only—when an extraordinary experience of war that vastly and excruciatingly surpassed their normal expectations forced such thoughts upon them. In a more than superficial way, this is true even for the first Great War remembered in western history. The Trojan War, historical in ancient Greek—though usually not in modern—perception, was long, intense, and brutal. It is no accident that the epic (the *Iliad*) dramatizing and heroicizing an episode of this war also pays remarkable attention to its devastating impact on those fighting it and the civilian population affected by it, to the desire for peace prevailing among the soldiers, and to efforts to preserve or restore peace.[23]

Two comments need to be added right away. First, the words "extraordinary" and "normal" are decisive here. Throughout history, and up to the recent past or even present, humans were usually not troubled by a "normal" amount of war: this was one of the common means to resolve conflicts, almost as old as humankind, and as such acceptable. Only wars that egregiously exceeded such "normal" experiences of war were able to trigger thought processes that encouraged the questioning of traditional concepts and norms, and the development of new ones. We need only think of the devastating effects of the wars of Napoleon III in the mid-nineteenth century and the two unprecedentedly destructive and murderous world wars in the twentieth that, not accidentally, motivated the creation of the International Red Cross, the League of Nations, and the United Nations, respectively.

Second, even so in the ancient world disastrous war experiences were perhaps a necessary but not a sufficient cause: they stimulated intensified thinking and debates about war and peace, but may not have sufficed to get those involved to take the next step and develop concepts or even theories of peace. One of the questions this volume tries to answer is what factors made this next step possible and why such factors seem to have been at work only in some societies and not in others, despite the ubiquity of intense war.

Efforts to preserve or restore peace and, if war proved inevitable, to claim the justice of one's cause are probably as old as the history of warfare. Such efforts also offer a long and sad story of futility and propagandistic deception. Yet we need not doubt in all cases the seriousness of such efforts. Warmongers often had to reckon among their peoples with a widespread desire for peace and justice. The remainder of this introductory chapter intends to pursue the question of what approaches may help us find evidence for concerns with peace in ancient societies, and to establish the following points. First, and briefly, wars in the ancient world were ubiquitous and brutal. Second, despite this uncontestable fact, visions of peace were widespread, even in imperial societies. Third, such visions crystallized in the religious sphere as well and found expression, in specific circumstances, in cults of peace. Fourth, in some societies peace was also an intense intellectual concern that in rare cases even influenced the practice of politics. I shall end this survey by formulating more precisely the questions this volume tries to answer.

The Prevalence and Brutality of War in the Ancient World

It goes without saying that wars were frequent and brutal in all ancient or early societies.[24] The label "Warring States," used for a period in early Chinese history, the pictorial reliefs in Neo-Assyrian palaces and Egyptian temples, the Mayan "Temple of the Skulls" in Chichen Itza, the images on Mayan, Aztec, and Moche reliefs and vases, and the scenes depicted on the Columns of Trajan and Marcus Aurelius in Rome offer graphic illustrations. Examples could be multiplied, from all corners of the globe. The quest for "peaceable societies" has yielded few and unimpressive results.[25] No wonder: the prevailing political culture tended to encourage war rather than peace. With few exceptions, the voices we hear from antiquity are those of the powerful, elites, and rulers. They were concerned primarily with legitimizing, securing, and extending their status and power. Kings and emperors found themselves under immense pressure to prove themselves, emulate their ancestors, and expand their domains, or, as in early American societies like the Maya and Aztecs, to produce a requisite number of war captives whose blood could "oil" the cosmic engine and keep it going.[26] Victory on the battlefield, riches gained in war, and imperial might enabled kings and generals to erect monuments, palaces, temples, and inscriptions that eternalized their glory; poets in their service sang their praise.

In city-states too, even in democratic Athens, the monumental cityscape reminded the citizens of their city's glory and power, achieved through victories in war and sacrifice for the community, and conditioned them to emulate their ancestors. Leaders found that policies based on action and intervention aroused emotions, easily proved attractive, and potentially paid huge dividends; policies of peace meant inactivity, lack of success, stagnation: nothing to fight and die for! As suggested before, Thucydides describes the Athenians as having been conditioned to be activists and interventionists, and this was reflected in their collective character, their way of life, and their policies. An inactive citizen was essentially useless to the community.[27]

In Rome, too, constant warfare over centuries molded society: the commoners learned to accept war as inevitable and profitable; the community used war to increase power and wealth, to impress others and to deter allies from revolts, to satisfy communal needs at the expense of the defeated, and to deflect internal conflicts toward the outside. In the aristocracy's value system, the path to status and glory led to success in war. In the ceremonial "triumph," the victorious general paid homage and thanks to Jupiter: in a fleeting moment of equality, the greatest mortal shook hands with the greatest god. *That* was worth dying for![28]

Visions of Peace

Despite all this, the elusive commodity called peace has left its traces in the extant record. Although space does not allow detailed discussion here, all large religious movements of antiquity grappled with visions of peace, not always successfully.[29] In ancient Israel, as attested by the Hebrew Bible, such visions broke through only rarely, perhaps most famously in Micah's and Isaiah's oft-cited prophecy that in the late 1980s provided the logo for the peaceful East German revolt against the communist regime: "They shall beat their swords into plowshares, and their spears into pruning hooks; nation shall not lift up sword against nation, neither shall they learn war any more."[30] Occupying an area that served as battle ground for the contests of great powers, and constantly challenged by their neighbors, the small states of Judah and Israel more often than not were forced to fight for their survival and thus relied on an ideology and a god that supported this fight: in important characteristics and perhaps in origin, Yahweh was a warrior god.[31] Early Christianity focused on another world and was soon confused by dogmatic infighting and its rise to state religion; it never succeeded in formulating a consistent response to the challenge of war vs. peace.[32] The Islamic "community of Believers" was initially tolerant of other monotheistic religions and ecumenical to a remarkable extent, but, preoccupied with empire building, civil wars, and dogmatic splits, it soon turned monopolistic and intolerant. Its expansion and imperial might were based on war, and war remained a defining obligation.[33] Buddhism was most explicit and uncompromising with regard to avoiding violence and causing pain to living creatures, but it tended to focus more on turning inward and achieving peace individually, omitted to address the problem of war explicitly, and was often unable to hold its ground against more aggressive and nationalist religions or interpretations of religion.[34] The "crown" for unwavering commitment to peace in the sense of nonviolence should perhaps be awarded to the Jains, a small but significant religious community found mainly in western India and dating back to the sixth century BCE.[35]

Even in ancient imperial societies, though, it is possible to find traces of an ideology of peace. The rock inscriptions of king Ašoka in India (circa 250 BCE) offer a good example.[36] Overwhelmed by the massive scale of suffering his conquests had caused, the king devoted himself "to the zealous study of morality." Hence, he advised his descendants against new conquests and urged them to be merciful, regarding "the conquest by morality as the only true conquest." Unfortunately, but not surprisingly, Ašoka's successors did not follow his example.

According to Achaemenid Persian royal ideology, the king, favored by the supreme god Auramazda, was capable of telling right from wrong and promoting justice, order, and peace. The policy of "Achaemenid Peace," however, though based on the deliberate pursuit of reconciliation and tolerance, required obedience and unwavering loyalty on the part of the subjects. As king Darius I wrote in the inscription on his great rock relief at Behistun that celebrated his victory over nine rebel kings,

> Says Darius the King: These are the countries which… were my subjects… Within these countries, the man who was loyal, him I rewarded well; him who was evil, him I punished well; by the favor of Ahuramazda these countries showed respect toward my law; as was said to them by me, thus was it done.[37]

The same was true of Roman peace (*Pax Romana*). Well into the Empire, the Romans concluded peace only under their own terms and only from a position of victory and strength. Augustus's "Altar of Peace" (*Ara Pacis*) and the closing of the Gates of Janus celebrated peace achieved by victories. In Augustus's report about his achievements (*Res gestae*) conquest became "pacification."

I quote from this document: "I made the sea peaceful (*pacavi*) and freed it from pirates… I extended the territory of all those provinces of the Roman people on whose borders lay peoples not subject to our government. I brought peace (*pacavi*) to the Gallic and Spanish provinces as well as to Germany… I secured the pacification of the Alps (*pacificavi*)…, yet without waging an unjust war on any people." In the *Aeneid*, Vergil defines the Roman imperial mission as *imposing* civilization (*mores*) upon peace: "Your skills, Romans, will lie in governing the peoples of the world in your empire, to impose civilization upon peace, to pardon the defeated, and to war down the proud."[38]

The beneficiaries of such generosity might have thought differently, and critics were not fooled. The historian Tacitus's ambivalence about the peace achieved by Augustus is well known. Moreover, he lets Gallic tribal leaders contemplating revolt be reminded that the Romans punish rebels with utmost severity but invite those who submit to share in the blessings of peace—and common servitude: "You must learn to love and foster peace and the city of Rome in which we all, vanquished and victors alike, have the same rights." Before a Roman general's final battle in Britain, the enemy leader famously says: victory "will mean the dawn of liberty for the whole of Britain," defeat submission to the most arrogant and exploitative rulers. "To robbery, butchery, and rape, they give the lying name of government; they create a desert and call it peace."[39] Still, the peace and prosperity granted the populations within the Roman Empire for two hundred years after Augustus (with only a few brief interruptions) and some more after the crisis of the third century—although of course not to be taken as absolute—were real enough and had profound and broad consequences that survived the empire by many centuries.[40]

We can pursue our search for evidence revealing concerns for peace in all kinds of directions: studying terminology and complementary as well as opposing words; and looking for conceptualizations, personifications, gods, cults, and monumental expressions of peace (not least in comparison with its opposite: war). I will illustrate this here by pursuing two related questions: Did peoples have deities of war and peace and what was their role in the pantheon? Were peace deities incorporated in monumental displays (statues, temples, inscriptions)?

Peace Cults

Of course, the question of cult applies only to polytheistic societies—although it is surely meaningful that Yahweh was a warrior god, while both the god and the savior of the Christians lacked martial attributes, however ambivalent

Christian attitudes toward war and violence may have been. The Hittites had a god of peace, the Mesopotamians and Egyptians apparently not.[41] Neither did early China, although there war was intimately connected with ritual and ancestor cults.[42] In Greece, Peace was personified very early and placed high in the divine hierarchy by the seventh-century poet Hesiod. The peace goddess, Eirēnē, was prominent on Athenian vases and in comedy and tragedy in the fifth century, clearly reflecting a reaction to the time's intense experience of war. Even so, Peace received an official cult in Athens only decades after the Peloponnesian War, in celebration of a victory over the Spartans in 375 BCE and of the Athenians' new role as "co-champions of peace" in a "Common Peace" agreement. A famous statue by a celebrated sculptor, perhaps the cult statue itself, shows the cheerful goddess with the boy Plutos (Wealth) in her arms.[43]

In the period of the Peloponnesian War, as we saw earlier, external war often went together with internal strife or civil war (*stasis*), which produced excesses of treachery and cruelty. Greek communities had known *stasis* all along, but in this intensity the experience was new, devastating, and shocking. Hence, a contrasting concept—concord (*homonoia*)—emerged and rose to political prominence in this period.[44] The concept was realized in a spectacular way in the Athenian "reconciliation and amnesty decree" of 403 BCE that ended the civil war between the supporters of an oppressive narrow oligarchy ruling with Sparta's support (the "Thirty Tyrants") and those of democracy and ushered in almost a century of domestic peace for Athens.[45] A cult for Homonoia followed in Athens a few decades later, still in the first half of the fourth century, although we do not know an exact date, place, or context. Like the concept of *homonoia* itself, this cult spread quickly throughout the Greek world. It was promoted by the Macedonian kings, Philip II and Alexander the Great, who used the concept to reactivate the memory of the great Greek victories over the Persians, especially at Plataea, and so to cement unity among the Greeks under their leadership in a new crusade against the Persians. The existing cult of Zeus Eleutherios (God of freedom) at Plataea, established after the battle of 479, apparently was enhanced by a link with Greek Homonoia. The latter played an important role in Alexander's campaign and during the Hellenistic period, and then served as the Greek equivalent to Roman Concordia in the Imperial period.[46]

In Rome, peace (*pax*) was conceptually important all along because every cult act had the purpose of securing "peace with the gods" (*pax deorum*), but personification and cult followed much later.[47] Interestingly, in contrast to Greece, in Rome the sequence of "peace" and "concord" was reversed. Internal peace or concord (*concordia*) was personified and received a temple or shrine in a prominent location above the Forum already in the fourth century BCE (reportedly in the context of compromises in the struggles between patricians and plebeians). This temple was rebuilt several times and joined by other shrines to Concordia, always in reaction to severe domestic strife and to demonstrate and celebrate restored civic unity.[48] After its splendid restoration by Tiberius and rededication as a Temple of Concordia Augusta in 10 CE, it served as a museum, exhibiting objects that symbolized peace and concord.[49]

Such prominence of Concordia, combined with the Romans' militaristic and imperialistic disposition, left little space for *pax* (peace). The latter rose to ideological, cultic, and monumental prominence only during and after the disastrous civil wars that destroyed the republic. At that time peace became the focus of urgent and widespread desire, expressed not least by the poets, and was imposed by the victors, eventually becoming "Augustan Peace" (*Pax Augusta*).[50] Caesar emphasized peace in word and action. The triumvirs placed Pax and Concordia on their coins. A celebratory medallion (cistophor) of 28 BCE praises Augustus as liberator of the Roman people and shows the figure and name of Pax on the reverse.[51] Augustus highlighted his accomplishment of establishing peace not only in his report on his accomplishments (mentioned before) and through the *Ara Pacis* (Altar of Peace), but also by linking this monument symbolically and monumentally with the great sundial adjacent to it (the *Solarium Augusti*) and with the sanctuary of Janus on the Forum, which served as "indicator of peace and war." When the shadow of the golden globe crowning the obelisk that served as the sundial's gnomon (and was dedicated on the same day as the Altar) moved on a straight line toward the door of the *Ara Pacis* on Augustus' birthday on the fall equinox, it was clear that the first emperor wanted to be seen as "born for peace."[52]

Yet, despite its splendor and the annual sacrifice offered there, the Peace Altar was no temple, and it was definitely intended to celebrate not so much Pax herself rather than Augustus as *the* Roman restorer of peace—it was an *Ara Pacis Augustae*.[53] The first temple dedicated to Peace was built only after another round of civil wars, by the emperor Vespasian, the conqueror of the Jews, in 75 CE.[54] Vespasian's Peace complex and Forum, praised as one of the most beautiful architectural designs in Rome, represents the fullest realization of the Roman peace concept, both monumentally and ideally. It comprises, apart from the magnificent temple and statue of Pax, a library and museum— places dedicated to peaceful occupations and recalling the library Augustus had attached to his new Temple of Apollo on the Palatine and the museum in the Temple of Concord. And just as Augustus's Peace complex on the Campus Martius was composed of victory monuments—the Altar celebrated Augustus's pacification of Spain and Gaul, the obelisk his conquest of Egypt—so too Vespasian's *templum pacis* was built with the spoils of his victory in the Jewish war, and the museum displayed the trophies his army had taken from Jerusalem and carried through the streets of Rome in Titus's triumph.[55] Obviously, then, even more than in Greece, in Rome the cultic and monumental elevation of peace came late and was prompted primarily by political and ideological motives.

War Cults

It is instructive to consider "war" in the same way. The Romans saw themselves as descendants of the war god Mars; his sacred animal, and the "totem animal" of the Romans, was the wolf, and statues of the wolf (with or without Romulus and Remus) were displayed prominently in the city. Bronze statuettes of the warrior god, who was connected with rituals of war, date back to early times.[56] Julius Caesar planned a grandiose temple for Mars, Augustus built it, for Mars Ultor (the Avenger) in his new Forum.[57] Moreover, Jupiter– and to some extent, Juno—were connected with war as well. When the conquest of Italy reached its climax, Roman generals began to use spoils to erect monuments and shrines, celebrating their victories and honoring the gods who had supported their achievement, including Salus (Salvation), Bellona Victrix (the victorious war goddess), Jupiter Victor, Venus Obsequens (Venus who imposes obedience), Victoria, Jupiter Stator (Jupiter who steadies the army), and Fors Fortuna (powerful Fortuna).[58] In subsequent centuries, the Capitol, Forum, Field of Mars, and adjacent areas became a vast "memorial space," shaping the Romans' identity and reminding ever new generations of the great deeds of their ancestors.[59]

By contrast, among the early Greeks the war god Ares enjoyed the worst possible reputation. The *Iliad* describes him as a "maniac who knows nothing of justice" and a "thing of fury, evil-wrought." Zeus, his father, acutely dislikes him because of his propensity for quarrelling and fighting. He is a coward and adulterer, ridiculed by the other gods. In Greek literary texts he is regularly associated with the most negative aspects of war.[60] It is perhaps not surprising, therefore, that the city of Athens did not have a sanctuary of Ares in the Classical Period—the temple that was erected in the Agora centuries later was brought there from one of the rural districts in Attica—although this should not be generalized: Ares and associated deities or personifications were worshipped in many places throughout the Greek world.[61]

As far as Athens is concerned, monuments and inscriptions celebrating victories proliferated in the city's center. The elegant little temple of Nikē (Victory) near the entrance of the Acropolis commemorated an important victory over

Sparta; statues of Nikē stood as akroteria on each wing of the magnificent Stoa (Portico) of Zeus the God of Freedom (Zeus Eleutherios) in the Agora; even the gold accumulated in the treasury of Athena was cast in Nikē statuettes. And the greatest temple of all, the Parthenon, served as a monument of Athens' Persian victories and imperial might.[62] The virgin goddess worshipped there was a warrior, and as such, leading her people to victory (*promachos*), she stood in a famous bronze statue (Athena Promachos) on the Acropolis, the greatest among many dedications commemorating Athenian victories. Moreover, monuments celebrating Athenian martial exploits stood also in the Agora and elsewhere, and the public tombs of the heroes fallen in Athens' wars formed a long "façade of honor" along the main road in the public cemetery outside the walls. By "monumentalizing and perpetuating with works of art the glory of her great citizens and their famous achievements, Athens gradually developed into a monument of her own historical identity."[63]

Fifth-century Athens was an imperial city, too, and not only the values and attitudes of its citizens but also its shrines, cults, and monuments reflected this. It is this collective enthusiasm for war and empire, the citizens' "aggressive activism" (mentioned earlier), that seems to have been responsible for keeping *eirēnē* down as a value concept, despite her early personification and an increasingly intense experience of war, and for the late establishment of a cult of Peace.

To take this to a more general level, it was the collective nature and competitive leadership characteristic of the governments of Athens and Rome that encouraged the celebration of victory through *communal* cults and public monuments highlighting individual events. While in oligarchic Rome the names of successful individuals were attached to such monuments, this was not the case during the height of democracy in fifth-century Athens; the demos as collectivity of citizens claimed the glory and bore the sacrifices for victories and defeats.[64] By contrast, in imperial monarchies victories were tied much more closely to the person of the monarch and the tutelary deities to whom he owed his power. The commemoration of victories thus was integrated (through inscriptions, sculptural reliefs, or paintings) into monuments that celebrated the monarch. Such monuments were dedicated to his memory, serving as funerary monuments, such as the Egyptian pyramids, the Mayan towers, or Augustus's mausoleum with the bronze pillars inscribed with his *Res gestae* (deeds); or they displayed the monarch's power while he was still alive—as did the famous Qin stelae or the central palace of the First Qin Emperor in China that replicated the palaces of all those states he had conquered, the Behistun relief of the Persian king Darius I, or the palaces of the Assyrian and Babylonian kings; or they enhanced the worship and acknowledged the power of the gods who made the king's rule and victory possible, such as the great temples in

Egypt.[65] In all these settings, imperial might and aspirations left no space for monumental expressions of peace.

To return to the list of things we could do to pursue our search for peace, we could examine rituals connected with peace, and efforts to avoid war and preserve or restore peace through intimidation, diplomacy, alliance, and arbitration, or to secure, in case such attempts failed, a just cause in war. We could discuss methods to stabilize peace, for example, through systems of honors, titles, or intermarriage among kings and dynasts, or through alliance systems and treaties. All this would be fascinating, and there is ample evidence for it across the ancient world.[66] But I want to turn to another subject that is crucial in the present context.

Intellectual Concerns with Peace

The modern world features an impressive array of leading intellectuals who thought and wrote about peace.[67] One of the prestigious Nobel Prizes annually honors and encourages efforts for peace.[68] What does the ancient world offer in this respect? Rather than developing a genre of narrative history, early Indian thinkers focused on theories, categories, and ideals. Thus the *Arthaśastra* or "Treatise on Worldly Gain" analyzes the arts of war and peace without primarily focusing on practical applications or historical examples.[69] In prevailing Indian ideologies, formulated, for instance, in the *Dharmaśastra*, the king was destined for activism, conquest, and rise to imperial rule. Inactivism was despised. In a world of petty kings and constant rivalry, the two primary conditions for peace were seen in forceful domination by one man and constant preparation for war. Only an emperor could be expected to bestow upon humankind the greatest gift possible, greater even than peace: *abhaya*, "freedom from fear."[70]

In China, centuries of ruthless warfare before the First Empire, the "warring state" period (mentioned above) prompted intense intellectual debates and the emergence of new ideas about the natural order, human society, power, war, and peace. Some authors saw moral improvement as an essential condition of peace: a ruler must perfect his own virtue before he can regulate his family, govern his state effectively, and bring peace to the entire realm. Others contemplated universal disarmament. Military treatises, however, wasted no thought on peace and focused only on ways to gain victory and destroy the enemy. Most thinkers agreed that lasting peace could only be established through the unification of all the contending states into a single empire. Still, the Chinese dossier on ideas about peace is exceptionally rich and sophisticated.[71]

In Rome, especially in the age of the civil wars and of Augustus, some of the greatest authors reflected in their works on the evils of the time and the momentous change from war to peace their age witnessed. The poets invoked a widespread desire for peace and praised Augustus for having achieved it.[72] In his report on the civil war of 49/48, Caesar emphasizes his great efforts to avoid this war or end it quickly through negotiations; two of his veteran colonies contain "peace" in their names, some of his late coinage features *pax*, and after his last victory in the civil wars, the senate decreed in his honor a temple to Concordia Nova (New Concord) because he had "restored peace in the state."[73] In his own summary of his achievements (*Res* gestae) and in the monumental imprint he left on Rome's cityscape, Augustus presented himself simultaneously as the greatest conqueror and greatest peacemaker.[74] Neither Livy's nor any other contemporaneous historian's books about the civil wars and their termination have survived, but allusions in later authors acknowledge Augustus's restoration of peace—though with surprisingly little emphasis and not always uncritically.[75] It is worth recalling the very different reaction of Velleius Paterculus, an equestrian officer (and thus not a member of the supreme elite) who had seen Augustus and served under Tiberius. In his universal history he writes, at the occasion of Octavian's return from Egypt in 29 BCE:

> There is nothing that man can desire from the gods, nothing that the gods can grant to a man, nothing that wish can conceive or good fortune bring to pass, which Augustus on his return… did not bestow upon the Roman state and people and the world. The civil wars were ended after twenty years, foreign wars suppressed, peace restored, the frenzy of arms everywhere lulled to rest; validity was restored to the laws, authority to the courts, and dignity to the senate… Agriculture returned to the fields, respect to religion, to mankind freedom from anxiety…
>
> (2.89; trans. F.W. Shipley)

It is a remarkable fact, though, that among the immense literary production of Greece and Rome not a single treatise "On Peace" or "On Concord" written before a famous chapter in Augustine's *City of God* has survived and we know of only few that were written: one, *On Concord* (*peri homonoias*), by the late fifth-century BCE sophist (philosopher and teacher of rhetoric) Antiphon, a second with the same title by a little-known philosopher, Demetrius of Magnesia, early in Caesar's civil war, and a third, *Pius de pace* (*Pius on Peace*), by M. Terentius Varro (mentioned earlier), perhaps at the occasion of the "Peace of Misenum" between Octavian and Sextus Pompey in 39 BCE.[76] One year earlier, the "Peace of Brundisium" between Antonius and Octavian had probably prompted Vergil to write his *Fourth Eclogue* with its vision of peace and the return of a Golden Age shining brightly in an age devastated by civil wars. At the time, peace "was in the air." We thus understand Varro's motive in writing his influential essay.

But Varro was a scholar, and one especially interested in antiquarian topics; his political career had been cut short by the civil wars. If we can trust the very fragmentary evidence that survives, why did the historians (with the exception of Velleius) not make more of Augustus's termination of the civil wars, and why did none of the leading politicians consider the topic worth his attention? If elite Romans engaged in scholarly or literary pursuits they usually did it in the realms of law or history. To a Roman senator it was counterintuitive to look at the issue of peace in an abstract or theoretical way, separated from practical politics. External peace, peace on the frontiers, certainly was good—and offered food for propaganda. Augustus realized this, emphasized the unprecedented three closings of the Gates of Janus during his principate, and tied his peace monuments to external victories—even if widespread unhappiness about the civil wars provided enough motivation to present himself as a peacemaker. After all, the *Ara Pacis* was decreed upon Augustus's return not from the termination of the civil wars but from the pacification of Spain and Gaul.[77] Domestic peace in the sense of an end to political violence and civil war, however, could not be celebrated without drawing undesirable attention to the civil wars themselves—an issue all those involved tried to avoid.[78] Thus, even for contemporary historians this issue was tricky, which may explain their reluctance to comment more emphatically on the termination of these wars.[79] For the senatorial class, and especially for those inclined to theoretical reflection, however, this issue was inextricably tied to a larger and more essential one: the restoration of a good and reliable order in communal affairs. If this could be achieved, domestic peace would follow. Hence, Cicero was interested in seeing (and perhaps writing) an essay on concord (*homonoia*) when he was considering a peace initiative early in Caesar's civil war (a plan that was soon overtaken by the events), but he wrote *The Republic* and *The Laws;* he emulated Plato, to be sure, but with a different purpose: his goal was to present a theoretical design not of an ideal state but of the Roman state restored to good "working condition." Augustus, appropriating some of Cicero's ideas, cloaked innovation in the garb of tradition and achieved peace by "restoring the republic."[80]

What about the Greeks? As I will show in my other chapter in this volume, they early on developed a serious discourse on questions of war and peace. In this respect they were not alone, although they may have done so more intensely—with the exception of early China—and certainly more publicly than others. In addition, like early Chinese thinkers, they went further, elevating the discourse on peace from the level of concern and conceptualization to that of theory. Under the impression of new and extraordinarily destructive forms of war, in roughly the last third of the fifth century, philosophers (called sophists) began to focus more specifically on the problem of how to contain both external war and civil strife (*stasis*). They proposed various solutions that ranged from moral improvement to constitutional theory. In Greek citizen communities (*poleis*) those who ruled (whether few, many, or all) had the power both to determine policies and shape their communal order. Hence, Greek thinkers found it easier to cope with *stasis* that took place within the polis and thus within the sphere over which the citizens had control, than with intercity war that essentially played out in an institutional no-man's-land.[81] Occasionally, such thinking and theorizing even had an impact on practical politics. More broadly, the philosophers' thoughts on war and peace, just as those on other urgent issues, were absorbed into a pool of ideas and theories that were shared among other intellectuals, debated intensely, and applied to other fields such as the analysis and interpretation of history. This is why, to mention but one example, we find in the works of Herodotus and especially Thucydides not only a pervasive concern with the issue of war and peace but also evidence for the use of philosophical theories in dealing with this issue.[82]

Conclusion

Rich evidence for war survives from many ancient or early societies around the globe. Evidence for concern about peace is much more limited, though in a variety of forms also recoverable from numerous societies. Such concerns became more urgent, and thinking about them intensified and sometimes took on new forms in societies that suffered especially intense and horrible experiences of war.

Specific evidence for concepts and theories of peace is rare. Few societies have left the kind of sources that would contain such evidence. Many that developed writing and even used it in sophisticated ways, for example to produce records of history or master scientific challenges (in mathematics, astronomy, or medicine), did apparently not engage in abstract or theoretical thinking in the spheres of politics or ethics (or at least did not commit such thinking to writing).[83] Despite the prolific written records they left, highly developed literate civilizations, such as the Egyptians, Mesopotamians, Hittites, Achaemenid Persians, or Maya, allow us to see that under certain conditions they preferred peace to war and knew how to prevent war and conclude or stabilize peace, but not whether they developed concepts or even theories of peace. For reasons discussed earlier, at least in monarchic and imperial states it seems unlikely that this happened. At any rate, it is only in societies that developed abstract and theoretical thinking, and thus forms of philosophical argument, that we can expect to find such thinking applied to the issues of war and peace as well.

Finally, as, for example, the cases of India (discussed elsewhere in this volume) or Rome (discussed above) show, cultural reasons, the general outlook of society, or the political and ideological needs of those who ruled could prevent the development of concepts or theories of peace even where this was intellectually possible. Much, it seems, would have depended on the social and professional status of those who engaged in theoretical or philosophical thinking. Personal involvement in politics, dependence on the ruler's (or rulers') patronage, social or even religious constraints might discourage the formulation of ideas that contradicted or challenged prevailing traditions, doctrines, or attitudes, while social and economic independence might encourage a thinker to explore more freely, push the boundaries, and try new solutions.

I suggest, therefore, that three conditions determined a society's ability to develop concepts or theories of peace: exceptionally harsh war experiences, which made peace an urgent need; capacity of abstract and philosophical thinking; and the political and critical independence of the thinkers. More factors, of course, may have played a role.[84] It is the purpose of the present volume to explore through four detailed case studies—all concerning highly developed ancient civilizations (China, India, Egypt, and Greece)—the conditions that encouraged (or prevented) the emergence of such concepts and theories, and shaped the forms these took.

Notes

1   Together with Raaflaub 2009 (see now also Chapter 5 in the present volume), 2011, and 2015, this essay is part of a series on ancient concepts of peace; it draws on the introduction to Raaflaub 2007. Earlier versions of this essay were published in Korea (*The Journal of Greco-Roman Studies* 40 [2010] 5–36), Serbia (K. Maricki-Gadjanski [ed.], *Antiquity, Modern World, and Reception of Ancient Culture.* Proceedings of the Serbian Society for Ancient Studies 6 [Belgrade 2012]: 306–30), and in a Japanese translation (Raaflaub, *War and Historiography in Ancient Greece* [preliminary title], ed. Akiko Moroo [Tokyo forthcoming]). I thank the editors for their permission to reuse parts of these essays for the present purpose.
2   The Wikipedia entry "*Hero* (2002 Film)" may serve as an introduction. See also the film's official website, http://trailers.apple.com/trailers/miramax/hero/ (accessed June 9, 2015). On the Warring State Period, see Lewis 1999.

3   See, e.g., Ebrey 1996: ch. 3; Lewis 2007; Portal 2007; Wood 2007, 2008; Pines et al. 2013.

4   The bibliography on war in the ancient world is immense (see, e.g., the chapters in *W&S* with good bibliographies). For peace, see Gilissen 1961–62; Zampaglione 1973; Sordi 1985; Binder and Effe 1989; Graeber 1992; Van Wees 2001; *W&P*; Meyer 2008b; Wilker 2012a (11 n.1 lists additional bibliography). Readers might also consult two encyclopedias of peace studies: Young 2010; Ager in preparation.

5   For more detailed analyses of the search for peace in individual ancient or early societies, see the chapters in *W&P*.

6   See Parker 1968; 1989: 403–6; Fenton 1998; Shenondoah and George 1998: 99–108; Crawford 1994 and in *W&P*; for the early date: Mann and Fields 1997. I am grateful to Neta Crawford and to Lisa Brooks (2014: 395–96) for drawing my attention to this remarkable achievement that may well be unparalleled in human history.

7   Opposing or rebellious tribes or nations were offered participation in the Great Peace; if they refused three times, war was opened and as a result of defeat they were destroyed or absorbed into the League's nations; see Parker 1968: 9–10.

8   Parker 1968: 17.

9   "I, Dekanawidah, and the confederate lords now uproot the tallest pine tree and into the cavity thereby made we cast all weapons of war. Into the depths of the earth,... we cast all weapons of strife. We bury them from sight forever and plant again the tree. Thus shall a Great Peace be established and hostilities shall no longer be known between the Five Nations but only peace to a united people" (Parker 1968: 9).

10 For Native American influence, through the The Great Law, on American ideas of confederacy and democracy, see Grinde 1977; Johansen 1982; Grinde and Johansen 1995; *contra:* e.g., Tooker 1990.

11 For detailed discussion, see Chapter 4 (Yates) in this volume. See also, e.g., Nivison 1999.

12 See relevant chs. in *CAH* IV and V; in addition, on the Persian Wars, Green 1996; on the Athenian empire, Meiggs 1972; on Athenian democracy, Raaflaub et al. 2007; on changes in warfare in the fifth century, Meier 1990b; Raaflaub 1999: 141–48; Hanson 2001; Tritle 2013. Pericles on Athens: Thuc. 2.35–46, esp. 37–41; Thucydides on civil strife: 3.69–84 with Price 2001; on the Athenian collective character, marked by *polypragmosynē* (literally, "doing a lot"), see n. 27 below.

13 Sakellariou 1996; Boedeker and Raaflaub 1998.

14 These efforts, and the Greek discourse on peace that begins with Homer, are discussed in Chapter 5 of this volume. On the emergence of *homonoia*, see below at n. 44.

15 See, for example, the narrative of Scipio Africanus the Younger in Cicero's *Republic*, Book 2, or the long rows of statues of *summi viri* (supreme leaders) decorating the porticoes in the Forum of Augustus (Zanker 1988: 210–15; Luce 1990).

16 On the formation of the Roman empire, see relevant chs. in *CAH* VII.2 and VIII, and summaries (with bibliog.) in chs. by Daniel Gargola and Arthur M. Eckstein in Rosenstein and Morstein-Marx 2006: 147–66, 567–89, as well as in relevant chs. of Flower 2004. On conditioning for war: Raaflaub 1996.

17   On the crisis of the Roman republic and the age of the civil wars, see relevant chs. in *CAH* IX and X; Jürgen von Ungern-Sternberg, in Flower 2004: 89–109, and chs. by C.F. Konrad and W. Jeffrey Tatum in Rosenstein and Morstein-Marx 2006: 167–89, 190–211.

18   See, e.g., Rawson 1985; Galinsky 1996.

19   For discussion, see below and ch. 5 (Raaflaub) of this volume.

20   On the famous but historically uncertain "sack of Rome" by the Gauls in 406 BCE, see Cornell 1995: 313–18. On Alaric's sack of Rome and its impact: *CAH* XIII (1998) 125–28; Kulikowski 2007.

21   Augustine, *Retractationes* 2.69.1; see Brown 2000.

22   Varro's *Pius de pace:* Katz 1985 (see further Raaflaub 2015: 111 n. 34). Augustine, *De Civitate Dei* 19.11–13. Fuchs 1965 argues for dependence on Varro. *Contra:* Laufs 1973. See also Wilhelm Geerlings, in Binder and Effe 1989: 191–203. For the ideas of Greek sophists on peace, see ch. 5 (Raaflaub) in the present volume.

23   On the *Iliad's* concern with these issues, see Chapter 5 in this volume.

24   For example, on violence in ancient Egypt, see Müller 2009; in ancient Greece, Van Wees 2000; in early China, Lewis 1990; among the Aztecs: Carrasco 1999.

25   On the discarded myth of the "peaceable Maya," see David Webster, *W&S* 336. The same, I suspect, will happen with the Indus Valley Civilization, still characterized as a "peaceable kingdom" by McIntosh 2000: 177–83. See also *W&P* 2–5, 9–10.

26   On human sacrifice in Mesoamerican societies, see Hassig 1988; Carrasco 1999; Tiesler and Cucina 2007.

27   On the active (*polypragmōn*) and passive (*apragmōn*) citizen: Thuc. 1.70; cf. 2.40, 61, 64; Raaflaub 1994; Christ 2006; Demont 2009. On Athenian attitudes toward war, see Meier 1990b; on conditioning for war: Raaflaub 2001; on the monumental cityscape of Athens: Hölscher 1998.

28   Conditioning for war in Rome: Nathan Rosenstein in *W&S*; Raaflaub 1996; Eckstein 2006. Triumph: Hölkeskamp 2006; Beard 2007.

29   See, generally, Nardin 1996; Smith-Christopher 1998; Fürst 2006; Hogan and Lehrke 2009.

30   Micah 4: 1–5; Isaiah 2: 2–5, with Thomas Krüger's chapter in *W&P* 161–71 (and Van Wees' comment in Chapter 6 below, at n. 11); see also Susan Niditch, ibid. 141–60; Henning Graf Reventlow, in Binder and Effe 1989: 110–22; Cohen and Westbrook 2008.

31   Yahweh as warrior god: Miller 1973; Lind 1980; see also von Rad 1991 (with a summary of the discussion triggered by this book's German publication in 1958 by Ben Ollenburger and an annotated bibliography on "War, Peace, and Justice in the Hebrew Bible" by Judith Sanderson); Erich Zenger, in Fürst 2006: 13–44, and, more generally on the motif of god as a warrior, Longman and Reid 1995. Furthermore, on the Near Eastern context of Israel's military practices, see Hasel 2005.

32   On Christian ideas on peace (or war), see Wengst 1987; Swartley 1996; Alfons Fürst's own ch. in Fürst 2006: 45–81; Louis J. Swift, in *W&P* 279–96; Wolfgang Wischmeyer, in Meyer 2008: 87–94.

33 On Islamic views on war and peace, see, e.g., Muhammad Kalisch, in Fürst 2006: 151–65; Fred Donner, in *W&P* 297–311.

34 On Buddhism, ancient India, and peace, see, e.g., Annette Wilke, in Fürst 2006: 83–150; Richard Salomon, in *W&P* 53–65, and especially Bronkhorst's detailed discussion in Chapter 3 below.

35 On the Jains, see Chapple 1998.

36 Thapar 1961; 2002: 174–208; Richard Salomon, in *W&P* 53–65 (whence the quotes), and the beginning of Chapter 3 (Bronkhorst) below.

37 Trans. Kent 1953; see Briant 2002: 125. On "Achaemenid Peace," see Josef Wiesehöfer, in *W&P* 121–40.

38 Augustus, *Res gestae* 25–26 (trans. Brunt and Moore); Vergil, *Aeneid* 6.850–53 (my trans.); on Roman peace: Carlin Barton, Nathan Rosenstein, in *W&P* 226–44, 245–55; Woolf 1993; Hardwick 2000; Raaflaub 2011; Cornwell 2015; in preparation. On the *Ara Pacis* and the Gates of Janus, see below n. 52.

39 Tacitus, *Annals* 1.2–4, 9–10; *Histories* 4.73–74 (trans. Fyfe and Levene); *Agricola* 30 (trans. Mattingly and Handford).

40 See, e.g., Strabo, *Geography* 6.4.2, end (with Dueck 2000: 115–22) or Aelius Aristides' speech *On Rome*, with Klein 1981; Harris and Holmes 2008: chs. 9–10.

41 On the Hittites, see Bryce 2002; Richard Beal, in *W&S* 81–97. Neither the *Reallexikon der Assyriologie* nor Bottéro 1991 or Black and Green 1992 contain a reference to "peace." For Egypt, see Chapter 2 (Bickel) in this volume.

42 Lewis 1990: esp. 15–96.

43 See Chapter 5 (Raaflaub) in this vol. on the prominence of peace themes in Athens. Cult of Eirēnē: Van Wees, Chapter 6 below, at n. 57; Parker 1996: 229–30; see also Simon 1986; Stafford 2000: ch. 6: Marion Meyer's own ch. in Meyer 2008: 61–86; Smith 2011: index. Statue of Eirēnē: e.g., Charbonneaux et al. 1969: fig. 399; Wünsche 2007: 79; Smith, ch. 10. On deities of peace in Greece and Rome, see Scheibler 1984; Simon 1988; on images of war and peace, Peter Kranz, in Binder and Effe 1989: 68–84. For a fuller comparative analysis of Greek and Roman peace cults, see Raaflaub 2015.

44 Civil strife (*stasis*): Lintott 1982; Gehrke 1985; Fisher 2000; see esp. Thuc. 3.69–84, 8.45–98 with Munn 2000: ch. 5; Price 2001. On the emergence and role of *homonoia*, see de Romilly 1972; Funke 1980.

45 This decree is discussed in detail in ch. 5 (Raaflaub) below, at n. 39.

46 On the cult of *homonoia*: Shapiro 1990; Thériault 1996; Smith 2011: 123–24 (and 60–61 on *harmonia* as a civic value). Zeus Eleutherios: Raaflaub 2004: 102–17.

47 *Pax deorum*: Sordi 1985: 146–54; Linderski 2007.

48 The original temple, now attested archaeologically as well, was dated to 367 or 304. For Concordia and her sanctuaries in Rome, see Hölscher 1990; Richardson 1992: 98–100; *LTUR* I: 316–21; Raaflaub 2011: 326. On the Roman concept of *concordia*, see now also Lobur 2008; Akar 2013.

49 Kellum 1990. This cult thus acknowledges Augustus's role as unifier after the civil wars.

50   See n. 38 above on *pax Romana* and Raaflaub 2011: 324–30 on the conditions
     that brought *pax* to the fore in Roman thought and politics. On the cult of Pax:
     Weinstock 1960: 44–52; Simon 1994; Scherf 2007.

51   Hölscher 1990; Simon 1994. Cistophor: e.g., *BMCRE* I: 112 with pl. 17.4;
     Simon 1994: 209 no. 38 (pl. 137/38). Caesar: below n. 73.

52   Altar of Peace: Weinstock 1960; Simon 1967; Zanker 1988: index under "Rome,
     Ara Pacis;" Richardson 1992: 287–89; Galinsky 1996: 141–55; *LTUR* IV: 70–74.
     Janus as "indicator of peace and war:" Livy 1.19.2; see Galinsky 1996: 294; Jeri
     DeBrohun, in *W&P* 256–78. Sundial of Augustus: Buchner 1982; Zanker 1988:
     144–45. Schütz 1990; Heslin 2007 are critical of Buchner's calculations and
     reconstruction but, as Haselberger 2011 (with the responses to his paper) demon-
     strates, Buchner's main insights are still valid. For the new cult of Pax Augusta, see
     soon also Stern forthcoming.

53   Accordingly, Van Wees suggests (conclusion of Chapter 6 below) that the dis-
     course of peace under Augustus was perhaps largely motivated by the consolida-
     tion of imperial power. For discussions of whether and how Pax was represented
     on this monument, see Simon 1967; for a summary, Raaflaub 2015.

54   Suetonius, *Vespasian* 9.1. On the civil wars of 68/69 CE, see Greenhalgh 1975;
     Wiedemann 1996. On Vespasian's Forum and Temple of Peace, see Anderson
     1984: 101–18; Richardson 1992: 286–87; *LTUR* IV: 67–70; relevant chs. in
     Coarelli 2009.

55   As represented on the relief panels of the Arch of Titus in the Roman Forum.

56   Mars: Simon 1984; Gordon 2006 with sources and bibliog.

57   Caesar's plan: Suetonius, *Caesar* 44. On the Forum of Augustus with the Temple
     of Mars Ultor, see, e.g. Zanker 1988; Richardson 1992: 160–62; Galinsky 1996:
     197–213; *LTUR* II: 289–95.

58   Monuments to war deities: *CAH* VII.2: 408.

59   Hölkeskamp 2004; Walter 2004; Stein-Hölkeskamp and Hölkeskamp 2006. See
     also above n. 15 on the *summi viri*.

60   *Iliad* 5.761, 831, 890–91 (trans. R. Lattimore); Burkert 1985: 169–70; Schachter
     2002.

61   Athenian Temple of Ares: Travlos 1971: 104–9; Camp 2001: 189–91. Cult places
     of Ares: Schachter 2002.

62   Temple of Nikē: Travlos 1971: 148–57; Stoa of Zeus Eleutherios: Travlos, 527–33.
     Parthenon: Osborne 1994; Beard 2003; Hurwit 2004: 106–54.

63   Dedications: Hurwit 2004: 79–84. See generally Hölscher 1998 (quote: 182);
     Raaflaub 2001.

64   Raaflaub 2001: 324. On Rome, see n. 59 above.

65   I formulate this here as a thesis, leaving a detailed investigation to another occa-
     sion. Specifically on the Qin stelae, see Kern 2008 (I thank Stephen Durrant for
     good advice).

66   For a brief survey, see *W&P* 17–21; the individual chapters in that volume offer
     rich material.

67 See, for example, Chanteur 1992.

68 For a list of Nobel Peace laureates, see http://en.wikipedia.org/wiki/Nobel_Peace_Prize (accessed June 9, 2015).

69 On the *Artaśastra*: Kautalya 1961; Boesche 2002; Whitaker forthcoming.

70 Derrett 1961, 1973, 1995. For further discussion of thoughts on peace in ancient India (including the works mentioned), see Chapter 3 (Bronkhorst) in this volume.

71 Moral transformation: Ebrey 1996: 46. Confucianism: Lun 1998. See, generally, Robin Yates, in *W&P* 34–52, and especially Chapter 4 (Yates) in this volume.

72 Poets: e.g., Vergil, *Eclogues* 4.4–17; Horace, *Epode* 7; *Odes* 4.5.5–24, 15.4–20; *Carmen Saeculare* 49–60; Tibullus 1.10.45–68; Ovid, *Fasti* 4.407–8. See Fuchs 1926; Zampaglione 1973: 131–84; Reinhold Glei, in Binder and Effe 1989: 171–90; Jeri DeBrohun, in *W&P* 256–78.

73 Caesar, e.g., *Civil War* 1.9–11, 32; for a detailed discussion, see Raaflaub 1974: 262–93. Temple of Concordia Nova: Dio Cassius 44.4; the dictator's death prevented its construction. On Caesar's peace colonies and coins, see Raaflaub 2011: 329.

74 On Augustus' statements and monuments concerning war and peace, see Gruen 1985; Rich 2003; Raaflaub 2011: 330–33; on Augustus the conqueror also Gruen 1990.

75 "Works of peace" in contrast to "deeds of war" in Nicolaus of Damascus' *Life of Augustus* §58 probably refers mainly to Augustus' reforms. (I thank Mark Toher for this reference.) Among later authors, see, e.g., Dio 65.39.1, 44.2; Tacitus (n. 39 above); on the assessment of Augustus by Dio and other authors, see Manuwald 1979.

76 Varro: above n. 22. On Antiphon, see ch. 5 (Raaflaub) in this volume, at n. 63. Demetrius's essay is mentioned by Cicero, *Letters to Atticus* 8.11.7; 9.9.2; on the person, see Montanari 2004 (with bibliog.).

77 *Res gestae* 12–13.

78 In his *commentarii*, Caesar with very few exceptions prefers words like "civil dissension" to "civil war," and Augustus, though mentioning "civil war" at the beginning of his *Res gestae*, otherwise avoids the word as well.

79 Livy supposedly published his books on the civil wars only after Augustus' death (*Periocha* of bk. 121), and in his young years the emperor Claudius was strongly advised to abstain from writing a history of the civil war (Suetonius, *Claudius* 41.2).

80 On Augustus' restoration of the republic, see, e.g., Millar 1973; Meier 1980, 1990a; Bleicken 1999: chs. 7–8.

81 For detailed discussion of this sphere, see recently Giovannini 2007; Low 2007.

82 For details, see Chapter 5 (Raaflaub) in this volume.

83 I suggest that this is an issue that scholars in these various disciplines should address much more directly. For valuable insights, see the essays in Raaflaub 2016.

84 See also the conclusion of Chapter 5 (Raaflaub). Some additional factors are highlighted in the conclusion of Chapter 6 (Van Wees).

Abbreviations

BMCR   *British Museum, Coins of the Roman Empire*
BNP   *Brill's New Pauly*
CAH   *Cambridge Ancient History*, 2nd edn.
LIMC   *Lexicon Iconographicum Mythologiae Classicae*
LTUR   *Lexicon Topographicum Urbis Romae*
W&P   *War and Peace* (Raaflaub 2007)
W&S   *War and Society* (Raaflaub and Rosenstein 1999)

References

Ager, S. (ed.). In preparation. *A Cultural History of Peace*, I: *Antiquity*. London.

Akar, P. 2013. *Concordia: Un idéal de la classe dirigeante romaine à la fin de la République*. Paris.

Anderson, J. C. 1984. *The Historical Topography of the Imperial Fora*. Brussels.

Beard, M. 2003. *The Parthenon*. Cambridge MA.

Beard, M. 2007. *The Roman Triumph*. Cambridge MA.

Binder, G. and Effe, B. (eds.). 1989. *Krieg und Frieden im Altertum*. Trier.

Black, J. and Green, A. 1992. *Gods, Demons and Symbols of Ancient Mesopotamia: An Illustrated Dictionary*. London.

Bleicken, J. 1999. *Augustus. Eine Biographie*. 3rd edn. Berlin.

Boedeker, D. and Raaflaub, K. (eds.). 1998. *Democracy, Empire, and the Arts in Fifth-century Athens*. Cambridge MA.

Boesche, R. 2002. *The First Great Political Realist: Kautilya and his Arthashastra*. Lanham MD.

Bottéro, J. 2001. *Religion in Ancient Mesopotamia*. Trans. T.L. Fagan. Chicago.

Briant, P. 2002. *From Cyrus to Alexander: A History of the Persian Empire*. Trans. P. T. Daniels. Winona Lake.

Brooks, L. 2014. "Corn and her story traveled: reading North American graphic texts in relation to oral traditions." In K. A. Raaflaub (ed.), *Thinking, Recording, and Writing History in the Ancient World*, 391–416. Malden MA and Oxford.

Brown, P. 2000. *Augustine of Hippo: A Biography*. Rev. edn. Berkeley.

Bryce, T. 2002. *Life and Society in the Hittite World*. Oxford.

Buchner, E. 1982. *Die Sonnenuhr des Augustus*. Mainz.

Burkert, W. 1985. *Greek Religion*. Cambridge MA.

Camp, J. M. 2001. *The Archaeology of Athens*. New Haven.

Carrasco, D. 1999. *City of Sacrifice: The Aztec Empire and the Role of Violence in Civilization*. Boston.

Chanteur, J. 1992. *From War to Peace*. Trans. S. A. Weisz. Boulder.

Chapple, C. K. 1998. "Jainism and nonviolence." In Smith-Christopher 1998: 13–24.

Charbonneaux, J., Martin, R., and Villard, F. 1969. *Grèce classique (480–330 av. J.-C.).* Paris.

Christ, M. R. 2006. *The Bad Citizen in Classical Athens.* Cambridge.

Coarelli, F. (ed.). 2009. *Divus Vespasianus. Il bimillenario dei Flavi.* Rome.

Cohen, R. and Westbrook, R. 2008. *Isaiah's Vision of Peace in Biblical and Modern International Relations: Swords into Plowshares.* New York.

Cornell, T. J. 1995. *The Beginnings of Rome.* London.

Cornwell, H. E. 2015. "The role of the peacemakers (*Caduceatores*) in Roman attitudes to war and peace." In G. Lee, H. Whittaker, and G. Wrightson (eds.), *Ancient Warfare: Introducing Current Research*, 331–48. Cambridge.

Cornwell, H. E. In preparation. *Pax terra marique: Rhetorics of Roman Victory, 50 BC–AD 14.*

Crawford, N. C. 1994. "A security regime among democracies: cooperation among Iroquois nations." *International Organization* 48.3: 345–85.

Demont, P. 2009. *La cité grecque archaïque et classique et l'idéal de tranquillité.* Paris.

Derrett, M. and Duncan, J. 1961. "The maintenance of peace in the Hindu world: practice and theory." In Gillissen 1961–62: I. 143–77.

Derrett, M. and Duncan, J. 1973. *Dharmasastra and Juridical Literature.* Wiesbaden.

Derrett, M. and Duncan, J. 1995. *Essays in Classical and Modern Hindu Law,* I: *Dharmasastra and Related Ideas.* New Delhi.

Dueck, D. 2000. *Strabo of Amasia: A Greek Man of Letters in Augustan Rome.* London.

Ebrey, P. B. 1996. *The Cambridge Illustrated History of China.* Cambridge.

Eckstein, A. M. 2006. *Mediterranean Anarchy, Interstate War, and the Rise of Rome.* Berkeley.

J. Edmondson (ed.). 2014. *Augustus.* Edinburgh.

Fenton, W. N. 1998. *The Great Law and the Longhouse: A Political History of the Iroquois Confederacy.* Norman OK.

Fisher, N. 2000. "Hybris, revenge, and stasis in the Greek city-states." In H. Van Wees (ed.), *War and Violence in Ancient Greece*, 83–123. London and Swansea.

Flower, H. (ed.). 2004. *The Cambridge Companion to the Roman Republic.* Cambridge.

Fuchs, H. 1926. *Augustin und der antike Friedensgedanke. Untersuchungen zum neunzehnten Buch der Civitas Dei.* Berlin. 2nd ed. 1965.

Funke, P. 1980. *Homonoia und Arche. Athen und die griechische Staatenwelt vom Ende des Peloponnesischen Krieges bis zum Königsfrieden (404/3–387/6 v. Chr.).* Wiesbaden.

Fürst, A. (ed.). 2006. *Friede auf Erden? Die Weltreligionen zwischen Gewaltverzicht und Gewaltbereitschaft.* Freiburg i. Br.

Galinsky, K. 1996. *Augustan Culture.* Princeton.

Gehrke, H.-J. 1985. *Stasis. Untersuchungen zu den inneren Kriegen in den griechischen Staaten des 5. und 4. Jahrhunderts v.Chr.* Munich.

Gilissen, J. (ed.). 1961–62. *La Paix.* 2 vols. Brussels.

Giovannini, A. 2007. *Les relations entre états dans la Grèce antique du temps d'Homère à l'intervention romaine (circa 700–200 av. J.-C.).* Stuttgart.

Gordon, R. L. 2006. "Mars." *BNP* 8: 397–401.

Graeber, A. 1992. "Friedensvorstellung und Friedensbegriff bei den Griechen bis zum Peloponnesischen Krieg." *Zeitschrift für Rechtsgeschichte* 109: 116–63.

Green, P. 1996. *The Greco-Persian Wars.* Berkeley.

Greenhalgh, P. A. L. 1975. *The Year of the Four Emperors.* New York.

Grinde, D. A. 1977. *The Iroquois and the Founding of the American Nation.* San Francisco.

Grinde, D. A. and B. E. Johansen. 1995. *Exemplar of Liberty: Native America and the Evolution of Democracy.* Los Angeles.

Gruen, Erich, S. 1985. "Augustus and the ideology of war and peace." In R. Winkes (ed.), *The Age of Augustus,* 51–72. Louvain.

Gruen, Erich, S. 1990. "The imperial policy of Augustus." In Raaflaub and Toher 1990: 395–416.

Hanson, V. D. 2001. "Democratic warfare, ancient and modern." In McCann and Strauss 2001: 3–33.

Hardwick, L. 2000. "Concepts of peace." In J. Huskinson (ed.), *Experiencing Rome: Culture, Identity and Power in the Roman Empire,* 335–68. London.

Harris, W. V. and Holmes, B. (eds.). 2008. *Aelius Aristides between Greece, Rome, and the Gods.* Leiden.

Hasel, M. G. 2005. *Military Practice and Polemic: Israel's Laws of Warfare in Near Eastern Perspective.* Berrien Springs MI.

Haselberger, L. 2011. "A debate on the horologium of Augustus: controversy and clarifications." *Journal of Roman Archaeology* 24.1: 47–73. With responses and additional remarks, 74–98.

Hassig, R. 1988. *Aztec Warfare.* Norman OK.

Heslin, P. 2007. "Augustus, Domitian and the so-called Horologium Augusti." *Journal of Roman Studies* 97: 1–20.

Hogan, L. and Lehrke, D. L. (eds.). 2009. *Religion and the Politics of Peace and Conflict.* Eugene OR.

Hölkeskamp, K.-J. 2004. "Capitol, Comitium und Forum. Öffentliche Räume, sakrale Topographie und Erinnerungslandschaften in der römischen Republik." In Hölkeskamp, *Senatus Populusque Romanus. Die politische Kultur der Republik,* 137–68. Stuttgart.

Hölkeskamp, K.-J. 2006. "Der Triumph—'erinnere Dich, dass Du ein Mensch bist'." In Stein-Hölkeskamp and Hölkeskamp 2006: 258–76.

Hölscher, T. 1990. "Concordia." *LIMC* 5: 479–98.

Hölscher, T. 1998. "Images and political identity: the case of Athens." In Boedeker and Raaflaub 1998: 153–83, 384–87.

Hurwit, J. M. 2004. *The Acropolis in the Age of Pericles.* Cambridge.

Johansen, B. E. 1982. *Forgotten Founders: Benjamin Franklin, the Iroquois, and the Rationale for the American Revolution.* Ipswich MA.

Katz, B. 1985. "Varro, Sallust, and the *Pius aut de pace*." *Classica & Mediaevalia* 36: 127–58.

Kautalya. 1961. *Arthasastra.* Trans. R. Shamasastry. 7th ed. Mysore (India).

Kellum, B. 1990. "The city adorned: programmatic display at the *Aedes Concordiae Augustae.*" In Raaflaub and Toher 1990: 276–307.

Kent, R. G. 1953. *Old Persian: Grammar, Texts, Lexicon.* 2nd ed. New Haven.

Kern, M. 2008. "Announcements from the mountains: the stele inscriptions of the Qin first emperor." In F.-H Mutschler and A. Mittag (eds.), *Conceiving Empire: China and Rome Compared*, 217–40. Oxford.

Klein, R. 1981. *Die Romrede des Aelius Aristides.* Darmstadt.

Kulikowski, M. 2007. *Rome's Gothic Wars.* Cambridge.

Laufs, J. 1973. *Der Friedensgedanke bei Augustinus.* Wiesbaden.

Lewis, M. E. 1990. *Sanctioned Violence in Early China.* Albany NY.

Lewis, M. E. 1999. "Warring States political history." In Loewe and Shaughnessy 1999: 587–649.

Lewis, M. E. 2007. *The Early Chinese Empires: Qin and Han.* Cambridge MA.

Lind, Millard, C. 1980. *Yahweh is a Warrior.* Scottdale PA.

Linderski, J. 2007. "Pax deorum (deum)." *BNP* 10: 659–60.

Lintott, A. 1982. *Violence, Civil Strife and Revolution in the Classical City (750–330 BC).* Baltimore.

Lobur, J. A. 2008. *Consensus, Concordia and the Formation of Roman Imperial Ideology.* London.

Loewe, M. and Shaughnessy, E. L. (eds.). 1999. *The Cambridge History of Ancient China: From the Origins of Civilization to 221 B.C.* Cambridge.

Longman III, T. and Reid, D. G. 1995. *God is a Warrior.* Grand Rapids MI.

Low, P. 2007. *Interstate Relations in Classical Greece.* Cambridge.

Luce, T.J. 1990. "Livy, Augustus, and the Forum Romanum." In Raaflaub and Toher 1990: 123–38. Repr. in Edmondson 2009: 399–415.

Lun, T. W. 1998. "Subverting hatred: peace and nonviolence in Confucianism and Daoism." In Smith-Christopher 1998: 49–66.

Mann, B. and Fields, J. L. 1997. "A sign in the sky: dating the league of the Haudenosaunee." *American Indian Culture and Research Journal* 21.2: 105–63.

Manuwald, B. 1979. *Cassius Dio und Augustus.* Stuttgart.

McCann, D. R. and Strauss, B. S. (eds.). 2001. *War and Democracy: A Comparative Study of the Korean War and the Peloponnesian War.* Armonk NY.

McIntosh, J. R. 2000. *A Peaceful Realm: The Rise and Fall of the Indus Civilization.* Boulder.

Meier, C. 1980. "Augustus. Die Begründung der Monarchie als Wiederherstellung der Republik." In Meier, *Die Ohmacht des allmächigen Dictators Caesar*, 225–87. Frankfurt/Main.

Meier, C. 1990a. "C.Caesar Divi Filius and the formation of the alternative in Rome." In Raaflaub and Toher 1990: 54–70.

Meier, C. 1990b. "Die Rolle des Krieges im klassischen Athen." *Historische Zeitschrift* 251: 555–605.

Meiggs, R. 1972. *The Athenian Empire.* Oxford.

Meyer, M. (ed.). 2008. *Friede: eine Spurensuche*. Vienna.

Millar, F. 2002. "Triumvirate and principate." In Millar, *The Roman Republic and the Augustan Revolution*, 241–70. Chapel Hill. Also in Edmondson 2009: 60–89.

Miller, P. D. 1973. *The Divine Warrior in Early Israel*. Cambridge MA.

Montanari, F. 2004. "Demetrios of Magnesia." *BNP* 4: 255.

Müller, M. 2009. "Facing up to cruelty." *Bulletin of the Australian Centre for Egyptology* 20: 115–42.

Munn, M. 2000. *The School of History: Athens in the Age of Socrates*. Berkeley.

Nardin, T. (ed.). 1996. *The Ethics of War and Peace: Religious and Secular Perspectives*. Princeton.

Nivison, D. S. 1999. "The classical philosophical writings." In Loewe and Shaughnessy 1999: 745–812.

Osborne, R. 1994. "Democracy and imperialism in the Panathenaic procession: the Parthenon frieze in its context." In W.D.E. Coulson et al. (eds.), *The Archaeology of Athens and Attica under the Democracy*, 143–50. Oxford.

Parker, A. C. 1968. "The constitution of the Five Nations." In W. Fenton (ed.), *Parker on the Iroquois*, Book Three. Syracuse.

Parker, A. C. 1989. *Seneca Myths and Folk Tales*. Ed. W. Fenton. Lincoln NE.

Parker, R. 1996. *Athenian Religion: A History*. Oxford.

Pines, Y., von Falkenhausen, L., Shelach, G., and Yates, R. D. S. (eds.). 2013. *Birth of an Empire: The State of Qin Revisited*. Berkeley.

Portal, J. (ed.). 2007. *The First Emperor: China's Terracotta Army*. Cambridge MA.

Price, J. 2001. *Thucydides and Internal War*. Cambridge.

Raaflaub, K. A. 1994. "Democracy, power, and imperialism in fifth-century Athens." In J. Peter Euben, J. R. Wallach, and J. Ober (eds.), *Athenian Political Thought and the Reconstruction of American Democracy*, 103–46. Ithaca NY.

Raaflaub, K. A. 1996. "Born to be wolves? Origins of Roman imperialism." In R. W. Wallace, and E. M. Harris (eds.), *Transitions to Empire: Essays in Greco-Roman History, 360–146 B.C., in Honor of E. Badian*, 273–314. Norman OK.

Raaflaub, K. A. 1999. "[War and society in] archaic and classical Greece." In *W&S* 129–61.

Raaflaub, K. A. 2001. "Father of all, destroyer of all: war in late fifth-century Athenian discourse and ideology." In McCann and Strauss 2001: 307–56.

Raaflaub, K. A. 2004. *The Discovery of Freedom in Ancient Greece*. First Engl. ed., revised and updated from the German. Trans. R. Franciscono. Chicago.

Raaflaub, K. A. (ed.). 2007. *War and Peace in the Ancient World*. Malden MA & Oxford.

Raaflaub, K. A. 2009. "Conceptualizing and theorizing peace in the ancient Greek world." *Transactions of the American Philological Association* 139: 225–50.

Raaflaub, K. A. 2011. "Peace as the highest end and good? The role of peace in Roman thought and politics." In G. Moosbauer and R. Wiegels (eds.), *Fines imperii— imperium sine fine: Römische Okkupations- und Grenzpolitik im frühen Prinzipat*, 323–38. Rahden Westfalen.

Raaflaub, K. A. 2015. "The politics of peace cults in ancient Greece and Rome." In T. R. Kämmerer and M. Kõiv (eds.), *Cultures in Comparison: Religion and Politics in Ancient Mediterranean Regions*, 103–29. Münster.

Raaflaub, K. A. (ed.). 2016. *The Adventure of the Human Intellect: Self, Society, and the Divine in Ancient World Cultures*. Malden MA and Oxford.

Raaflaub, K. A., Ober, J. and Wallace, R. W. 2007. *Origins of Democracy in Ancient Greece*. With chapters by Cartledge, P. and Farrar, C. Berkeley.

Raaflaub, K. A. and Rosenstein, N. (eds.). 1999. *War and Society in the Ancient and Medieval Worlds*. Washington D.C.

Raaflaub, K. A. and Toher, M. (eds.). 1990. *Between Republic and Empire: Interpretations of Augustus and His Principate*. Berkeley.

Rawson, E. 1985. *Intellectual Life in the Late Roman Republic*. Baltimore.

Rich, J. W. 2003. "Augustus, war and peace." In L. de Blois, P. Erdkamp, O. Hekster, et al. (eds.), *The Representation and Perception of Roman Imperial Power*, 329–57. Amsterdam. Repr. in Edmondson 2009: 137–64.

Richardson Jr, L. 1992. *A New Topographical Dictionary of Ancient Rome*. Baltimore.

de Romilly, J. 1972. "Vocabulaire et propagande ou les premiers emplois du mot *homonoia*." In A. Ernout (ed.), *Mélanges de linguistique et de philologie grecques offerts à Pierre Chantraine*, 199–209. Paris.

Rosenstein, N. and Morstein-Marx, R. (eds.). 2006. *A Companion to the Roman Republic*. Malden MA and Oxford.

Sakellariou, M. 1996. *Colloque international: Démocratie athénienne et culture*. Athens.

Schachter, A. 2002. "Ares." *BNP* 1: 1047–50.

Scheibler, I. 1984. "Götter des Friedens in Hellas und Rom." *Antike Welt* 15.1: 39–57.

Scherf, J. 2007. "Pax." *BNP* 10: 657–59.

Schütz, M. 1990. "Zur Sonnenuhr des Augustus auf dem Marsfeld." *Gymnasium* 97: 432–57.

Shapiro, H. A. 1990. "Homonoia." *LIMC* 5: 476–79.

Shenondoah, J. and George, D. M. 1998. *Sky Woman: Legends of the Iroquois*. Santa Fe.

Simon, E. 1967. *Ara Pacis Augustae*. Tübingen.

Simon, E. 1984. "Mars." *LIMC* 2: 505–59.

Simon, E. 1986. "Eirene." *LIMC* 3: 700–5.

Simon, E. 1988. *Eirene und Pax. Friedensgöttinnen in der Antike*. SB Wiss. Ges. Joh. Wolfg. Goethe-Univ. Frankfurt/Main 24.3. Frankfurt/Main.

Simon, E.1994. "Pax." *LIMC* 7: 204–12.

Smith, A. C. 2011. *Polis and Personification in Classical Athenian Art*. Leiden.

Smith-Christopher, D. L. (ed.). 1998. *Subverting Hatred: The Challenge of Nonviolence in Religious Traditions*. Maryknoll NY.

Sordi, M. (ed.). 1985. *La pace nel mondo antico*. Milan.

Stafford, E. 2000. *Worshipping Virtues: Personification and the Divine in Ancient Greece*. London and Swansea.

Stein-Hölkeskamp, E. and Hölkeskamp, K.-J. (eds.). 2006. *Erinnerungsorte der Antike: die römische Welt*. Munich.

Stern, G. 2016. "The new cult of Pax Augusta 13 BC–AD 14." Forthcoming in *Acta Antiqua Academiae Scientiarum Hungaricae* 56.

Swartley, W. M. 1996. "War and peace in the new testament." In W. Haase (ed.), *Aufstieg und Niedergang der römischen Welt*, II.26.3: 2299–2408. Berlin.

Thapar, R. 1961. *Aśoka and the Decline of the Mauryas*. London.

Thapar, R. 2002. *Early India from the Origins to AD 1300*. Berkeley.

Thériault, G. 1996. *Le culte d'Homonoia dans les cités grecques*. Lyon and Quebec.

Tiesler, V and Cucina, A. 2007. *New Perspectives on Human Sacrifice and Ritual Body Treatment in Ancient Maya Society*. New York.

Tooker, E. 1990. "The United States constitution and the Iroquois League." In J. A. Clifton (ed.), *The Invented Indian: Cultural Fictions and Government Policies*, 107–28. New Brunswick NJ.

Travlos, J. 1971. *Pictorial Dictionary of Ancient Athens*. New York.

Tritle, L. A. 2013. "Democracy at war." In J. P. Arnason, K. A. Raaflaub, and P. Wagner (eds.), *The Greek Polis and the Invention of Democracy*, 298–320. Malden MA and Oxford.

Van Wees, H. (ed.). 2000. *War and Violence in Ancient Greece*. London and Swansea.

Van Wees, H. 2001. "War and peace in ancient Greece." In A. V. Hartmann and B. Heuser (eds.), *War, Peace and World Orders in European History*, 33–47. London.

Von Rad, G. 1991. *Holy War in Ancient Israel*. Grand Rapids MI.

Walter, U. 2004. Memoria *und* res publica. *Zur Geschichtskultur im republikanischen Rom*. Frankfurt am Main.

Weinstock, S. 1960. "Pax and the 'Ara Pacis'." *Journal of Roman Studies* 50: 44–58.

Wengst, K. 1987. *Pax Romana and the Peace of Jesus Christ*. Trans. John Bowden. Philadelphia.

Whitaker, J. 2016. "Ancient India." Forthcoming in B. Meissner, K. A. Raaflaub, and R. Yates (eds.), *The Cambridge History of War,* I. Cambridge.

Wiedemann, T. E. J. 1996. "From Nero to Vespasian." *CAH* X: 256–82.

Wilker, J. (ed.). 2012a. "Introduction." In Wilker 2012b: 11–24.

Wilker, J. (ed.). 2012b. *Maintaining Peace and Interstate Stability in Archaic and Classical Greece*. Mainz.

Wood, F. 2007. *The First Emperor of China*. London.

Wood, F. 2008. *China's First Emperor and His Terracotta Warriors*. New York.

Woolf, G. 1993. "Roman peace." In J. Rich and G. Shipley (eds.), *War and Society in the Roman World*, 171–94. London.

Wünsche, R. 2007. *Glyptothek, Munich: Masterpieces of Greek and Roman Sculpture*. Trans. Rodney Batstone. Munich.

Young, N. J. (ed.). 2010. *The Oxford International Encyclopedia of Peace*. Oxford.

Zampaglione, G. 1973. *The Idea of Peace in Antiquity*. Trans. Richard Dunn. Notre Dame.

Zanker, P. 1988. *The Power of Images in the Age of Augustus*. Trans. Alan Shapiro. Ann Arbor.

Zuntz, G. 1955. *The Political Plays of Euripides*. Manchester.

2

Concepts of Peace in Ancient Egypt

SUSANNE BICKEL

If we inquire about the conditions that can lead a society to develop a concept of peace or an explicit peace discourse, it seems that at least two factors need to be considered. A society can develop a certain predisposition to reflecting on peace in the frame of its general world view, in the context of cosmology or theology, and in the sphere of moral values and its vision of ideal human conduct. A society can also work out a peace discourse in reaction to a particular stimulation or out of necessity to engage in such reflection. These two approaches correspond to an ideal or principle of peace on the religious and conceptual level on the one hand and, on the other, to the possibility of a peace discourse on a political or social level. The two factors may also be interdependent: the political discourse of a specific culture relies greatly on its conceptual predispositions and on the available terminology. Yet a successful political concept can also have an impact on, and shape, religious conceptions and actions as well as the semantics of terminology.

Peace can be a value or condition opposed either to war and conflict or to aggressiveness and violence. It can be negotiated and agreed upon by two previously opposed parties, or it can be imposed and enforced by one party on the other.

Peace in the Ancient World: Concepts and Theories, First Edition. Edited by Kurt A. Raaflaub.
© 2016 John Wiley & Sons, Inc. Published 2016 by John Wiley & Sons, Inc.

It is important to stress that peace, although seemingly obvious, is neither a universal and uniform concept nor the result of natural aspiration; rather, it is a cultural product. Conceptions and valuations of peace as a cultural phenomenon vary greatly from one culture to another and from one period to another. Our contemporary definitions do therefore not necessarily apply to other historical or cultural entities.

It is the aim of the following investigation to examine ancient Egyptian conceptions of peace within two different frames: world view and cultural valuation on the one hand, and political behavior and historical reality on the other. It will become apparent that these two levels of reasoning were intensely interwoven but did not always coincide.

The Egyptian World View: Conflict and Equilibrium

The ancient Egyptian world view was largely unprepared to consider a state without opposition. From the earliest periods, antagonism was an essential aspect of the Egyptian comprehension of the world and seen as a major force driving the universe as well as society. Myths relate this view in various ways. The creation of the universe was initially imagined as an essentially nonviolent process of diversification. The concept of an original fight between the creator god and an opposing power emerged only in the first millennium BCE. Much earlier, however, from the late third or early second millennium, the two principal antagonistic factors that existed within the created world were mythologically described as the serpent demon Apophis who embodied a permanent threat to creation, and the god Seth who represented all sorts of trouble within divine or human society.

Apophis was not seen as a deity with a specific character but as a mere power that constantly sought to oppose the principles of creation and the cosmic cycles.[1] The creative and constructive forces—embodied by the sun god and his entourage—had to repel this powerful opponent in a common and permanent effort. Apophis's attack could only be countered by utmost violence and magic power. Mythology situated this clash in the middle of the night, at the turning point toward the rebirth of the sun and the beginning of a new day. Apophis was cruelly defeated every night, but never annihilated. His role was to provoke a new creative effort, to trigger new cosmogonic momentum that guaranteed the permanence of creative power and of the universe's structures and cycles. This mythical conflict situation could not be settled or pacified but had to be fought out again and again: as a permanent hostile threat, it was part of the world order and of its regenerating processes.

Seth is a much more complex divine personality, as ambiguous and versatile as human nature.[2] He stands in the center of the most elaborate, multifunctional, and prevalent mythological complex of ancient Egypt. From various textual sources, we gain the following main outline: eager for power, Seth had murdered his brother, Osiris, who was the ruler over the world. Once Osiris's posthumous son Horus had grown up, a long struggle for the succession in divine kingship began. The young and vulnerable Horus opposed the strong and experienced Seth. The myth questions the justification of two models of succession, the generally accepted concept of patrilinear succession versus that of collateral succession, which in this particular case also corresponds to the principle of "might is right." The assembly of all gods and goddesses tried to arbitrate the dispute but remained undecided on the issue of legitimacy. The myth describes two methods by which the conflict was carried out. One is the direct physical confrontation of the two opponents, narrated in many phases of combat, sometimes with crude details and varying results, the wit of the younger contender often winning over the strength of the older. The other consists of endless deliberations of the gods' assembly, as in a trial. In many sources that refer to the myth, the violent and the argumentative approach are interwoven.

In the myth, neither fights nor discussions produced a clear-cut and definitive solution. Finally, the gods decided to acknowledge Horus as victor and successor in the kingship, without, however, declaring Seth a loser. He was offered various compensations, such as the kingship over foreign countries or even a kind of partition of power in Egypt. He was explicitly integrated into the structure of divine governance: his strength and aggressiveness were needed. Horus and Seth as representatives of royal power and of Egypt as a political unit were set in a subtle balance of complementarity and productive antagonism. The final result, which the myth presented as a model for royal governance on earth, was, however, not peaceful coexistence but an equilibrium through tension.

Cosmic and social order were both perceived as fundamentally unstable and exposed to disruptive conflicts. The created order constantly and actively needed to be kept in balance. The principle that was able to maintain or reestablish the equilibrium was called Maat. Maat represented order and justice as well as cohesion within the universe and society. Personified as a goddess, Maat came into being, according to myth, at the outset of creation, parallel to the principle of Life.[3] As the basic condition of all existence and coexistence, she personified values of paramount importance to Egyptian thinking. Maat represented the concept of vertical solidarity between gods and men and of horizontal solidarity within society.[4] Maat was a dynamic principle: it had to be realized actively by the king and all humans in order to guarantee the functioning of the created world structures. Through the realization of Maat, the disruptive forces, often represented by Seth, could be neutralized.

As a moral value and factor of social cohesion, including aspects such as justice, harmony, and respectful behavior, the concept of Maat could come close to a modern concept of peace. However, nonviolence and nonaggression were not its main concerns. Justice and cohesion were defined within a cultural context that considered outside opposition inherent in the world's and society's structures and explicitly allowed violent behavior to counter this opposition. In certain political circumstances, violent actions and the repression of opponents were explicitly justified as being in conformity with Maat.

As the cosmos and the divine sphere were persistently exposed to disruptive and destructive forces, so was the world that men expected to enter after death. This was no paradise of peace and harmony but a world full of dangers and aggressive and malevolent opponents where the deceased constantly had to reaffirm their status and rightfulness. Men hoped to be admitted close to the great gods by proving their moral conduct on earth. The proximity to the sun god Ra and to the king of the netherworld Osiris would place the deceased in the center of the regenerative forces and set them in a favorable position to fight for the realization of Maat, who kept the universe in balance.

Tension held together the world as the ancient Egyptians perceived it; antagonism was constitutive of the world order. Fighting out this intrinsic antagonism and gaining control over the opposing forces was a means of realizing Maat. This fight set free a new creative impetus and a state of cohesion, which could only endure through new conflict. These general concepts, through which the functioning of the cosmos was apprehended, were also transposed, as will be shown below, into the earthly political sphere.

The dynamic character of the principle of Maat and the concept of cyclical renewal through tension and conflict left little room for the development of a more static concept of peace. Peace as opposed to aggression and violence did not fit into the ancient Egyptian world view, since the latter were considered essential factors of the creation's continuity.

Peacefulness as Moral Value

This general world view, which considered aggression a necessary impulse, was not applicable to social relations and even stands in clear contrast to moral values such as they were taught—at least among the elite—and are known to us through literary texts, the so-called "teachings." Here, the wise man is portrayed as a silent, respectful, and peaceful man. Arrogance and aggressiveness are assessed very negatively: they characterize the uneducated man or uncontrolled temperament. Nonviolence was certainly a social ideal and moral value. The pupil was not instructed, however, always to be silent but rather to keep his self-control and to respect the social status conventions even when dealing with a hot-tempered and aggressive man. The ideal of a man's self-control and well-tempered character could be referred to with composite expressions that contain terms related to the semantic field of peace: a man can be described as "peaceful-hearted" or as "one who pacifies/satisfies the heart" (*ḥtp jb*) of his superior, of the king, or the gods.[5]

For instance, the teaching of Ptahhotep from the beginning of the second millennium says:

> People's schemes do not prevail,
> God's command is what prevails;
> Live in the midst of peacefulness,
> What they give comes by itself.[6]

The advice given here implies a state of internal peacefulness based on confidence in divine guidance and a certain distance from human affairs and their general importance. Such internal peacefulness appears as a personal goal of instructed men; it was also implicitly considered a reward for moral and pious behavior. A roughly contemporaneous teaching states: "Open is the tent for the silent one, wide is the place for the peaceful one."[7] Aggressiveness was considered a positive quality only in a king and only in certain instances; in all other humans it was valued very negatively.

The gods also grant peacefulness or reward the peaceful man. Thus, for instance, Ptah "gives life to the peaceful one, death to the criminal."[8] In the inscription on their funerary stela, two brothers express their hope to receive offerings in the netherworld "when they implore peace from Osiris."[9] What they hope to obtain is a status in their future existence that will keep them from being attacked by gods and dangerous beings of the netherworld. As will be seen, the same expression "to implore peace" has an eminently political meaning in other types of contemporaneous New Kingdom sources.

These examples show clearly that "peace" designates a personal attitude as well as a state of being. It refers to nonaggressiveness as opposed to the behavior of the hot-tempered or the criminal, and it also describes the condition of being safe or protected from attack. The moral concept of peace therefore had both active and passive implications.

Cultural Valuation of War and Peace

The impact of war can vary from individual distress and grief to collective and cultural shock. Whereas in the former case the social or political consequences are minimal, in the latter these can comprise massive collective trauma and stimulate far-reaching reactions. Even the threat of a major war that recalls past experiences can prompt such reactions. Intensified reflection on the usefulness of war and a new valuation of peace might result from such trauma, prompting the development of a peace discourse. This seems to have occurred in fourth-century Greece with the emergence of the concept of "common peace" (*koinē eirēnē*) in an effort to avoid continuing major conflicts.[10] In the more recent past, the Moscow-Washington hotline might be considered a similar posttraumatic and preventive measure.

In the ancient Egyptian world view and state conception, war was considered a necessary action to maintain balance in the created order. In very explicit terms, the king's role as guarantor of state order was analogized to the sun god's role as guarantor of cosmic order and connected with the inevitability— that in turn was mythologically reinforced—of subduing opposing forces. The necessity of regular military campaigns was hardly ever questioned. Very few texts thus reflect a critical or even negative attitude towards warfare. Hardly any extant source can be considered a factual report on military events, since all texts are profoundly marked by the underlying conceptions of world view and royal discourse, the validity of which was never overtly questioned during the long Egyptian history.[11]

According to the definition of his ritual and political roles, the king was considered brave and victorious; because of his strength and superiority, he was regularly associated with the lion or with the bull. Accordingly, bravery as a personal value was less central in Egyptian than in other societies; even men with long military careers generally remain somewhat modest in emphasizing their accomplishments and rather stress their fidelity and proximity to the king.[12] Victory was always the king's success; his army at best contributed to it.[13]

The Ramesside period (thirteenth to eleventh century BCE) was an era of renewed and intensified imperialism when Egypt sought to establish control over extended territories in Western Asia. An increasingly massive army was led—often by the kings themselves—to regular campaigns through these regions.[14] Royal ideological discourse focused most intensely on the king's military success as proof of his efficiency in maintaining the world order and as illustration of the divine protection he enjoyed, which in turn was taken to demonstrate the legitimacy of Pharaonic rule. During the same period, a series of texts, used mainly in the training of young scribes, developed an extremely negative picture of the soldier's profession and quality of life. His fate is depicted as so painful that "he is dead while yet alive."[15] Although these texts sound as if they stood in sharp opposition to the official representation of war as a necessity and blessing, they do in fact neither reflect an alternative to official ideology nor any antimilitaristic attitude or implicit appeal for peace. This literary tradition essentially devalued the profession of the soldier in order to enhance the advantages of being a scribe, although the two professions were not on the same social level and probably rarely posed real alternatives.[16]

Whether or not peace was valued depended entirely on the context. Modesty, a cool-tempered character, and peacefulness were paramount ideals of the educated man; they granted success on the level of social relations. On the political level, however, during most periods of Egyptian history there was no concept that attributed high value to a peaceful attitude towards neighbors. World view and economic interests rather favored a dominant and militant approach to external relations.

Terminology

The Egyptian vocabulary has no word for "war"; it uses more specific words for campaign, battle, army, etc. It also lacks a word corresponding precisely to the modern concept of "peace;" terms generally translated with "peace" refer basically to notions like quietness, satisfaction, or mercy.[17] There are mainly two word stems that in certain instances come close to the notion of peace: *hrw* (*heru*) and *htp* (*hotep*). Both can be used to designate a state opposed to "fighting" and "agitation."

The stem *hrw* basically means "to be quiet," "to be content." Its nominal derivatives (*hrt, hrw-jb*) mean "quietness," but also "peace, peacefulness." In the teaching of the sage Ptahhotep (mentioned above), this is the word used to recommend peaceful behavior and inner peacefulness as a moral value or at least a recommendable way of living. In its causative form (*shr* –"make quiet") the word can take on a political dimension, especially when it is used in royal names that have a programmatic character. The name "Who pacifies the land" was used particularly in periods striving for the reunification of the country after periods of fragmentation or foreign occupation and the reestablishment of political unity after civil wars. Antef I of the eleventh and Kamose of the seventeenth dynasties took this name to express the state of contentment and (slightly anticipated) recovery of interior peace.[18] Similar names with *shtp* were used by Teti, Amenemhat I, and Piye who all stood at the beginning of a new dynasty or even a new era.

The word *shr* is frequently used to describe royal action and also to qualify prominent men who make the land of Egypt, a city, or humankind content and peaceful. It does not necessarily mean to bring peace after a conflict, but rather to guarantee a state of quietness and bliss. The pharaoh Hatshepsut "is the one who pacifies/makes content the land through her words."[19] The expression can also be used in more bellicose contexts in the sense of "keep quiet" or "enforce peace;" thus, in the prophecy of Neferty, the powerful and protective uraeus-snake of the future king will "keep quiet (*shr*) the wrecked-ones, when one will build the 'wall of the prince' so that the Levantines will not enter Egypt."[20] In a religious text the god Thot "imposes peace (*shr*) upon the two fighters [Horus and Seth] in their moment of fury."[21]

The polysemous word stem *ḥtp* (*ḥtpw, ḥtpt*) can take the sense of "peace," with several nuances. Very often it has the concrete meaning of subsistence or offering of provisions. It thus basically describes the state of well-being, subjective satisfaction, and peacefulness achieved in gods and men through the enjoyment of food. It can consequently also take the meaning of "to rest, to lie down." The word appears in the opening of every divine or funerary offering formula. "To satisfy" or "to bring about a state of well-being" (the causative form *sḥtp*) is the purpose of many rituals, specifically those performed for goddesses feared for becoming furious and destructive. They had to be brought to or kept in a mood of satisfaction, equilibrium, and peace, a state that was ritually achieved not only through food but also through flowers and music. In addition to this sense of physical contentment, the word also has the meaning of peacefulness or peace: "The sky is at peace, the earth is in joy, for they have seen that the king has set right (Maat) in the place of evil."[22]

Beginning with Old Kingdom texts from the end of the third millennium, *ḥtp* is used in a political and military context, mainly to express the state of the army's satisfaction and integrity after battle. This can take the form of a refrain as in the following victory song:[23]

> The army has returned in peace,
> After having annihilated the sand dwellers (beduins).
> The army has returned in peace,
> After having plundered the land of the sand dwellers…

The word *ḥtp* can also be opposed to the notion of violence. In a royal eulogy, one of the benefits of the accession of Ramesses IV is that "those who were agitated in this country have become peaceful (*m ḥtp.y*)."[24] In a calendar of lucky and unlucky days that are mostly characterized by mythological features, a specific day is "good, good, good, the peace-(making) of Horus and Seth has been ordered."[25] The word *ḥtp* here describes a state that is opposed to conflict and combat, and guarantees both parties a well-balanced relationship.

In the middle of the second millennium, the word also entered political contexts and descriptions of international relations. Several expressions like "to implore peace" (*dbḥ ḥtp(w)*), "to make peace" (*jrj ḥtp*) or "to offer peace" (*rdj ḥtp*) are ascribed to foreign and subdued areas and refer to a unilateral concept of peace, the terms of which were dictated by Egypt as the stronger party. This concept also underlies statements such as the following in a description of foreigners bringing tribute to Ramesses II: "the great ones of all inaccessible and unknown countries came in order to pacify (*sḥtp*) the heart of the strong bull [that is, the pharaoh] and to implore peace from him (*dbḥ ḥtpw ḥr=f*)."[26] The same text states "that all foreign countries are under peace" (*ḥrj ḥtpw*), a phrase that, through its preposition, clearly indicates that the subdued were under a regime imposed by the victor.

During the Ramesside period, the Semitic word "*shalom/salam*" (in Egyptian group writing, *š3-r3-m3*) was imported and used exclusively in political contexts, mostly to refer to the surrender of opponents in a military conflict. In the text commemorating the first Libyan war of Ramesses III, the losers "sue for peace (*shalom*), coming humbly through fear of him [pharaoh]".[27]

In most political contexts the words chosen describe a state of more or less nonviolent but definitely unequal relations, an agreement of mercy against obedience. During the New Kingdom, "peace" designated a political situation that Egypt granted to subdued cities and countries in exchange of well-defined economic advantages. This concept probably came close in several respects to the much later *Pax Romana*.[28]

That there was no word in the Egyptian language of all periods covering the double sense of nonviolence and personal interior peace is demonstrated by the fact that the Coptic translations of biblical texts, as well as Coptic funerary inscriptions, always adopted the Greek loan word *eirēnē*.[29]

Internal Strife and its Conceptual Treatment

Several periods of Egyptian history saw the disintegration of the central royal power and the emergence of competing regional centers. Those are the so-called intermediate periods (the first circa 2125–1975, the second circa 1760–1520, the third circa 1075–723). Territorial and political disintegration also prompted the emergence of regional leaders and their armies.

Liberated from centralized royal guidance and its strong dependence on decorum and ideology, these intermediate periods were all very innovative in cultural expression. They were not always characterized by political and social turmoil, but wars between various regions of Egypt were frequent. These civil wars were struggles for power led by regional chiefs or kinglets, but in their final phase and in the view of the winner, they appeared as wars of reunification, reintegrating the entire territorial state and inaugurating a new era of overall royal power.

The civil wars did not fit into the conceptual scheme of the divinely protected pharaoh repelling evils and outside threats against creation and order. None of the regional chiefs and kinglets could legitimize his ambitions within the framework of traditional cosmology and royal ideology—a conceptual framework that applied unquestionably only to the Egyptian territory and population as a whole. Participants in those wars do not, in their extant monuments, reflect on the question of civil war; they speak of battles and of loyalty towards their leaders. By contrast, in the eras following the first and second intermediate periods, we find profound concerns with the phenomenon of civil war in literary compositions that dealt explicitly with the issue.[30] According to the ideal of a unified political and cultural entity, kept in balance by Maat thanks to the joined efforts of the king, of humankind, and the gods, a different reality could only be explained as a form of chaos characterized by the absence of divine protection and intervention. The lack of territorial unity maintained by a common ruler was interpreted as the gods' withdrawal from Egypt and the cessation of the principle of Maat. "Ra had turned his back to Egypt," "they had governed without Ra," are expressions to characterize *a posteriori* the epochs of division and civil war—which also brought up questions about human responsibility in this kind of conditions.

In sum, whereas aggression against neighboring areas was entirely compatible with the Egyptian world view, and even a duty of the king, internal conflict could not be integrated into the concept of world order. It was considered a phenomenon outside the created and divinely ruled sphere, a phase during which the gods were absent.

Political Behavior and Foreign Policy

Representations of aggression and domination occur already in Neolithic iconography on several types of objects. The demonstration of force and the oppression of enemies were central elements of cultural expression even before the time of the constitution of the Egyptian territorial state at the beginning of

the third millennium.[31] The rhetoric of power and dominion remained fundamental throughout Pharaonic culture. Gradually, however, during the third
millennium, royal ideology began to concentrate entirely on the repression of
opposition from outside its territorial borders. Internal opposition soon became
a taboo subject, whereas dealing with external foes emerged as one of the principal royal actions: the emblematic expression of the king's sacred function.
The king's subduing of foreign enemies was conceptually equaled to the sun
god's repelling all menace to creation and order. Egypt's neighboring peoples
were assimilated to the mythical threat to the divine world order. With an
aggressive attitude the king had to assure his control over all potentially dangerous areas beyond Egypt's natural borders.

This ideology led to an utterly ambivalent attitude towards neighboring
populations. During most periods, the integration of foreigners into all hierar-
chic levels of Egyptian society is amply attested. At the same time, Egyptian
troops regularly undertook campaigns into the Levant and Nubia in order to
seize raw materials and manpower, or to impose the regular payment of commodities in the form of tribute. Until the middle of the second millennium this
policy did not constitute any major risk for Egypt nor require massive military
actions. With relatively small armies, composed partly of Egyptians partly of
Nubian mercenaries, Egypt secured an uncontested hegemony over the loosely
organized eastern and southern neighbors. Some of the dominated areas, such
as Nubia, were kept under permanent military control and integrated into the
Egyptian administrative system. Most Near Eastern areas were not occupied
militarily and administratively, while the Egyptians aimed primarily at imposing
control, obedience, and payments. Their motives were both economical and
ideological.

Keeping the ever-present menace off Egypt's borders was one of the pharaoh's main duties. The boundary stela Sesostris III erected at his southern
frontier in Semna illustrates this ideological scheme: Sesostris is

> merciless to the foe who attacks him,
> one who attacks him who would attack,
> who stops when one stops,
> who replies to a matter as benefits it.
> To stop when attacked is to make bold the foe's heart,
> attack is valor, retreat is cowardice,
> a coward is he who is driven from his border.
> Since the Nubian listens to the word of mouth,
> to answer him is to make him retreat.
> Attack him, he will turn his back,
> retreat, he will start attacking.

> They are not people one respects,
> they are wretches, craven-hearted.
> My majesty has seen it, it is not an untruth.[32]

In Egyptian understanding as reflected in royal discourse, these campaigns against Nubia and the Levant were essentially defensive or preventive: they aimed at countering an intensely felt menace. Based on conceptions of world view and religion, and certainly also on political interest, the *topos* of attacks from neighboring populations was constantly propagated as endangering Egyptian stability and order.

The prevailing cultural setting defined Egypt as a peaceful and divinely organized country regularly attacked by wicked enemies but protected by a powerful godlike king. The following passages of a rock stela near Aswan illustrate this world view:

> His majesty was in Thebes in the precinct of Karnak, his arms being pure in divine purity after he had satisfied (*sḥtp*) his father Amon... Then one came to announce to his majesty: "The Nubian has come down to the area of Wawat having planned rebellion against Egypt. He has associated all vagabonds and rebels of another country." Then the king proceeded in peace to the temple in the morning to bring great offerings to the father who had created his perfection... He ordered to prepare the army immediately and sent it in bravery and strength. Then his majesty set out to slay the one who attacked him in Nubia, being brave in his golden ship like Ra when he places himself into the morning bark... the king sailed upstream like Orion...[33]

Warfare was not only part of the king's duties, it also had a ritual character, being executed regularly and following a predefined scheme of roles and attitudes. In the passage just quoted, the identification of the king's military journey with the sun god Ra's travel in the solar bark is explicit and the reader would have understood that, like Ra, the king will successfully slay his foes and guarantee the created order. During the New Kingdom, a solemn military campaign immediately followed the coronation of most kings in their first regnal year.[34]

In real politics, occasional intrusions of Nubians in the South or Bedouins in the East Delta would probably have been of little concern to Egypt's security and culture. Moreover, the presence of foreign people (such as Palestinian shepherds in the Delta marshes) was often tolerated, or even actively favored (as in the case of the settlement of Nubian soldiers in Upper Egypt). Yet the justification to set out for war was sought neither in actual political situations nor in historical models and arguments.[35] War was perceived as an obvious and necessary aspect of royal action undertaken in the name of the gods and for the sake of Maat and world stability. The passages cited above reflect the principle of equilibrium through tension, which underlies mythological explanations of world order. From this perspective, like creation as a whole, the land of Egypt needed attacks and conflicts in order to regenerate its strength and power. Regular attacks by external foes were constructed and their subjugation by the king staged as a ritual and conceptually essential action. In this conceptual frame and under the given political circumstances there was neither need nor reason to develop ideas of peace as an alternative to warfare.

For over a millennium, real politics seems to have corresponded to this principle. On the international political scene the dominant position of Egypt was not challenged before the second half of the second millennium. By that time, other powers arose in Western Asia that showed interest in the same areas and economic resources Egypt had so far controlled. These changed conditions necessitated the creation of a massive Egyptian army that quickly gained much social and political influence.[36] The role of the king as a warlord became central, and the successes of the frequent campaigns repelling opposing forces from Egypt turned into a major theme of cultural self-presentation and valuation, both in discourse and temple decoration. In reality, too, this issue gained increased pertinence since, for the first time in Egypt's history, the menace to its interests, though not to the country itself, became serious. The wars were no longer simple demonstrations of supremacy or easy conquests but conflicts of power over political and economic control. Some of these armed conflicts were severe, but Egypt remained largely in control of the international situation. These conditions prevailed during the eighteenth and early nineteenth dynasties (fifteenth to fourteenth century) when Thutmose III and his successors opposed the powerful kingdom of Mitanni, and Seti I contested the expansion of the Hittite empire, when conflicts were still mainly decided in uneven encounters of the Egyptian army with those of individual cities or small states that were tempted to abandon the status of Egyptian vassal.

Many inscriptions on official royal monuments commemorate the campaigns that allowed Egypt to establish and maintain its hegemony over Western Asia. Smaller opponents were forced to accept the conditions of surrender and tribute payment Egypt imposed on them in order to avoid the destruction of their city and the deportation of their population. Their acceptance was often expressed as a request for peace or an offer to make peace.

From the time of Hatshepsut, the expression "to implore peace from the king" (*dbḥ ḥtp(w)*) is frequently used of foreign regions who demonstrate their inferiority. For example, Syrian princes bring tribute to Thutmose III "to implore peace from his majesty, that the breath of life may be given to their nose."[37] In the annals relating the wars of the same king and the booty he acquired, a list mentions two towns that were seized and three other towns that "made peace" (*jrj ḥtp*). This, like the expression "to give peace," (*rdj ḥtpw*) used in similar circumstances, probably means that they offered their capitulation before being annihilated.[38] Following an attack where men and cattle were killed, "peace was offered to his majesty by this city."[39] Both parties were aware that the destruction of a city and the deportation of its surviving population were a realistic alternative. In these contexts, "peace" designated a situation of (temporary) nonviolence obtained through the political and economic surrender of the vanquished. This terminology reflects not only the uneven balance of power, but also the Egyptian ideology that presented external opponents self-evidently as the attackers and the Egyptian response as a means of restoring Maat.

Ramesses II was the first to be confronted with a potentially superior opponent. The famous battle he almost lost at Kadesh in year five (circa 1275 BCE) against the Hittite king Muwatalli became the topic of a major enterprise of ideological processing and cultural revaluation. The conflict ended sixteen years later in a remarkable international peace treaty (discussed below).[40] Merneptah, the successor of Ramesses II, had a victory over the Libyans recorded on a commemorative stela that offers an excellent example of the prevailing royal discourse. By crashing the enemy, the king pleased the gods, restored divine order on earth, and brought the surrounding populations into a state of dependence and obedience. The final section is famous for its mention of Israel but also interesting for its use of the Semitic word for peace and its clear indication of how the notion of peace was applied in ideological speech.

> The princes are prostrate saying: "Shalom!"
> Not one of the Nine Bows lifts his head:
> Tjehenu [Libya] is vanquished, Hatti at peace,
> Canaan is captive with all woe.
> Ashkalon is conquered, Gezer seized,
> Yanoam made nonexistent;
> Israel is vasted, bare of seed,
> Khor [Syria] has become a widow for Egypt,
> all the countries are at peace...[41]

The final statement, "all the countries are at peace," is rather common. To be "at peace" (*m ḥtp*) here indicates a state of surrender to the conditions imposed by Egypt.

During the first two and a half millennia of its Pharaonic history, Egypt did not suffer any international conflict on its own territory and only few serious international conflicts at all. As the leading regional power and with its ideologically driven militant attitude, Egypt carried war abroad. With the exception of some internal conflicts that, as mentioned above, were conceptualized in a very different manner and led to other types of reactions and discourses, the inhabitants of Egypt were not confronted directly with the torments of war. Losses of soldiers abroad were, overall, marginal and did not have any known social, political, or conceptual impact. There was thus little stimulation to develop a concept of peace based on parity as a political value, nor to expand on a concept that would have set two parties on an equal level, granting each party political and economic independence.

The prevailing Egyptian discourse defined peace as a state in which the opponents were vanquished, obliged to "implore peace" or to "say shalom," and made incapable, politically and economically, of constituting any kind of menace for Egypt. "All countries are at peace" means that they were overpowered and thus had to accept the imposed conditions and to refrain from "planning rebellion." According to the Egyptian world view, combat was always the reaction to an attack or "rebellion" on the part of foreign countries. At least ideally, the state of peace therefore implied that these countries would not be attacked again as long as they refrained from engaging in an attack themselves. Hence, in this context the notion of peace again contains both an active and a passive aspect: nonaggression and not being attacked.

The definition of peace as a favor granted by the stronger party was still valid in the eighth century BCE. A long inscription presents the systematic conquest of Egypt by the Nubian king Piye who aimed at the country's reunification under one sovereign after three centuries of territorial partition. One after the other, all the local chiefs and kinglets accepted the leadership of the new pharaoh. The most serious opposition came from the chief Tefnakhte who controlled the western part of the Delta. He offered his final surrender in a letter addressed to Piye, which begins with the words: "Peace from you. I cannot see your face in the days of shame; I cannot stand before your flame."[42] It is again the loser who begs for peace, asking primarily for the cessation of military attacks and a settlement guaranteeing his survival.

By the second part of the first millennium, the international balance of Western Asia changed and Egypt lost its independence. Persian, Macedonian, and Roman invasions swept over the country and led to various types of foreign domination, none of which left Egypt any room to negotiate for peace and autonomy.[43] Persian and Hellenistic rule—together covering almost five centuries—with their massive military presence and administrative constraints caused deep frustration among the Egyptian intellectual elite. The result was a gradual cultural introversion and a reinforcement of traditional religious values. This intellectually driven movement provoked an era of intense cultural production (temple constructions, religious and literary texts).

However, it also stimulated larger, culturally and politically motivated "nationalistic" upheavals and a climate of frequent revolts and repressions during the second and first centuries BCE. Even so, these did not produce an actual and prolonged situation of war and had no substantial impact on the development of a peace concept as an alternative value.

The peace treaty between Egypt and the Hittites

For almost seventy years in the thirteenth century BCE, the Hittites and the Egyptians fought numerous wars in an intense struggle for leadership in Western Asia. None of them was decisive or brought about any major political change in the area. One battle, however, which was certainly not very successful, perhaps even near-disastrous, for pharaoh Ramesses II, provoked deep cultural reactions in Egypt. We will probably never know what really happened on the shores of the Orontes, near the city of Kadesh, in year five of Ramesses II. The Egyptian sources, although exceptionally abundant, are each in its own way so strongly committed to reaffirm the core values of the Egyptian world conception and royal ideology that the "true" course of historical events is hard to reconstruct. Each of the literary and visual compositions developed new forms of expression and found innovative solutions to promulgate an admittedly unsuccessful campaign as a personal triumph of the king, obtained with the help of the god Amun. These biased retrospectives flourished for more than a decade after the crucial event and are related to the peace treaty concluded between Egypt and Hatti in year 21 of Ramesses II (circa 1259).[44]

This treaty between Ramesses II and Hattusili III is probably rightly considered "unique in being a true 'parity treaty' between real equals in terms of both rank and power."[45] It was concluded in Akkadian, the *lingua franca* of the period, originally engraved on two silver tablets, one for each party. The Egyptian silver tablet was probably deposited in the temple of Ra in Heliopolis.[46] The text of the treaty is preserved on several clay tablets found in the Hittite capital Hattusha/Bogazköy and in Egyptian translation and hieroglyphic script engraved on the walls of two Theban temples, Karnak and the Ramesseum. The Akkadian and Egyptian versions largely correspond in their wording.[47] The notion of peace is of course central, and the Egyptian version consistently uses the word *ḥtp*. The formula "in good peace and good brotherhood" occurs numerous times. This formulation, hitherto unknown, "good peace" (*ḥtp nfr*), might suggest that it referred to a phenomenon that was unfamiliar to Egyptian political practice: a form of equitable agreement. The word "brotherhood" (*snsn*) underlines the parity of rank between the two contractors, another feature never before acknowledged by the Egyptians. The parties agreed on mutual nonaggression, respect of their territory, and defense against aggression by a third. They also stipulated the repatriation of fugitives and guaranteed their amnesty.[48] Finally, the treaty was designed to last forever: the children's children of Ramesses II and Hattusili III were to respect the agreement: "they (the descendants) shall remain in our state of brotherhood, in our state of peace, and the land of Egypt and the land of Hatti shall be peaceful and brotherly like us for ever."[49]

The treaty was indeed effective, and there were no more conflicts between the two empires. The equal status of the two powers was also acknowledged in the official correspondence between the two kings, where Ramesses calls Hattusili his brother, referring to their agreement.[50] In a letter to the king of an Anatolian vassal state, Ramesses mentions the treaty and the "good brotherhood and good peace" that unite Egypt and Hatti.[51]

Some thirteen years after the treaty and following an intense exchange of diplomatic letters,[52] the Hittite king Hattusili offered his daughter in marriage to Ramesses II who in turn sent Hattusili prestigious goods. The treaty was still in force some 50 years later when Egypt sent grain to supply the Hittite empire that suffered a severe food shortage in year five of Merneptah's reign.[53] It lost its raison d'être only when the Hittite empire collapsed at the end of the twelfth century.

In real politics, Egypt thus seems to have agreed to an alliance based on a contract concluded on fair and equal terms, and even to have supplied its partner in difficult years. Yet the period in the reign of Ramesses II during which the treaty was negotiated and concluded—a process that took several years, considering the distance the messengers had to cover back and forth—also corresponded to a time of abundant cultural expression through intense building activity: Abu Simbel, the pylon at the Luxor temple, and parts of the Ramesseum (to cite only the extant monuments) were erected at that time and largely decorated with scenes and texts recalling the conflict with the Hittites and the battle of Kadesh. The Egyptian copies of the treaty were also set up in temples; they were thus included in the presentation of culturally relevant actions undertaken by the king, and placed in sacred spaces to confirm their timeless validity. Next to the proclamation of "good peace and good brotherhood," however, battle scenes and accompanying texts boasted about

Egyptian supremacy and the "miserable foe begging for peace." In the Egyptian cultural context, the assertion of superiority was such a traditional and central concern that it came up prominently in every text and in parallel to the parity treaty that governed real politics.

A large literary composition (nowadays called "The Poem") reflects the Kadesh battle; it was inscribed on papyrus as well as on several temple walls and contains a statement attributed to the Hittite King Muwatalli that says: "Peace is more useful than fighting. Do give us breath."[54] The first sentence seems to define a condition without violence such as the relationship achieved through the treaty. Interestingly, some versions use the word *ḥrt*, others *ḥtp*, which perhaps offers a further hint at the fact that the Egyptians had no well-defined concept and terminology of nonviolence based on equal status. The plea of the Hittite king for air to breathe, however, pulls his statement back into the scheme of Egyptian world conception.

In the temple of Karnak, the copy of the peace treaty itself, which insists on the parity of "good peace and good brotherhood," is introduced by a preamble stating twice that Hattusili had sent the silver tablets with the treaty to Ramesses in order to "implore peace from the majesty of the king of Upper and Lower Egypt."[55] The stela commemorating the marriage of Ramesses II with Hattusili's daughter, which in fact was an exchange of goods and gifts, begins with: "Words spoken by the great ruler of Hatti: 'I have come to you, I adore your beauty... I am under your feet eternally and forever, along with the entire Hatti-land'."[56] In another text dated from year 35 of Ramesses II, the god Ptah cites a long list of blessings that he accorded to the king. He describes the arrival in Egypt of the Hittite princess as a sign of submission and refers to the treaty with the following words: "Unknown was the situation of Hatti at one mind with Egypt. See, I ordained them slain under your feet, to sustain your name eternally."[57] This formulation very clearly summarizes the situation in which the two empires had agreed on a common solution of mutual respect and equality: they were "at one mind." And again the second sentence draws the description back into the frame of traditional ideology, emphasizing Egypt's superiority and total control over the outside world.

Although an exception, a peace agreement based on parity was possible in Egyptian political reality, but it remained inconceivable in ideology and in narratives related to ideal governance and kingship. Egypt's superiority and determination to drive off menacing external forces remained a dominant concern that informed most types of cultural expression. Within the frame of this discourse, peace was neither a state of mutual acceptance nor an agreement based on nonviolence; rather, it described a situation obtained by the unconditional surrender of other peoples to the power of pharaoh.

Conclusion

Their world view and belief system did not prepare the ancient Egyptians to envisage a state without opposition. Both the gods and the king, assisted by the people through ritual actions, were obliged to react aggressively to hostile forces that were imagined as permanently present and endangering world order. Subduing these opponents, the king contributed to restore the world to its original equilibrium and helped set free new creative powers, only to see them soon endangered again.

A peaceful attitude was, however, considered a core value in the sphere of individual social behavior and morals. In contrast, peacefulness was not an ideal on the level of political conceptions and royal discourse. Political ideology, intimately linked to the religious belief system and world view, considered an aggressive attitude towards the exterior—that by definition represented a constant menace—essential to safeguarding Egypt as a cultural and political entity.

Not only these conceptual predispositions, but also the reality of Egypt's long history offered hardly any opportunity to reflect about peace as a political value. Over a very long period of time Egypt was in a solidly dominant position and could afford to act according to its ideology: external opponents had to be countered forcefully and kept under control. Neither the conceptual frame nor the political situation ever encouraged the development of an ideal of tolerance and nonviolence or a consideration of others as equals.

The imperial period of Egypt—the second half of the second millennium—was marked by regular campaigns in Western Asia. The rather frequent use of the word "peace" in official royal documents of this period reflects the ideological and political reality very clearly. Peace was a state that the weaker side had to implore; "to make peace" referred to what we would call capitulation. "To implore peace" was the weaker political entity's last chance for survival and implied the total acceptance of the imposed conditions. In the Egyptians' view, peace was a favor the king could grant to opponents he could also have annihilated totally.

The only period when Egypt was confronted with an equivalent adversary was the thirteenth century when it fought repeatedly with the Hittites and both parties developed an interest in achieving a treaty based on parity that defined peace as a state of nonviolence, nonaggression, and mutual respect and aid. Both parties were able to negotiate and found advantages in such a treaty. The agreement led to a situation that was new for the Egyptians and which they termed "good peace." But even during this process, ideological prejudices and biases are visible in every Egyptian source: the traditional world view prevailed; its persistence created an acute discrepancy with the peace efforts in the reality of politics.

As a whole, the international context in which Egypt evolved and formed its political coherence and culture was—with the rare exception of the treaty with the Hittites—not favorable to the development of a concept of peace as a state of parity and mutual respect. There was no *necessity* to create such a concept, nor even an *interest* in doing so, because (during the third and second millennium) Egypt was much more powerful than its neighbors and potential opponents, and later (in the first millennium) there was no *possibility* because the opposing forces overpowered Egypt and integrated the country into their political entities.

Notes

1   Morenz 2004.
2   Velde 1967; Mathieu 2011.
3   Bickel 1994.
4   Assmann 1989, 1990.
5   Doxey 1998: 60–64, 144; see also Lichtheim 1992.
6   Pap. Prisse 6.9–10, after Lichtheim 1973–80: I. 65.
7   Teaching to Kagemni: Lichtheim 1973–80: I. 59–61.
8   The so-called Memphite Theology: Lichtheim 1973–80: I. 55.
9   Stela of Suti and Hor: London BM 826, in Sethe 1961: 1944 (*Urk.* IV: 1943–1946).
10 Vidal-Naquet 1993: 56–57; Tritle 2007: 180–81; see also ch. 5 (Raaflaub) in this volume, at nn. 17–32.
11 See Bestock in preparation.
12 Gnirs 1996: xx.
13 That the king was exclusively credited with success had important consequences for the process of decision-making; see Liverani 2002.
14 Assmann 2003.
15 Lichtheim 1973–80: II. 172.
16 Spalinger 2006.
17 Assmann 1984: 175–231; Gnirs 2009: 67.
18 Helck, *LdÄ* II: 331.
19 Tomb of Ineni: Dziobek 1992: 52–54.
20 Helck 2000: 56–60.
21 Book of the Dead, chapter 182: Faulkner 1985: 181.
22 Pyramid Texts, PT 627, §1775a–b: Faulkner 1969: 260.
23 Autobiography of Uni: Gnirs and Loprieno 2009: 245.
24 Bickel and Mathieu 1993: 41–43.
25 Leitz 1994: 58 (Pap. Sallier IV. 3, 6–7).
26 KRI II: 241.
27 KRI V: 25.11; Kitchen 2008: 22.
28 Raaflaub 2007: 7–8; see also ch. 1 (Raaflaub) in this volume, at n. 38.
29 Förster 2002: 231–32.

30 Gnirs 2006: 210–12.
31 Davis 1992.
32 Lichtheim 1973–80: I. 119; Eyre 1990.
33 Konosso Stela of Thutmoses IV: Sethe 1961 (*Urk.* IV: 1545–1548).
34 Hornung 1971.
35 Gottlieb 2000.
36 Spalinger 2005: 70–82; Gnirs 2009.
37 Sethe 1961: 907 (*Urk.* IV 907.8); Lorton 1974: 144–47.
38 Sethe 1961: 704 (*Urk.* IV 704.6).
39 Sethe 1961: 1304 (*Urk.* IV 1304.15); Lorton 1974: 77.
40 Bell 2007.
41 Kitchen 1982 (KRI IV): 19; Lichtheim 1973–80: II. 77; Kaplony-Heckel 2005 (with bibliography).
42 Lichtheim 1973–80: III. 79.
43 Bestock in preparation.
44 For general descriptions of the period, e.g. Klengel 2002; Pernigotti 2010.
45 Kitchen 1999: 140. Roth 2005. We know of the existence of a preceding treaty between the two powers, but no details: Davis 1990; Sürenhagen 2006.
46 Edel 1994: 77.
47 Edel 1997. For the legal value of certain Egyptian expressions, see Harari 1990.
48 A nuanced interpretation of this aspect in Allam 2010. For the Hittite preoccupations and political agenda Bryce 2006.
49 Kitchen 1970–1979: 227 (KRI II: 227).
50 Edel 1994: 125.
51 Edel 1994: 75.
52 Bryce 2003.
53 Kitchen 1982: 5 (KRI IV.5).
54 Kitchen 1970–1979: 95 (KRI II: 95.6).
55 Ibid. 226 (KRI II: 226.8, 10).
56 Ibid. 235 (KRI II: 235).
57 Ibid. 276 (KRI II: 276); see also Goelet 1993.

Abbreviations

KRI   Kitchen, *Ramesside Inscriptions*
LdÄ   *Lexikon der Ägyptologie*

References

Allam, S. 2010. "Der Vertrag Ramses' II. mit dem Hethiterkönig Hattusili III." In M. Lang, H. Barta, and R. Rollinger (eds.), *Staatsverträge, Völkerrecht und Diplomatie im Alten Orient und in der griechisch-römischen Antike*, 81–116. Wiesbaden.

Assmann, J. 1984. "Krieg und Frieden im Alten Ägypten: Ramses II. und die Schlacht bei Kadesch." *Mannheimer Forum* 1983/1984: 175–231.

Assmann, J. 1989. *Maât, l'Egypte pharaonique et l'idée de justice sociale.* Paris.

Assmann, J. 1990. *Ma'at: Gerechtigkeit und Unsterblichkeit im Alten Ägypten.* Munich.

Assmann, J. 2003. *The Mind of Egypt: History and Meaning in the Time of the Pharaohs.* Cambridge MA.

Bell, L. 2007. "Conflict and reconciliation in the ancient Middle East: the clash of Egyptian and Hittite chariots in Syria, and the world's first peace treaty between 'superpowers'." In Raaflaub 2007: 98–122.

Bestock, L. In preparation. "One waded in their blood as in water: Egyptian sources for warfare in the first millennium BC." In K. Raaflaub and B. Meissner (eds.), *Early Iron Age Land Warfare in West Asia and the Mediterranean: Problems and Perspectives* (working title).

Bickel, S. 1994. "Un hymne à la vie. Essai d'analyse du Chapitre 80 des Textes des Sarcophages." In C. Berger, G. Clerc, and N. Grimal (eds.), *Hommages à Jean Leclant*, I: 81–97. Cairo.

Bickel, S. and Mathieu, B. 1993. "L'écrivain Amennakht et son enseignement." *Bulletin de l'Institut français d'archéologie orientale* 93: 31–52.

Bryce, T. R. 2003. *Letters of the Great Kings of the Ancient Near East: The Royal Correspondence of the Late Bronze Age.* London.

Bryce, T. R. 2006. "The 'eternal treaty' from the Hittite perspective." *British Museum Studies in Ancient Egypt and Sudan* 6: 1–11.

Chaunu, P. (ed.). 1993. *Les fondements de la paix. Des origines au début du XVIIIᵉ siècle.* Paris.

Davis, D. 1990. "An early treaty of friendship between Egypt and Hatti." *Bulletin of the Australian Centre for Egyptology* 1: 31–37.

Davis, W. 1992. *Masking the Blow: The Scene of Representation in Late Prehistoric Egyptian Art.* Berkeley.

Doxey, D. M. 1998. *Egyptian Non-royal Epithets in the Middle Kingdom.* Leiden.

Dziobek, E. 1992. *Das Grab des Ineni, Theben Nr 81.* Mainz.

Edel, E. 1994. *Die ägyptisch-hethitische Korrespondenz aus Boghazköi in babylonischer und hethitischer Sprache.* Opladen.

Edel, E. 1997. *Der Vertrag zwischen Ramses II. von Ägypten und Hattuschili III. von Hatti.* Berlin.

Eyre, C. J. 1990. "The Semna Stelae: quotation, genre, and functions of literature." In Israelit-Groll 1990: I. 134–65.

Faulkner, R. O. 1969. *The Ancient Egyptian Pyramid Texts.* Oxford.

Faulkner, R. O. 1985. *The Ancient Egyptian Book of the Dead.* London.

Förster, H. 2002. *Wörterbuch der griechischen Wörter in den koptischen dokumentarischen Texten.* Berlin.

Gnirs, A. M. 1996. *Militär und Gesellschaft: ein Beitrag zur Sozialgeschichte des Neuen Reiches.* Heidelberg.

Gnirs, A. M. 2006. "Das Motiv des Bürgerkriegs in Merikare und Neferti. Zur Literatur der 18. Dynastie." In G. Moers, H. Behlmer, K. Demuß, and K. Widmaier (eds.), *jn.t dr.w: Festschrift für Friedrich Junge*, 207–65. Göttingen.

Gnirs, A. M. 2009. "Ägyptische Militärgeschichte als Kultur- und Sozialgeschichte." In Gundlach and Vogel 2009: 67–141.

Gnirs, A. M. and Loprieno, A. 2009. "Krieg und Literatur." In Gundlach and Vogel 2009: 243–308.

Goelet, O. 1993. "The Blessing of Ptah." In E. L. Bleiberg (ed.), *Fragments of a Shattered Visage, The Proceedings of the International Symposium on Ramesses the Great*, 28–37. Memphis Tenn.

Gottlieb, G. 2000. "Geschichte als Argument für Krieg und Frieden im alten Griechenland." In J. Burkhardt (ed.), *Krieg und Frieden in der historischen Gedächtniskultur*, 17–30. Munich.

Gundlach, R. and Vogel, C. (eds.). 2009. *Militärgeschichte des pharaonischen Ägypten. Altägypten und seine Nachbarkulturen im Spiegel aktueller Forschung*. Paderborn.

Harari, I. E. 1990. "The historical meaning of the legal words used in the treaty established between Ramesses II and Hattusili III, in Year 21 of the reign of Ramesses II." In Israelit-Groll 1990: I. 422–35.

Helck, W. 2000. *Die Prophezeiung des Nfr.tj*. Wiesbaden.

Hornung, E. 1971. "Politische Planung und Realität im alten Ägypten." *Saeculum* 22: 48–58.

Israelit-Groll, S. (ed.). 1990. *Studies in Egyptology presented to Miriam Lichtheim*. 2 vols. Jerusalem.

Kaplony-Heckel, U. 2005. "Die Israel-Stele des Mer-en-Ptah." In *Texte aus der Umwelt des Alten Testaments*, n.s. I.6: 544–52.

Kitchen, K. A. 1970–1979. KRI II*: Ramesside Inscriptions, Historical and Biographical*, II: *Ramesses II, Royal Inscriptions*. Oxford.

Kitchen, K. A. 1982. KRI IV: *Ramesside Inscriptions, Historical and Biographical*, IV. Oxford.

Kitchen, K. A. 1983. KRI V: *Ramesside Inscriptions, Historical and Biographical*, V. Oxford.

Kitchen, K. A. 1999. *Ramesside Inscriptions. Ramesses II: Royal Inscriptions, Notes and Comments*, II. Oxford.

Kitchen, K. A. 2008. *Ramesside Inscriptions, Translated & Annotated: Translations*, V. Oxford.

Klengel, H. 2002. *Hattuschili und Ramses: Hethiter und Ägypter – ihr langer Weg zum Frieden*. Mainz.

Leitz, C. 1994. *Tagewählerei: das Buch "hat nhh ph.wy dt" und verwandte Texte*. Wiesbaden.

Lichtheim, M. 1973–80. *Ancient Egyptian Literature*. 3 vols. Berkeley.

Lichtheim, M. 1992. *Maat in Egyptian Autobiographies and Related Studies*. Freiburg (Switzerland) and Göttingen.

Liverani, M. 2002. "The cautious advisers of the Amarna Pharaoh." *Vicino Oriente Quaderno* 3.1: 289–94.

Lorton, D. 1974. *The Juridical Terminology of International Relations in Egyptian Texts through Dyn. XVIII.* Baltimore.

Mathieu, B. 2011. "Seth polymorphe: le rival, le vaincu, l'auxiliaire." *ENIM (Egypte Nilotique et Méditerranéenne)* 4: 137–58.

Morenz, L. 2004. "Apophis: on the origin, name, and nature of an ancient Egyptian anti-god." *Journal of Near Eastern Studies* 63.3: 201–5.

Pernigotti, S. 2010. *L'Egitto di Ramesse II fra guerra e pace.* Brescia.

Raaflaub, K. (ed.). 2007. *War and Peace in the Ancient World.* Malden MA and Oxford.

Roth, S. 2005. "'In schönem Frieden befriedet und in schöner Brüderschaft verbrüdert'. Zu Motivation und Mechanismen der ägyptisch-hethitischen diplomatischen Kontakte in der Zeit Ramses' II." In D. Prechel (ed.), *Motivation und Mechanismen des Kulturkontaktes in der späten Bronzezeit,* 179–226. Florence.

Sethe, K. 1961. *Urkunden der 18. Dynastie.* Urkunden des ägyptischen Altertums, Abteilung 4. Berlin.

Spalinger, A. 2005. *War in Ancient Egypt.* Oxford.

Spalinger, A. 2006. "The paradise of scribes and the Tartarus of soldiers." In Spalinger, *Five Views on Egypt,* 5–49. Göttingen.

Sürenhagen, D. 2006. "Forerunners of the Hattusili-Ramesses treaty." *British Museum Studies in Ancient Egypt and Sudan* 6: 59–67.

Tritle, L. A. 2007. "'Laughing for joy': war and peace among the Greeks." In Raaflaub 2007: 172–90.

Velde, H. te. 1967. *Seth, God of Confusion: A Study of His Role in Egyptian Mythology and Religion.* Leiden

Vidal-Naquet, P. 1993. "La guerre, la Grèce et la paix." In Chaunu 1993: 51–61.

3

Thinking about Peace in Ancient India

JOHANNES BRONKHORST

Aśoka

Indian history begins, in a certain way, in the third century BCE with the inscriptions of Aśoka.[1] These inscriptions are among the earliest surviving written testimony from the subcontinent. Their contents are surprising, to say the least. They are messages for his subjects from Emperor Aśoka, who calls himself "the beloved of the gods." And they tell us a lot about the emperor himself, especially about his religious and generally moral attitudes. We know from these inscriptions that Aśoka turned to Buddhism at some point in his life, and that he considered himself a lay Buddhist. Not unrelated, but of more immediate interest for our topic, are the regrets that Aśoka expresses about the violence he had perpetrated during the conquest of a region in eastern India, Kaliṅga. We find this in the so-called thirteenth Major Rock Edict, extracts of which I present here in the somewhat free rendering of Romila Thapar:

> When he had been consecrated eight years the Beloved of the Gods, the king Piyadassi, conquered Kaliṅga. A hundred and fifty thousand people were deported, a hundred thousand were killed and many times that number perished. …

Peace in the Ancient World: Concepts and Theories, First Edition. Edited by Kurt A. Raaflaub.
© 2016 John Wiley & Sons, Inc. Published 2016 by John Wiley & Sons, Inc.

On conquering Kaliṅga the Beloved of the Gods felt remorse, for, when an independent country is conquered the slaughter, death, and deportation of the people is extremely grievous to the Beloved of the Gods, and weighs heavily on his mind. What is even more deplorable to the Beloved of the Gods, is that those who dwell there, whether brahmans, śramaṇas, or those of other sects, or householders who show obedience to their superiors, obedience to mother and father, obedience to their teachers and behave well and devotedly towards their friends, acquaintances, colleagues, relatives, slaves, and servants—all suffer violence, murder, and separation from their loved ones. Even those who are fortunate to have escaped, and whose love is undiminished [by the brutalizing effect of war], suffer from the misfortunes of their friends, acquaintances, colleagues, and relatives. This participation of all men in suffering, weighs heavily on the mind of the Beloved of the Gods. ... Today if a hundredth or a thousandth part of those people who were killed or died or were deported when Kaliṅga was annexed were to suffer similarly, it would weigh heavily on the mind of the Beloved of the Gods.[2]

Aśoka tries to remedy the situation by promoting the victory of Dharma, which approximately translates "righteous rule, correct behavior." It covers, for Aśoka, a variety of virtues, including generosity, medical care for humans and animals, religious tolerance, and much else. Virtually all his Rock Edicts deal with the propagation of Dharma within and beyond his empire. The thirteenth Major Rock Edict continues:

The Beloved of the Gods considers victory by Dharma to be the foremost victory. And moreover the Beloved of the Gods has gained this victory on all his frontiers to a distance of six hundred yojanas [i.e. about 1500 miles], where reigns the Greek king named Antiochus, and beyond the realm of that Antiochus in the lands of the four kings named Ptolemy, Antigonus, Magas, and Alexander; and in the south over the Colas and Pāṇḍyas as far as Ceylon. Likewise here in the imperial territories among the Greeks and the Kambojas, Nābhakas and Nābhapanktis, Bhojas and Pitinikas, Andhras and Pārindas, everywhere the people follow the Beloved of the Gods' instructions in Dharma. Even where the envoys of the Beloved of the Gods have not gone, people hear of his conduct according to the Dharma, his precepts and his instruction in Dharma, and they follow Dharma and will continue to follow it.[3]

We should not conclude from this that Aśoka had renounced all use of violence. Indeed, as Hans Bakker points out, "he is not slow to add that those subjugated by him 'should be told of the power (to punish them) which Devānāṃpriya [i.e. Aśoka, JB] (possesses) in spite of (his) repentance, in order that they may be ashamed (of their crimes) and may not be killed'."[4]

Aśoka is no doubt a unique and perhaps also extreme case in the ancient world. His empire stands at the beginning of the political history of classical

India. Its memory bequeathed to subsequent rulers and thinkers an ambiguous message.[5] This will be clear from the following passage, which I quote from Hartmut Scharfe's book *The State in Indian Tradition*:

> Even though Indians admired heroes and glorious conquests throughout their history, the ideal kingdom of the epic and classical texts was seen as a state of permanent peace. The notion of a single state for the whole "world," (i.e. the Indian subcontinent) could satisfy from the time of the Brāhmaṇa-texts on the thirst for ultimate glory and, at the same time, put an end to the perpetual wars between a multitude of competing dynasties. No Hindu ruler ever achieved that goal, and the attempts to reach it led to numerous and bloody conflicts. Each king is potentially and ideally a *vijigīṣu* "desirous to conquer [the world]" and aspires to be a *sārva-bhauma* "[king] ruling the whole world" or a *cakravartin*.[6]

The ultimate aim of permanent and universal peace led in practice to ceaseless and relentless war.

Brahmanism

It makes sense to distinguish two major currents in the post-Mauryan intellectual history of India: the Brahmins and the Buddhists. The thinkers of these two currents dealt quite differently with the inherited ideal of permanent and universal peace.

The Brahmanical thinkers, to begin with, were pragmatic in their approach. This is clear from the Brahmanical texts that deal, as a whole or in part, with statecraft. The one called *Arthaśāstra* ("Treatise on Statecraft") is no doubt the oldest surviving Brahmanical text that exclusively deals with such issues. Let me say a few words about it.

Brahmanical tradition ascribes the authorship of the *Arthaśāstra* to a person variously called Cāṇakya and Kauṭalya/Kauṭilya. Still according to Brahmanical tradition, this person was a Brahmin who advised King Candragupta, Aśoka's grandfather and the founder of the Mauryan empire, which Aśoka inherited and expanded. This Brahmin, moreover, was such a cunning politician that without him Candragupta would not have succeeded in creating his empire.[7]

The identification of the two persons—the minister of Candragupta and the author of the *Arthaśāstra*—is no doubt apocryphal.[8] The fact that no writing was used in India at the time of Candragupta Maurya is one reason to think so.[9] Another is the fact that the *Arthaśāstra* presupposes a kingdom that can be surrounded by more powerful rivals, whereas the empire of Candragupta and his successors could not be encircled.[10] Then there is the obvious advantage which more recent Brahmins could derive from the claim that the Mauryan empire—which had not been sympathetic to them—had really been created by a Brahmin, using the methods which those more recent Brahmins promoted among the rulers that were their contemporaries.[11]

The *Arthaśāstra* (13.4.55–63) distinguishes four possible ways of conquering the world.[12] It does not waste words on this final goal. Most of the text deals with concerns—such as ruling a state and taking maximum advantage from the relative strengths and weaknesses of neighboring kings—that come up when conquering the world is still a distant dream. It does so matter-of-factly, with few theoretical digressions or justifications. One may assume that the final goal of permanent and universal peace is to be considered a hidden justification for the sometimes doubtful recommendations that the text contains, but if so, the text does not say so. One has the feeling that the Brahmins who composed the *Arthaśāstra* were less interested in dreams than in securing and safeguarding their own position at and around the royal courts.

This does not mean that the *Arthaśāstra* is not interested in ordinary peace, the kind of peace that may reign between neighboring kingdoms or within a kingdom. However, this kind of peace is not always an aim in itself. Frequently, it is, as so many other things in this text, a means to an end; that is, to the intermediate end of maintaining power and, of course, of maintaining the social order in which Brahmins occupy a privileged position. The idea, for example, that kings should look after the well-being of their subjects is not unknown to the text. Typically, it does not present this as a duty of the king, but as a topic that secret agents in disguise should discuss in public places in order to restrain the common people and to find out who among them might feel critical of the present king (1.13.1–14).[13] And peace with a neighboring king is but a temporary ploy, to be abandoned once one has the means to overthrow or conquer him. Peace is also useful for creating confidence in one's neighbor, whose power can then be undermined by secret manipulations and occult means (7.1).[14]

Another classical Brahmanical text—the so-called *Laws of Manu* (*Manusmṛti* or *Mānava Dharmaśāstra*)—dedicates some of its chapters to matters of state. Like the *Arthaśāstra*, it unabashedly describes the task of kings as acquiring with military force what they have not yet acquired, to preserve with vigilance what they have acquired, to augment what they have preserved through profitable investments, and to distribute through gifts what has been augmented in this manner (7.101). The recipients of the gifts, to be sure, are the Brahmins. The *Laws of Manu* is not in favor of war, but the reason is not the promotion of peace as such, but rather the consideration that war brings risks that may be avoided by trying out other means first (7.198–200):

> He [the king] should strive to triumph over his enemies through conciliation, gifts, and fomenting dissension, employed collectively or separately, but never through war. Victory and defeat in battle are uncertain for the two combatants; he should, therefore, avoid war. When the aforementioned three strategies fail, then let him, always on guard, pursue war in such a manner that he will triumph over his enemies.[15]

War remains an honorable occupation, as the following verse shows (7.89):

> When kings fight each other in battles with all their strength, seeking to kill each other and refusing to turn back, they go to heaven.

The *Pañcatantra*, to give one more example, though presenting its political advice in charming fables, is no more peace-minded than the two preceding works. The title of its first book—"On causing dissension among allies" in Olivelle's translation—reveals its cynical attitude, while book III—"On war and peace"—explains with the help of stories how wit can be used to attain one's goals without resorting to war.[16] No idealism here, only calculation.

The Brahmanical political tradition, then, was not actively in search of peace. Quite on the contrary, it impressed upon rulers that the expansion of their realms was part of their duty and that war in the service of that aim was justified, even obligatory. This is not just the attitude of books that are, wholly or in part, political manuals, such as the *Arthaśāstra*, the *Laws of Manu* and the *Pañcatantra* just considered. It also finds expression in such texts as the *Bhagavadgītā*, arguably the most popular book of Hinduism until today. The *Bhagavadgītā* contains the teaching imparted by God to the warrior Arjuna, just before a battle in which Arjuna is going to destroy many friends and family members. Arjuna's scruples are presented in detail, but they are discarded with the argument that it is a warrior's duty to fight. Political peace in the sense of avoidance of war is not part of the ideology of this text, as it is not part of most other texts belonging to the Brahmanical tradition.[17]

Brahmanical political thought succeeded in exerting ever-greater influence on the rulers of the numerous kingdoms that the South Asian subcontinent has known. Countless panegyrics that survive in inscriptions—especially from the time of the Guptas onward, that is, from about the fourth century CE—praise rulers for the conquests they have made, and for the harm they have been able to inflict upon their neighbors and competitors.[18] These inscriptions are depressing reading and could not be more different in their general tone from the inscriptions of Aśoka with which we began. The victory of Brahmanism in the realm of religious, social, and political ideas expressed itself in what might be called a celebration of war, both in reality and in rhetorical contexts.

Still, we should not conclude from what precedes that Brahmins did not want to live in peace. Other things being equal, we must assume that everyone, with the possible exception of born and committed warriors, wishes to live in peace. But Brahmins wanted peace in conditions that were favorable to them. This meant in practice that often they encouraged warfare—not least because, in the general political situation of their day, kings who were ready to engage in war were more likely to stay in power than those who were not. Brahmanism's success was in part due to the fact that it did not hesitate to promote war. By doing so, it betted on the right horse, so to say. Conversely, this political ideology suited ambitious kings, and the kings who adopted this ideology may, on the whole, have had less inner resistance to war and therefore greater chances of staying in charge or even extending their power.

The pragmatic attitude of the Brahmanical texts with regard to the realities of war and peace has much to do with the fact that Brahmanism, as it managed to impose itself during the centuries following the collapse of the Mauryan empire, was primarily a vision of society. Brahmanism was no religion that attempted to make religious converts. Indeed, if we look upon the ideas found in the Vedic corpus of texts as being the religious doctrines of Brahmanism, we must conclude that Brahmanism kept its doctrines secret: large portions of the population had no right whatsoever to hear (or read) the Veda. The Brahmins themselves were barely interested in those doctrines. Brahmanism, I repeat, was primarily a vision of a highly stratified society, in which Brahmins occupied the highest position and kings were there to create and expand kingdoms. Brahmanism succeeded over time in imposing itself on large parts of the South Asian subcontinent and beyond. Not least among the reasons of its success was its capability to help rulers by giving them the pragmatic advice they needed.

What about the *ahiṃsā* ("nonviolence") for which India has become so famous? The answer is given in the following passage, which I borrow from an article by Jos Gommans:

> The ultimate aim for both Brahmins and kings was not earthly power but eternal salvation; the way thither was not conquering the world but renouncing it. This pursuit also involved the well-known Indian ideal of *ahiṃsā* or non-injury to life. As it was only the ascetic who could really live up to it, world-renouncement and *ahiṃsā* had to be internalized by those whose dharmic role could not escape the evil consequences of worldly action. As such, this second-best option was most fitting for kings and warriors wielding earthly power. Hence, their *hiṃsā* (violence, JB) had to be detached, without self-interest; *ahiṃsā* only serving to calm their inner world. This

also explains why even martial sects of ascetic warriors saw no problem at all in sub-scribing to the vow of *ahiṃsā* … In any case, it is clear that *ahiṃsā* was not meant to establish peace in the public realm as had been the prime objective of the European peace movements.[19]

Buddhism

Buddhist thinkers were not quite as pragmatic as their Brahmanical confrères. This is hardly surprising. Buddhism did not start out as a vision of society, even less as a model to be followed in ruling a state. It taught a path to escape from rebirth, and following this path implied leaving society and surviving hence-forth by begging. The nature of the society left behind was of little concern to the early followers of the Buddha.[20]

This initial situation did not last long. Buddhism soon became the victim of its own success. The community of monks and nuns organized itself, and mon-asteries were created. Questions regarding the interaction between the Buddhist community and society at large became inevitable, all the more so since the core members of the Buddhist community, the monks and nuns, had few or no worldly possessions. In order to build monasteries and places of worship, a steady stream of gifts from donors was required. The Buddhists could not for-ever go on hiding their heads in the sand as far as questions of society and its political organization were concerned. But the challenge they were confronted with was too great to deal with.

Consider first an early text, part of the Buddhist canon, that deals with the organization of society and explains how it came to be as it is. This text, the *Aggañña Sutta*, criticizes the Brahmanical vision of society and rejects the notion according to which Brahmins are fundamentally different from all other mem-bers of society. Brahmins had justified their claim to superiority with the help of a myth, which recounts that Brahmins, unlike all other human beings, were born from the mouth of the Creator God. The *Aggañña Sutta* does not accept this and presents a creation story of its own. In this alternative story, differences between people only came about as a result of different behavior in some unspec-ified past. Brahmins, for example, are the descendants of people who meditated or compiled books; the text hastens to add that Brahmins have a common ances-try with all other classes of society. The kingly class came about when people chose one from among themselves to impose order on society. Once again the text emphasizes the common origin of the king with the other classes.[21]

The *Aggañña Sutta*, while reacting to Brahmanical ideas, adopts some of them. It criticizes the fundamental difference between the four classes of society taught by the Brahmins, yet accepts this division of society as real. It also accepts without discussion that kings behave the way kings do. In the words of the *Aggañña Sutta*, a king is a being who, appointed by the rest of the population, "would show anger where anger was due, censure those who deserved it, and banish those who deserved banishment."[22]

Yet this is where the shoe pinches. Buddhism teaches a path that leads to liberation. This path is open to all human beings, not just Brahmins or some other group. Buddhism is therefore bound to encourage behavior that, in the long or short run, leads to that goal. The strong-arm tactics that worldly rulers use (and may be compelled to use) do not lead in that direction. In fact, they do the opposite. The Brahmins could maintain that a certain class of people, the warriors, were born with the obligation to use violence in appropriate circumstances. They could point out that a warrior who did *not* use violence in such circumstances might expect to be punished for this omission, in this or in a next life. For Buddhists this was harder to maintain. They recognized no separate class of warriors, fundamentally different from other human beings, with different obligations and different fates. For Buddhists there was no fundamental difference between a monk and a warrior. If violence was wrong for the one, it was wrong for the other.

This is the conundrum in which Buddhist theoreticians of political power found themselves. Was there a right way of ruling a country, without violence? In answering this question, the memory of the Mauryan empire, and especially of its emperor Aśoka, appears to have made itself felt. Aśoka, as we have seen, talked about the victory of Dharma, that is, of "righteous rule, correct behavior." The notion of Dharma in connection with political power had great appeal to the Buddhists. They thought and spoke about a Dharma-king, who conquered the world in an unobjectionable manner. The *Cakkavatti-Sīhanāda Sutta*, another canonical text, describes what happened to one such righteous king to whom one day a Wheel appeared:[23]

> Then, rising from his seat, covering one shoulder with his robe, the king took a gold vessel in his left hand, sprinkled the Wheel with his right hand, and said: "May the noble Wheel-Treasure turn, may the noble Wheel-Treasure conquer!" The Wheel turned to the east, and the king followed it with his fourfold army. And in whatever country the Wheel stopped, the king took up residence with his fourfold army. And those who opposed him in the eastern region came and said: "Come, Your Majesty, welcome! We are yours, Your Majesty. Rule us, Your Majesty." And the king said: "Do not take life. Do not take what is not given. Do not commit sexual misconduct. Do not tell lies. Do not drink strong drink. Be moderate in eating." And those who had opposed him in the eastern region became his subjects.

Then the Wheel turned south, west, and north... (as before). Then the Wheel-Treasure, having conquered the lands from sea to sea, returned to the royal capital and stopped before the king's palace.[24]

We do not know how many Buddhist monarchs waited in vain for a Wheel-Treasure to appear and help them in the task of conquering the world. Without a Wheel-Treasure the task became much harder, and would inevitably breach the rules that the king was supposed to promulgate, especially the ones about not taking life and not taking what is not given. In spite of these drawbacks, there were always volunteers to carry out the job, even without Wheel-Treasure. The question is, what advice could their Buddhist counselors give them?

The answer is, very little. We possess some works whose stated aim is to give advice to (sometimes identifiable) kings. One of these is a letter sent to the young King Kaniṣka by the Buddhist scholar Mātṛceṭa in the second century CE. It is not clear to which Kaniṣka the letter was addressed (several kings bore that name), nor indeed whether it was really sent to a king of that name.[25] However, the most famous Kaniṣka (Kaniṣka I) was a king of the Kuṣāṇa dynasty, about whom the Indian historian Romila Thapar writes: "The Kushana dynasty was in the ascendant in central Asia under Kanishka, whose relationship to the earlier kings has been confirmed by the recent discovery of an inscription in Afghanistan. In this he claims that he conquered *hindo*/India, i.e. the better-known north-west of India, and proclaimed his conquest in all the cities as far as Champa (in the middle Ganges Plain)."[26] Perhaps the most striking feature of Mātṛceṭa's letter, addressed as it is to the successor, descendant, and namesake of a king known for his conquests (if not to that king himself), is its emphasis on saving the life of *animals*. Nothing at all is said about the killing of *humans*.[27]

Nāgārjuna was more or less a contemporary of Mātṛceṭa.[28] His *Precious Garland* contains advice for kings. Some of the passages involved show that Nāgārjuna's political ideas were still very close to those that we found in the canonical texts studied above. Consider the following verse: "Through proper honoring of stūpas, honorable beings, Superiors, and the elderly, you will become a Universal Monarch, your glorious hands and feet marked with [a design of] wheels."[29] A Universal Monarch is the same as the Dharma-king whom we met earlier. Like the Dharma-king, the Universal Monarch is associated with wheels, with the difference that this time wheels appear as marks in his hands. Universal kingdom, here as well as there, is presented as the outcome of virtue. Violent conquest, the verse suggests, can be avoided.

Other passages from the *Precious Garland* are no more practical, even though the pious and virtuous intentions of its author cannot be doubted. No one would be averse to living in a country ruled by Nāgārjuna's ideal king. Whether such a king would remain in charge for long is a different question. It seems that even Nāgārjuna himself had some doubts, for he ends his political advice with the following verse: "However, if from the unrighteousness of the world it is difficult to rule religiously, then it is right for you to become a monastic for the sake of practice and grandeur."[30] In other words, trying to be a good and virtuous king may turn out to be impossible. In that case the Buddhists have no further advice to offer, except that it is time to turn one's back to the world and become a monk.

The *Letter to King Gautamīputra*, attributed to the same Nāgārjuna, is even less practical in its advice than the *Precious Garland*, and even more insistent that a king really finds himself in the wrong place: "[In choosing] between the one who conquers [attachment to] the ever unsteady and momentary objects of the six sense-organs and the one who conquers the enemy's army in battle, the wise know the first to be a far greater hero."[31] The advice it gives is, as the text itself admits, more suitable to monks than to kings: "It is difficult even for a monk in isolation to follow the counsel which has been given to you; [yet] make this life meaningful through cultivating the quality of the essence of any of these practices."[32]

It is conceivable, though not certain, that Mātrceta and Nāgārjuna had read Aśvaghoṣa's *Life of the Buddha* (*Buddhacarita*).[33] Aśvaghoṣa puts the following assessment of kingship in the mouth of the future Buddha after he has left home but before he has reached enlightenment:

> In what way could it be right for a wise man to take sovereignty on himself? It is the abode of delusion in which are to be found fearfulness, the intoxication of pride, weariness and loss of Dharma by the mishandling of others. For kingship is at the same time full of delights and the vehicle of calamity, like a golden palace all on fire, like dainty food mixed with poison, or like a lotus-pond infected with crocodiles. ... For it is better to eat herbs in the forest, embracing the highest contentment as if one were concealing a jewel, than to live with the dangers to which sovereignty is exposed, as if with loathsome black snakes.[34]

We may assume that Aśvaghoṣa, one of the first Buddhist authors to compose works in Sanskrit, addressed a courtly audience, as did Mātrceta and Nāgārjuna. The topic he is dealing with in his poem allows him to be even more outspoken than the other two, and he does not mince his words.

To conclude this discussion I will cite one more Buddhist text, Vasubandhu's *Abhidharmakośa Bhāṣya*, which dates from the fourth or fifth century CE. This text mentions kings, judges (*daṇḍanetr*), and ministers (*vyāvahārika*) as self-evidently (*arthataḥ*) belonging to the group of indisciplined people along with fishermen, hunters, bandits, executioners, jailors, and others.[35] No comments are called for.

Indian Buddhism, then, did not develop much in terms of thought about political peace, not at least during the period under discussion. And yet the Buddhists, including the Buddhist thinkers who developed so much acuity in other areas of thought, had to live in the real world in which political peace was of the greatest importance to them. How do we explain their lack of imagination in this crucial realm?

The answer presents itself, I believe, if we look at some more recent developments in South Asia and project our findings back into the period under consideration. Recall, to begin with, that there was in India a joint presence of Brahmins and Buddhists for many centuries. These two competed with each other in several areas.[36] The history of Indian philosophy during the first millennium CE, for example, can be thought of as the history of a long debate between Brahmanical and Buddhist thinkers. The competition between the two was not confined to philosophy. They competed for royal favors in a variety of ways and areas. An enumeration is not necessary at this point. There were, however, some areas in which the two did *not* compete, which the Buddhists abandoned to the Brahmins, and which they had apparently abandoned from an early date onward. An example is the field which combines astrology, astronomy, and mathematics, but which is jointly thought of as one single field in the Indian tradition. This is a field in which a succession of authors made some important contributions. These authors were often Brahmins, sometimes Jainas, but never Buddhists.[37] The explanation appears to lie in the circumstance that Buddhists refused to be associated with anything that had the remotest connection with predicting the future, including astrology. And indeed, the people who, according to an ancient legend, predicted the future of the Buddha soon after he was born, were Brahmins. The Buddhists, it appears, were ready to have their future predicted, at least in certain circumstances; they were not ready to do the predicting themselves. As a result, they cut themselves out of the market of all future developments in the area of astronomy and mathematics.

Surprising as it may seem, it appears that the Buddhists also left matters relating to statecraft to Brahmins. This is most clearly visible in certain Southeast Asian countries which, though Buddhist, kept Brahmins at the court to advise the king. Thailand does so until today. In Ceylon, the Buddhist kings voluntarily took advice about governing from Brahmanical texts, including the ones we have considered, the *Arthaśāstra* and the *Laws of Manu*.[38] Here and elsewhere the Brahmins presented themselves as specialists, with sophisticated manuals at their disposal and useful advice for the practicalities of governance. The Buddhists had no such tradition and, as we have seen, had major difficulties creating one. In this area, it appears, the Buddhists did not enter the competition. They left this area to the Brahmins, conceding that the latter were the specialists in this domain.

This situation did not last indefinitely. The later history of Buddhism in India shows that a variety of modifications permitted this religion to enter into competition with the Brahmins after all, even in realms that directly concerned the state. The difficulty, as we have seen, was that Buddhism found it difficult to present a picture of and a justification for a society in which there was place for real kings and realistic policy.[39] Worse, Buddhism did not have much place for positions people might occupy in society outside the monastery. It concentrated on encouraging people to become monks and nuns. Failing this, it encouraged them to become lay followers—*upāsaka*s or *upāsikā*s—but the obligations it imposed upon them, and the further vows that these lay followers were expected to make, put them in a category quite distinct from the ordinary citizen and excluded them from many occupations.[40] For others, most notably those involved in ruling the country, Buddhism had but little advice. Those others should somehow fit into the dominant vision of society, that of the Brahmins. As long as Buddhism had nothing of its own on offer, it could not but accept that vision, no doubt with regrets. The pressure to come up with something more satisfactory must have been great. It led to developments, which we will now briefly consider.

Let us first look at the so-called Jātakas. These are stories that tell what the most recent Buddha had gone through and done in earlier lives. These deeds had contributed to his ultimate victory, that of becoming a Buddha. However, the most recent Buddha is not the only Buddha there has been, or will be. Already in canonical times, Buddhists had come to believe that there had been Buddhas before the most recent one, and that there will be others in the future. Obviously, the highest aim these Buddhists could aspire to was that of becoming a Buddha themselves. This aim, they thought, was to be preferred to the simpler and more self-centered one of becoming an enlightened Arhat (liberated Buddhist saint). Some of these Buddhists actually made a resolve to become a Buddha. This resolve is known by the name *bodhicitta*.[41] Those who have generated it are henceforth Bodhisattvas, future Buddhas. These new Bodhisattvas drew inspiration from the Jātakas and tried to imitate the deeds there recounted to the extent possible.[42] This in its turn had interesting consequences; for example, a serious and committed Buddhist did not have to be a monk, he might stay in society and play a role in it, just as the most recent Buddha had occupied various positions in society in earlier lives.[43]

This last point is illustrated in an early text belonging to the Mahāyāna branch of Buddhism, *The Inquiry of Ugra* (*Ugraparipṛcchā*). Half of this text gives advice to householder Bodhisattvas, including the following:

> The householder Bodhisattva seeks wealth according to the Dharma; he does not seek it according to what is non-Dharmic. He seeks it fairly, not unfairly. He pursues right livelihood, not wrong livelihood. ... not desiring happiness for himself, he causes all beings to attain happiness. Unmoved by profit or loss, fame or infamy, praise or blame, happiness or suffering, he transcends worldly things. He does not become arrogant because of amassing profit and wealth, nor is he discouraged by the absence of profit, fame, or praise. ... With respect to his undertakings, he is firm in his sense of obligation.[44]

Furthermore:

> The householder Bodhisattva who lives at home, by being free of attachment and aversion, should attain equanimity with respect to the eight worldly things. If he succeeds in obtaining wealth, or a wife, or children, or valuables, or produce, he should not become proud or overjoyed. And if he fails to obtain all these things, he should not be downcast or distressed.[45]

Note that the householder Bodhisattva depicted in this text passes his time seeking wealth. It is true that there are limits to the methods he can use in doing so, but as long as he observes these, he can participate in economic life. He can also marry and have children, that is to say, participate in ordinary social life.

Another Mahāyāna text that especially addresses lay people is the *Sūtra on Upāsaka Precepts* (*Upāsakaśīla Sūtra*). This text admonishes the lay Bodhisattva to take a number of vows, some of which concern future lives. The following are of special interest in the present context:

> I vow that wherever I am reborn, I shall not take rebirth as a woman, as one without sexual organs, or with both [male and female] sexual organs, or as a slave. ... [I vow] not to be born in a bad country or borderland but to be born into a noble family with outstanding physical appearance and great wealth.[46]

Once again we hit upon the theme of wealth, this time inherited wealth. Clearly, there is nothing wrong with wealth according to the author of this passage. Quite on the contrary, wealth may accrue to a person because he has taken a Bodhisattva vow in an earlier existence.[47] But acquired wealth also befits a lay Bodhisattva:

> The Bodhisattva has to perfect eight dharmas to benefit himself and others. What are they? [They are:] (1) a long life, (2) superior appearance, (3) great physical strength, (4) noble birth, (5) *much wealth*, (6) being a male, (7) eloquence, and (8) fearlessness when facing great assemblies of people.[48]

And how does one perfect these dharmas?

> The Bodhisattva *mahāsattva* has compassion and does not kill for immeasurable lives; for this reason he obtains a long life. In measureless lives he constantly gives away clothing and lamps, and for this reason he enjoys a superior appearance. In measureless lives he always destroys arrogance, and for this reason he is born in a noble family. In measureless lives he always gives food to others, and for this reason he obtains great physical strength. In measureless lives he always takes delight in speaking the Dharma, and for this reason he obtains great wealth. In measureless lives he loathes the female body and for this reason he is born as a man. In measureless lives he keeps precepts sincerely, and for this reason he is eloquent. In measureless lives he makes offerings to the Three Treasures, and so he is fearless in the assembly.[49]

Wealth, and all the other advantages that certain people have with respect to others, are here presented as a virtue, or rather as the outcome of virtue in earlier existences.

Let me emphasize the importance of the development here sketched. Buddhism had from the beginning presented itself as a path leading to the end of suffering and rebirth. This path consisted in saying farewell to the world and dedicating oneself to the spiritual practices taught by the Buddha. Monks and nuns actually did so (or were supposed to do so), *upāsakas* and *upāsikās* did so to a considerable degree. Those who did not do so and remained in the world had an ill-defined position in the Buddhist scheme of things. They might feel sympathetic toward the Buddhist teaching and community, but it was not clear whether and to what extent they could be thought of as partaking in the Buddhist path.

Non-monastic Buddhists could not forever remain in limbo. They found a place for themselves by laying stress on the importance of accumulating merit. Recall what, according to authors like Nāgārjuna, one had to do in order to become a Universal Monarch. The answer is: acquire merit. One verse spells out what kind of merit is meant: "Through proper honoring of stūpas, honorable beings, Superiors, and the elderly, you will become a Universal Monarch, your glorious hands and feet marked with [a design of] wheels." In other words, accumulating merit is the most secure way to acquire a kingdom, or whatever else one wishes to acquire in a future life. The Jātakas show that accumulating merit is also essential for reaching the highest aim there is, that of becoming a Buddha. Innumerable inscriptions confirm that the advice to accumulate merit was taken to heart by rulers and subjects, by monastics and lay people alike.

If we now return to the Jātakas, it will be clear that these stories could become examples of ideal behavior for all those who wished to increase their stock of merit, including those who had not decided to become Buddhas themselves. These stories often emphasize the generous or compassionate aspect of this or that earlier incarnation of the Buddha. But they do more. They show that one can be a totally committed Buddhist, even a future Buddha, while yet continuing to occupy a role in society. Living in the world is compatible with being a Buddhist in the strictest sense of the term. But living in the world also means living in accordance with the norms of society. Depending on the position one occupies, one may even be obliged to kill. In this way, the question that must have occupied many Buddhists: "Can one be a Buddhist and live in society?" found its most poignant expression in the question "Can one be a Bodhisattva and kill?" This last question is discussed in a number of texts belonging to the movement that was particularly interested in the careers of Bodhisattvas, and which came to be known as the Bodhisattva-yāna or Mahā-yāna.[50] Not surprisingly, this issue raises a number of questions, for example about the state of mind of the Bodhisattva and that of his victim while the former kills the latter.[51]

Related to the question of killing is that of whether war is ever justified. The Mahāyāna *Mahāparinirvāṇa Sūtra* states in so many words that lay Buddhists must protect Buddhist teaching, if necessary with the help of arms. It further states that killing certain people—those who reject Mahāyāna and adhere to particularly unwholesome views and practices—is less bad than killing animals; what is more, it constitutes no infringement of the prohibition to kill.[52] Enemies of Buddhism, the *Sarvadurgatipariśodhana Tantra* adds, should be killed where possible.[53] The *Bodhisattvabhūmi* points out that a Bodhisattva who is king commits a serious transgression if he does not threaten severe punishment in order to impose virtuous behavior on his subjects, even against their will.[54]

Once Buddhism had resolved the issue of how one could be a layman in society and yet be counted as a devout Buddhist, its competition with Brahmanism took a different shape. Brahmanism had always had the great advantage of being able to counsel political rulers in a most practical fashion. It had been able to assure those rulers that the violence they sometimes had to commit was in keeping with their position in society and was indeed part of their duty. Now that the Buddhists had come to realize that the Buddha himself had been king in earlier existences,[55] and had competently ruled the kingdoms he had been in charge of, they could no longer blame present rulers for carrying out their task using the means required. This opened up new possibilities.

They might henceforth aspire to the position of royal counselor in political matters, just as the Brahmins had done so far.[56]

A beautiful example of a Buddhist minister who justifies the kingship of his ruler in Buddhist terms comes from the kingdom of Aṅkor, in present-day Cambodia.[57] The ruler concerned is Jayavarman V, who ruled from 968 to 1001 CE. From his realm a considerable number of inscriptions have been preserved, one of which, the so-called Vat-Sithor inscription, merits our attention. The Buddhist minister called Kīrtipaṇḍita figures prominently in this inscription, which contains some Buddhist propaganda. For our present purposes it is most interesting that both the king and his minister Kīrtipaṇḍita are characterized as Bodhisattvas whose deeds are guided by the unique concern to lead their subjects to heaven and liberation. What the king expects from his subjects, moreover, is in agreement with the true teaching (*dharma, saddharma*) of the Buddha, and conducts his subjects to better rebirths and liberation. Rulers could thus compare themselves to Bodhisattvas, or even to a Buddha. When the Pāla ruler Devapāla gained the throne, he repeatedly stated that he did so just as a Bodhisattva obtains the position of a Buddha, following the *parinirvāṇa* of the previous teacher of the world.[58]

Once it had become possible for Buddhists to act as counselors of the king, they could profit from the experience and expertise that the Brahmins had acquired in the course of time. More particularly, they might use the manuals that had been composed by Brahmins, among them the *Arthaśāstra* and the *Laws of Manu*. Evidence illustrating this comes from Sri Lanka. The rulers of this island and their Buddhist counselors used these Brahmanical texts for running the country.[59]

There is no need to search for further examples. Whether or not the Buddhists succeeded in becoming political counselors at the royal courts, they could now legitimately aspire to such positions. They could do so because they had come to accept society as a legitimate place to live in, not just as something to flee from. This new development reduced the gap between Buddhists and Brahmins to a considerable extent. However, the Brahmins had one more trump card. They did not just offer political counseling. They also offered the magical protection, which only they, as possessors of traditional Vedic lore, could provide. It seems a fair bet that many rulers appreciated this magical protection as much as they did the political counseling, if not more so. In the realm of magical protection, traditional Buddhism had not much to offer. Neither the ascetic practices laid down in the ancient texts nor the rationalized doctrines, which Buddhists defended in their Sanskrit debates, provided magical protection in any form whatsoever. Certain Buddhists may have come to experience this as a drawback, one that might deprive them of the political support that they yet desperately needed.

It is no doubt in this context that we have to understand the ever-stronger tendency in Buddhism to use rites and spells. This tendency was not confined to Buddhism, to be sure, nor was it limited to rites and spells that might be of use to the royal court.[60] It would not be correct either to say that there was once a time when Buddhism was completely without them. Protective spells are a common feature of Mahāyāna, and they appear to have been in use already in earlier phases of Buddhism.[61] Philosophically inclined Buddhists held various views about the nature and value of mantras.[62] Yet it seems clear that there was an upsurge of rites and spells from the seventh century CE onward.[63] It is customary to speak in this connection of Tantric Buddhism. The available evidence suggests that Tantric Buddhism borrowed extensively from non-Buddhist religious currents, most notably Śaivism.[64]

In a recent article, Alexis Sanderson enumerates a number of factors that contributed to the success of the relevant form of Śaivism. One of these is "that the Śaivism of the Mantramārga developed in practice a thorough accommodation of the brahmanical religion that it claimed to transcend, thus minimizing, even eliminating, the offence it gave as a tradition whose scriptures, like those of the Buddhists, were seen to be, and claimed to be, outside the corpus of the Vedas. These Śaivas were to accept that the brahmanical tradition alone was valid in the domain it claimed for itself and that they were bound to follow its prescriptions and incorporate its rituals beside their own wherever practicable."[65] This process sometimes worked in the opposite direction, as Sanderson points out in another article: in order to respond to the altered expectations of their royal clients, Brahmins of the *Atharvaveda* added "Śaiva and Vaiṣṇava rituals to their repertoire, composing or appropriating texts that prescribe them and adding these to the corpus of their sacred literature."[66] Evidence for this is provided by certain ancillary tracts included in the *Atharvavedapariśiṣṭa*.

Another factor, the most vital according to Sanderson, "is that the religion succeeded in forging close links with the institution of kingship and thereby with the principal source of patronage."[67] It did so in various ways. For instance, Śaiva officiants occupied the office of Royal Preceptor (*rājaguru*) and in this position gave Śaiva initiation (*dīkṣā*) to the monarch followed by a specially modified version of the Śaiva consecration ritual (*abhiṣeka*) as an empowerment to rule beyond that conferred by the conventional Brahmanical royal consecration (*rājyābhiṣeka*). They provided a repertoire of protective, therapeutic, and aggressive rites for the benefit of the monarch and his kingdom. They developed Śaiva rituals and their applications to enable a specialized class of Śaiva officiants to encroach on the territory of the Rājapurohita, the Brahmanical expert in the rites of the *Atharvaveda* who served as the personal priest of the king,[68] warding off all manner of ills from him through apotropaic rites, using sorcery to attack his enemies, fulfilling the manifold duties of regular and occasional worship on his behalf, and performing the funerary and other postmortuary rites when he or other members of the royal family died.[69]

The Śaivas were not, however, the only ones to attempt to forge links with royalty in this manner. Buddhists tried to imitate them in this respect, too. Sanderson gives some examples:

> We see similar cases of regularization of rites of royal protection in our evidence for the Buddhist Way of Mantras. The *Rgya gar chos 'byun*, the Tibetan history of Indian Buddhism completed by Tāranātha in AD 1608, reports that in order to protect his dynasty, expand its rule, and spread the Buddhist religion the Pāla king Dharmapāla (r. c. 775–812) had a fire-sacrifice performed regularly for many years by Tantric officiants under the direction of his Guru Buddhajñānapāda at an overall cost of 902,000 tolas of silver.

> An inscription of the reign of Jayavarman V (r. c. 968 – c. 1000/1) reveals a similar arrangement in the Khmer court of Angkor. It tells us that one Kīrtipaṇḍita, a Mahāyānist scholar and adept of the Buddhist Yogatantras, who had been adopted by the royal family as their Guru, was frequently engaged by the king to perform apotropaic, restorative and aggressive Mantra rituals within the royal palace for the protection of his kingdom.[70]

We met the Kīrtipaṇḍita here mentioned earlier: this Buddhist minister was apparently appreciated at the Khmer court for his ability to perform even violent and aggressive Mantra rituals.[71] There is not much direct evidence from South and Southeast Asia to show that the new emphasis on incantations and rites had as one of its aims to secure a place for Buddhists at the royal court, apart from the cases just considered. It is worth mentioning here the description of a war machine in an Indian Buddhist Tantric text, the *Kālacakra Tantra*.[72] This description, unexpected in a Tantric text, may find a partial explanation in the fact that this text foresees a final and definitive battle between Buddhism and Islam in which the latter will be destroyed. It also shows the proximity that was felt to exist between Buddhism and the political powers that were to make use of this war machine.

Brahmanical literature is full of stories about ascetics with powers far exceeding those of any king. Tantric Buddhism, too, came to have its powerful ascetics, often called *siddha*s ("accomplished ones"). This topic cannot be explored here, but one story from Abhayadatta's *Caturaśītisiddhapravṛtti* may be presented by way of illustration:

In the city of Kansati, Virūpa bought wine from a tavern girl; she gave him a glass of wine and a plate of rice, which he greatly enjoyed. He continued eating and drinking. For the space of two days and a night, he prevented the sun from moving and the king, amazed, exclaimed: "Who is it who performs such a miracle?" In answer, the goddess of the sun appeared to the king in a dream and said, "A yogin has pledged me as payment to a tavern girl." The king and his subjects paid the price of the wine, which came to a million glasses, and Virūpa disappeared.[73]

Geoffrey Samuel, who cites this story, comments: "What is ... notable about this story is the implicit comparison of Virūpa's Tantric power and the king's temporal power."[74] Indeed—as is the case in many Brahmanical stories—it is clear that the king's power cannot compare with that of the ascetic. In other words, Tantric Buddhism, like Brahmanism before it, claimed great powers, which the king would be wise to respect and honor.

If the evidence from South Asia concerning the political role that Buddhist rites and spells were meant to play is limited, it is known that Buddhism owed much of its attraction in China, Japan, and elsewhere to its supposed capacity to defend the state against danger. It may be true, as Ronald Davidson points out, that "Indian esoteric Buddhism did not arise for the express purpose of converting the courts and appealing to the intelligentsia of Tibet, China, Japan, Burma, or elsewhere," but it is equally true that "its success was ... dramatic in these areas".[75] The Tantric master Amoghavajra, to take an example, helped to defeat the invasion of China in 742 CE by a combined force of Tibetans, Arabs, Sogdians, and others. He did this through certain rituals derived from a Buddhist text specifically concerned with the protection of the state.[76] Buddhist monks in China were exempted from military service, but were expected to execute Tantric Buddhist rites that would provide protection against natural and other disasters, most in particular against war and enemies.[77] In Japan, in 940 CE, the state was threatened by a rebellion. The Shingon priest Kanjo was directed by the Emperor to bring an image of Fūdō, a Tantric deity, to Narita in order to defeat the rebellion. After three weeks of continual fire offerings, the leader of the rebellion, Taira no Masakado, was killed by the Emperor's forces and peace was restored. At least some of the credit was given to the Fūdō rituals.[78] Geoffrey Samuel presents an interesting argument to show that one of the reasons why Tibet adopted Buddhism in the eighth century was identical with or similar to that which attracted the Chinese and the Japanese, that is, to secure the state and the position of the king.[79] Also, later, rituals were used in Tibet to secure the subjugation or annihilation of enemies.[80] It follows from these and other examples that there are plenty of reasons to think that the Tantric turn of Buddhism opened up a niche that had so far been inaccessible to this religion, and which the Buddhists had been accustomed to leave to the Brahmins.

There is another feature of Tantric Buddhism that might be taken as evidence for the political role that its rites and spells were meant to play. Tantric Buddhist ritual, as Ronald Davidson points out, is full of political metaphors. This imperial metaphor, as Davidson calls it, finds expression in the explicit relationship between the initiatory ritual of the *abhiṣeka* and the coronation ritual of kingship.[81] The maṇḍalas that serve as objects of meditation, moreover, "are implicitly and explicitly articulations of a political horizon in which the central Buddha acts as the Rājādhirāja [Supreme Overlord, JB] in relationship to the other figures of the maṇḍala." Moreover, "Buddhists derived their maṇḍala forms and functions ... from their immediate observation at the disposition and execution of realpolitik in their environment." These and other examples show that esoteric Buddhism internalized the political models of medieval India. Davidson suggests that, in this way, "the great litterateurs and teachers of North Indian monasteries [were] trying to sanctify the world as they received and accepted it." The mission of Buddhist cloisters, he adds, "was a consensual effort at sanctifying society."[82] This, if true, is of course of the greatest interest in our present context. Buddhism had always abstained from justifying society in any of its forms, not to speak of sanctifying it. Davidson's analysis suggests that the Buddhist attitude to society had changed most radically.

Does this mean that Buddhism had now succeeded in freeing itself from the weight of Brahmanism? For many centuries, though not right from the beginning, subcontinental Buddhism had conceded to a form of cohabitation with Brahmanism in which the latter was responsible for matters of state, society, and much else. It took Buddhists many centuries to emancipate themselves from this tutelage. Had they finally succeeded now that they could admit that Buddhists, too, could play roles in society, including the role of ruler or counselor to the ruler? And that they could compete with Brahmins even in the domain of rites and incantations? To some extent, the answer is no doubt *yes*. Buddhists could now develop ideas about the way the state should be run, and they could now offer the kind of supernatural protection that had always been provided by Brahmins.[83] However, the Buddhists remained indebted to Brahmanism in various ways. This can be seen as follows.

The Buddhists of South Asia had not developed any realistic ideas about statecraft of their own. They had slowly come to accept many of the Brahmanical ideas. They themselves never produced more than modified versions of these Brahmanical ideas. The Buddhist concept of the ruler as a Bodhisattva was new, to be sure, as was the accompanying view that rulers acted for the soteriological well-being of their subjects. In practical terms, however, I know of no evidence that might show that Buddhists in South and Southeast Asia really struck out on their own. The Brahmanical model was and remained the basis of their political thought.

In the realm of supernatural protection by means of rites and spells, one might expect a greater distance from the Brahmanical tradition. Buddhists underwent in this area the influence of Śaivism, which was itself in competition with traditional Brahmanism. In spite of this, Tantric Buddhism contains many features that were directly taken from the orthodox Brahmanical tradition. Shrikant Bahulkar has shown, in a private communication, that Vedic concepts, practices, and even a Ṛgvedic mantra found a place in this form of Buddhism. Its texts do not even hesitate to mention the Brahmanical division of society into four classes (*varṇa*), whose existence they clearly take for granted. As an example of this last feature we may consider three parallel Buddhists texts dealing with a rite called the Ahorātravrata. All three of these texts contain detailed stipulations as to the ways Brahmins, Kṣatriyas, Vaiśyas, Śūdras, and those belonging to lower castes should perform their worship. The lowest castes are discouraged from worshipping at all, or at the very least they are told to stay far away from the object of veneration.[84]

South Asian Buddhists, then, have had little opportunity to reassert themselves against the Brahmins who had been their rivals for so long. Their ultimately unsuccessful attempts at doing so took them far from the ideas and practices they had adhered to during the early centuries of their religion, and dangerously close to their much-detested rivals. Most notably, their competition with the Brahmins offered no opportunity to develop ideas about political peace. Quite on the contrary, where Indian Buddhism had originally looked with disapproval upon all forms of violence, including political violence, in the course of time they found ways to justify and contribute to it.

Conclusion

What does all this mean? In one sentence, it means that Indian antiquity has produced no credible ideas about *political* peace. This may look surprising in a civilization in which *mental* peace played such an important role. Mental peace is central in Buddhism and in many manifestations of Brahmanism. To be sure, there may be an element of rhetoric in this claimed interest in mental peace, but it seems undeniable that it represented a real concern to at least some Brahmins and Buddhists. Typically, the standard way to attain this mental peace was by leaving human society altogether. Human society, even in periods of political peace, was often rejected as not conducive to mental peace. This does not change the fact that many of those in search of *mental* peace would have benefited from a society in which there was *political* peace: they usually depended upon the gifts provided by members of society. However, thinkers did little to promote political peace. Those Brahmins whose influence was felt at the court were too occupied with promoting their own interests, and many of the others (primarily the Buddhists), having first left this responsibility to those Brahmins, ended up trying to imitate them. In this way they entered into competition with the Brahmins even in the realms that they had initially ceded to them. The result was that war was endemic in India for all but the few periods in which one kingdom succeeded in uniting a major part of the subcontinent under a single ruler. Thinking about political peace did not play a credible role in ancient India and never exerted a noticeable influence.

The Christian priest Charles Freer Andrews, a friend and admirer of Mahatma Gandhi, wrote to the latter in 1918, praising Indians who "as a race did repudiate bloodlust." Gandhi did not agree with his friend, and it will be interesting to cite his words:

> Is this historically true? I see no sign of it either in the Mahabharata or the Ramayana, not even in my favourite Tulsidas… The incarnations [of God] are described as certainly bloodthirsty, revengeful and merciless to the enemy. They have been credited with having resorted to tricks also for the sake of overcoming the enemy. The battles are described with no less zest than now, and the warriors are equipped with weapons of destruction such as could be possibly conceived by the human imagination. The finest hymn composed by Tulsidas in praise of Rama gives the first place to his ability to strike down the enemy… The code of Manu prescribes no such renunciation that you impute to the race. Buddhism, conceived as a doctrine of universal forbearance, signally failed, and, if the legends are true, the great Shankaracharya did not hesitate to use unspeakable cruelty in banishing Buddhism out of India… Even among the Jains the doctrine has signally failed. They have a superstitious horror of blood(shed), but they have as little regard for the life of the enemy as a European.[85]

Gandhi had no illusions about the nonviolent nature of his own "race." Perhaps characteristically, it was a foreigner who attributed to India the tendency to nonviolent politics, and the modern apostle of nonviolence *par excellence*, Gandhi, who knew better.

Notes

1 Especially at the beginning of this chapter, there is some overlap with Richard Salomon's "Ancient India: Peace within and War without" (2007).
2 Thapar 1963: 255–56.
3 Ibid. 256.
4 Bakker 2006: 29.

5   I believe that Cristina Scherrer-Schaub (2007: 762 n. 14) must be right in thinking that the memory of the "epigraphical" Aśoka survived him for many centuries. The fact that both Rudradāman (ca. 150 CE) and Samudragupta (two centuries later) left inscriptions in places where there were already inscriptions of Aśoka (Falk 2006: 118–19, 158–59) may be understood as supporting this belief. Far from being "curieux" and "peu digne d'un grand souverain" (Fussman 2007: 707), is it not possible that these rulers thus augmented their glory through association with the great former emperor? The "literary" Aśoka exerted an influence on more recent rulers, most notably Kaniṣka; see Deeg 2012.

6   Scharfe 1989: 51.

7   See Trautmann 1971: 10–68 for an analysis of the story of Cāṇakya and Candragupta in the various sources. Further McClish & Olivelle 2012: xi ff.

8   For the most recent enumeration of arguments against this identification, see Olivelle 2013: 31–38.

9   Note that the *Arthaśāstra* (2.10 and elsewhere) is familiar with writing and scribes (*lekhaka*).

10   Fussman 1987–1988: 46.

11   The surviving *Arthaśāstr*a is, as a matter of fact, a composite text, dating from "the first or perhaps the second century A.D." (Scharfe 1993: 293), "100 BCE–100 CE" (McClish & Olivelle 2012: xx–xxi). See further Trautmann 1971: 174ff.; Bronkhorst 1991; 2011: §2.3.

12   McClish & Olivelle 2012: 156.

13   Ibid. xlvii.

14   Ibid. 123.

15   Trans. Olivelle 2005.

16   Trans. Olivelle 1997; 2006.

17   See Fussman 1980: 387: "L'Inde ancienne ne connaît pas de distinction entre guerre juste et guerre injuste, entre guerre d'agression et guerre défensive. La guerre n'a pas à être justifiée. Elle est le devoir du *kṣatriya*—et sa raison d'être."

18   They are accessible in the many (42) volumes of the *Epigraphia Indica* and other such collections.

19   Gommans 1999: 305.

20   In his contacts with contemporary kings, the Buddha abstained from giving them political advice, if the early sources are to be trusted: Bareau 1993: 38.

21   Meisig 1988: 142ff.

22   Trans. ibid. 413.

23   For the parallel in Chinese translation, see Warder 1980: 165–66.

24   Walshe 1987: 397–98.

25   Hartmann 1987: 36–37.

26   Thapar 2002: 221.

27   Hahn 1999: 38–39.

28   Mātṛceṭa was the intellectual "grandchild" of Nāgārjuna according to Bu ston and Tāranātha, but the value of this testimony is dubious (Hartmann 1987: 36). Another Buddhist author belonging roughly to the same time is Āryadeva, who

wrote critically about kings in the fourth chapter of his *Catuḥśataka*; see Lang 1986: 46–47; 1992.

29 Hopkins 1998: 118.

30 Ibid. 148.

31 Jamspal et al. 1978: 14.

32 Ibid. 65.

33 Johnston (1936: II. xiv) provides a piece of evidence, which he does not press, suggesting that Mātṛceṭa is somewhat later in date than Aśvaghoṣa.

34 *Buddhac* 9.40–41, 43.

35 *Abhidh-k-bh(P)* 4.36, p. 221 l. 13–15; *Abhidh-k(VP)* vol. 4 p. 91.

36 For the sometimes violent forms that this competition took, see Verardi 2011.

37 See the historical surveys by Pingree (1981) and Plofker (2007, 2009); further Bronkhorst 2007.

38 Lingat 1989: 152–53; Bronkhorst 2010.

39 The Jainas, here as elsewhere, adjusted more easily, as may be clear from the following (Flügel 2007: 3–4): "Jaina texts on kingship, statecraft and personal law were composed in contexts where individual Jain mendicants exercised personal influence over one or other 'Hindu' king or local official. The majority of the texts were created by monks of the Digambara tradition which had a sustained influence on the ruling dynasties in the Deccan between the eighth and twelfth centuries. The most significant Jaina works on statecraft are the *Ādipurāṇa* of Ācārya Jinasena (ca. 770–850 CE) and the *Nītivākyāmṛtam* (ca. 950 CE) and the *Yaśastilaka* (959 CE) of Ācārya Somadeva Sūri. Both authors were associated with the rulers of the Rāṣṭrakūṭa empire. The *Ādipurāṇa* belongs to the genre of universal history. It tells the life story of the first Jina, the legendary first king and law-giver Ṛṣabha, in the manner of a Jaina *Mahābhārata*, and for the first time offers blueprints for Jain social rituals and Jain kingship through the Jainization of Brāhmaṇical prototypes. The *Nītivākyāmṛtam*, by contrast, is an entirely secular text on statecraft modelled on the *Arthaśāstra* of Kauṭilya … with barely noticeable emphasis on Jaina morality." This last text "barely shows any Jain traits at all" (Dundas 1991: 176).

40 La Vallée Poussin 1925; 1927: 47–48.

41 Wangchuk 2007.

42 Jātakas also inspired people who did not wish to become Buddhas themselves, perhaps already at a time when the Bodhisattva ideal did not yet exist; see Walters 1997: 166.

43 Bodhisattvas characterize primarily Mahāyāna (on which below), but not exclusively so; see Samuels 1997; Appleton 2010: 91–108.

44 Nattier 2003: 223, 225, 226.

45 Ibid. 246.

46 Shih 1994: 35.

47 It goes without saying that a Bodhisattva keeps his wealth in order to benefit others: "A bodhisattva is not covetous of his body, life, or wealth. If he protects his body, life, and wealth, it is to regulate sentient beings" (ibid. 54).

48 Ibid. 57.

49 Ibid.

50 It may be useful to recall Skilling's (2005: 270–71) observation that Śrāvakayāna and Mahāyāna are "[t]wo of the most overworked categories in Buddhist studies": "we have reified the categories and treated Śrāvakayāna and Mahāyāna as discrete historical agents and movements, when they are meant to describe related processes of intellectual interaction, often intense dialogue and debate, within a single (but infinitely variable) imagination, Buddhism. The categories are meant to provide a background, to help us sort out our data, but they have marched on to the stage and taken over the show."

51 See Schmithausen 2007; also 1996: 76–77; 1999: 59; further Kleine 2003: 246–47.

52 Schmithausen 1996: 75; 1999: 57–58. The Mahāyāna *Aṇgulimālīya Sūtra* expresses itself similarly: Schmithausen 2003.

53 Schmithausen 1996: 76; 1999: 58; Skorupski 1983: 66, 218.

54 Schmithausen 2003: 42–43.

55 Many hundreds of times the Buddha had been a universal ruler (*rājā cakkavattī*), already according to the *Aṅguttara Nikāya* (*AN* IV p. 89).

56 Note that "the *Rājadharma-nyāya-śāstra*, part of the massive *Yogācārabhūmiśāstra* ascribed to Maitreya and Asaṅga (early centuries CE), puts kingship into the larger scheme of a Bodhisattva's development as accepted by the Yogācāra school; it strongly emphasizes morality, though the urge for world conquest is not quite reconciled with non-violence" (Scharfe 1989: 22, with a reference to Jan 1984).

57 Mertens 2000.

58 Davidson 2002: 89.

59 Lingat 1989: 152; Bechert 1966: 24.

60 Some certainly were. Gray (2007: 252) gives an example from the *Cakrasaṃvara Tantra* of "a fierce *homa* rite for the purpose of subduing a rival kingdom."

61 See Snellgrove 1987: 121–22; Bongard-Levin et al. 1996: 30–31; Skilling 1997: 63–64; 2007; Davidson 2002: 144–45. The *gāndhārī vidyā* (Pāli *gandhārī nāma vijjā*) "spell (?) from Gandhāra" (Tucci [1963: 147–48] proposes: "a magical formula connected with or placed under the control of Gāndhārī [the Devī from Gandhāra]") is already referred to in the *Kevaddha Sutta* of the *Dīgha Nikāya* (*DN* I p. 213). Early *dhāraṇīs* are found in the texts from Gilgit; see Hinüber 1981.

62 Braarvig 1997; Eltschinger 2001, 2008.

63 Davidson 2002: 116–17.

64 Sanderson 1988: 678–79; 1994; but see White 2005: 8–9.

65 Sanderson 2005: 231–32; see also Sanderson 2007b: 231–32.

66 Sanderson 2007a: 196.

67 Sanderson 2005: 232; see also Gupta and Gombrich 1986; Sanderson 2007b: 241–42, 288–89.

68 On the precise qualifications of Purohitas and their historical development, see Inden 1992.

69 Sanderson 2005: 233, 238–39.

70 Ibid. 238.

71   Kīrtipaṇḍita was mentioned above at n. 57. On the expression of violence in
      Buddhist Tantric mantras, see Verhagen 1999.
72   Grönbold 1996.
73   Samuel 1993: 431, citing from Robinson 1979: 29.
74   Samuel, ibid.
75   Davidson 2005: 23–24.
76   Samuel 2002: 10, with a reference to Chandra 1992. For the activities of Tantric
      Buddhists at and around the imperial court, see Strickmann 1996: 213–14.
77   Demiéville 1957: 355; see also Shen 2004.
78   Samuel 2002: 11.
79   Samuel 2002.
80   Schmithausen 1996: 80–81. On the not altogether idyllic nature of traditional
      Tibetan society, see Parenti 2007; Trimondi and Trimondi 1999: 478–79. Western
      notions of Tibet are exposed in Lopez 1998.
81   Davidson 2002: 123–24.
82   Quotes: ibid. 131, 139, 160, 161.
83   One would think that they might even occupy themselves with astrology and
      related sciences. It is in this connection interesting to note that Amoghavajra, the
      Tantric Buddhist master in China whom we met before (at n. 76 above), is also
      reported to have been the author of a text on Indian astrology (Yano 1987).
84   Handurukande 2000: xvii, 22–23, 75–76, 88, 107–8, 120, 125.
85   Letter of July 6, 1918: Gandhi 1965: 474–75.

Abbreviations

Abhidh-k-bh(P)   Vasubandhu, *Abhidharmakośabhāṣya*. Ed. P. Pradhan. 2nd rev. ed. by
                   Aruna Haldar. Patna 1975.
Abhidh-k(VP)   Vasubandhu, *Abhidharmakośa*, traduit et annoté par Louis de La
                   Vallée Poussin. 6 vols. Paris 1923–1931.
AN   *Aṅguttara-Nikāya*. Ed. R. Morris and E. Hardy. 5 vols. London
                   1885–1900; vol. 6 (Indexes, by M. Hunt and C.A.F. Rhys Davids).
                   London 1910.
Buddhac   Aśvaghoṣa, *Buddhacarita*. Ed. and trans. E.H. Johnston. Calcutta 1935.
DN   *Dīghanikāya*. Eds. T.W. Rhys Davids and J.E. Carpenter. 3 vols. Patna
                   1890–1911.

References

Aggañña Sutta. See Walshe 1987: 407–15; also Collins 1993.
Appleton, N. 2010. *Jātaka Stories in Theravāda Buddhism: Narrating the Bodhisatta
      Path*. Farnham.
Arthaśāstra. See Kangle 1969; Olivelle 2013.

Bakker, H. 2006. "The Hindu religion and war." In King, A. S. (ed.), *Indian Religions: Renaissance and Renewal*, 28–40. London.

Bareau, A. 1993. "Le bouddha et les rois." *Bulletin de l'École française d'Extrême-Orient* 80.1: 15–39.

Bechert, H. 1966. *Buddhismus, Staat und Gesellschaft in den Ländern des Theravāda-Buddhismus*, I: *Allgemeines und Ceylon*. Frankfurt/Main.

Bongard-Levin, G., Boucher, D., Fukita, T., and Wille, K. 1996. "The Nagaropamasūtra: an apotropaic text from the Saṃyuktāgama. A transliteration, reconstruction, and translation of the central Asian sanskrit manuscripts." In F. Fumio Enomoto, J.-U. Hartmann, and H. Matsumura (eds.), *Sanskrit-Texte aus dem buddhistischen Kanon: Neuentdeckungen und Neueditionen*, III: 7–131. Göttingen.

Braarvig, J. 1997. "Bhavya on mantras: apologetic endeavours on behalf of the Mahāyāna." *Studia Indologiczne* 4: 31–39.

Bronkhorst, J. 1991. "Two literary conventions of classical India." *Asiatische Studien / Études Asiatiques* 45.2: 210–27.

Bronkhorst, J. 2007. "Science and religion in classical India." *Indologica Taurinensia* 33: 183–96.

Bronkhorst, J. 2010. "The spread of Sanskrit." In E. Franco and M. Zin (eds.), *From Turfan to Ajanta. Festschrift for Dieter Schlingloff on the Occasion of his Eightieth Birthday*, I: 117–39. Bhairahawa, Rupandehi.

Bronkhorst, J. 2011. *Buddhism in the Shadow of Brahmanism*. Leiden.

Cakkavatti-Sīhanāda Sutta. See Walshe 1987: 395–405.

Chandra, L. 1992. "Tantras and the defence of T'ang China." In Chandra, *Cultural Horizons of India*, II: 257–66. New Delhi.

Collins, S. 1993. "The discourse on what is primary (Aggañña-Sutta): an annotated translation." *Journal of Indian Philosophy* 21.4: 301–93.

Davidson, R. M. 2002. *Indian Esoteric Buddhism. A Social History of the Tantric Movement*. New York.

Davidson, R. M. 2005. *Tibetan Renaissance. Tantric Buddhism in the Rebirth of Tibetan Culture*. New York.

Deeg, M. 2012. "Aśoka, model ruler without a name?" In P. Olivelle, J. Leoshko, and H. Prabha Ray (eds.), *Reimagining Aśoka: Memory and History*, 362–79. New Delhi and Oxford.

Demiéville, P. 1957. *Le bouddhisme et la guerre*. In Renondeau and Demiéville 1957: 347–85.

Dundas, P. 1991. "The Digambara Jain warrior." In M. Carrithers and C. Humphrey (eds.), *The Assembly of Listeners: Jains in Society*, 169–86. Cambridge.

Eltschinger, V. 2001. *Dharmakīrti sur les mantra et la perception du supra-sensible*. Vienna.

Eltschinger, V. 2008. "Dharmakīrti on mantras and their efficiency." In *Esoteric Buddhist Studies: Identity in Diversity*, 273–89. Koya-mati.

Falk, H. 2006. *Aśokan Sites and Artefacts. A Source-book with Bibliography*. Mainz.

Flügel, P. 2007. "A short history of Jaina law." *International Journal of Jaina Studies* 3.4: 1–15.

Fussman, G. 1980. "Le concept d'empire dans l'Inde ancienne." In M. Duverger (ed.), *Le concept d'empire*, 379–96. Paris.

Fussman, G. 1987–1988. "Central and provincial administration in ancient India: the problem of the Mauryan empire." *Indian Historical Review* 14: 43–72.

Fussman, G. 2007. "Les Guptas et le nationalisme indien." *Cours et travaux du Collège de France*, Résumés 2006–2007: 695–711.

Gandhi, M. 1965. *The Collected Works*, XIV: *October 1917 – July 1918*. Delhi.

Gommans, J. 1999. "The embarrassment of political violence in Europe and South Asia c. 1100–1800." In Houben and van Kooij 1999: 287–315.

Gray, D. B. 2007. "Compassionate violence? On the ethical implications of tantric Buddhist ritual." *Journal of Buddhist Ethics* 14: 239–71.

Grönbold, G. 1996. "Kriegsmaschinen in einem buddhistischen Tantra." In F. Wilhelm (ed.), *Festschrift Dieter Schlingloff zur Vollendung des 65. Lebensjahres*, 63–97. Reinbek.

Gupta, S. and Gombrich, R. 1986. "Kings, power and the goddess." *South Asia Research* 6.2: 123–38.

Hahn, M. (trans.). 1999. *Invitation to Enlightenment: Letter to the Great King Kaniṣka by Mātṛceṭa & Letter to a Disciple by Candragomin*. Berkeley.

Handurukande, R. 2000. *Three Sanskrit Texts on Caitya Worship in Relation to the Ahorātravrata*. An edition and synopses in English. Tokyo.

Hartmann, J.-U. (ed., trans.). 1987. *Das Varṇārhavarṇastotra des Mātṛceṭa*. Göttingen.

Hinüber, O. von. 1981. "Namen in Schutzzaubern aus Gilgit." *Studien zur Indologie und Iranistik* 7: 163–71.

Hopkins, J. (ed., trans.). 1998. *Buddhist Advice for Living & Liberation: Nāgārjuna's Precious Garland*. Ithaca NY.

Houben, J. E. M., and Kooij, K. R. (eds.). 1999. *Violence Denied: Violence, Non-Violence and the Rationalization of Violence in South Asian Cultural History*. Leiden.

Inden, R. 1992. "Changes in the Vedic priesthood." In A. W. van den Hoek, D. H. A. Kolff, and M. S. Oort (eds.), *Ritual, State and History in South Asia: Essays in Honour of J. C. Heesterman*, 556–77. Leiden.

Jamspal, L., Chophel, N. S. and della Santina, P. 1978. *Nāgārjuna's Letter to King Gautamīputra*. Delhi.

Jan, Y.-H. 1984. "Rājadharma ideal in Yogācāra Buddhism." In P. Jash (ed.), *Religion and Society in Ancient India: Sudhakar Chattopadhyaya Commemoration Volume*, 221–34. Calcutta.

Johnston, E. H. (ed., trans.). 1936. *The Buddhacarita or Acts of the Buddha*. 2 parts. Lahore. Reprint Delhi, 1984.

Kangle, R. P. 1965, 1969, 1972. *The Kauṭilīya Arthaśāstra*. 3 parts. Bombay. Reprint Delhi, 1986–1988.

Kauṭilya: *Arthaśāstra*. See Kangle 1965–1972.

Kleine, C. 2003. "Üble Mönche oder wohltätige Bodhisattvas?" *Zeitschrift für Religionswissenschaft* 11: 235–58.

Lang, K. (ed., trans.). 1986. *Āryadeva's Catuḥśataka: On the Bodhisattva's Cultivation of Merit and Knowledge*. Copenhagen.

Lang, K. 1992. "Āryadeva and Candrakīrti on the dharma of kings." *Asiatische Studien / Études Asiatiques* 46.1: 232–43.

La Vallée Poussin, L. de. 1925. "Notes bouddhiques, VI §3: Les fidèles laïcs ou upāsakas." *Bulletins de la classe des lettres et des sciences morales et politiques, Académie Royale de Belgique,* 5th ser. 11: 15–34.

La Vallée Poussin, L. de. 1927. *La morale bouddhique.* Paris. Repr. Paris, 2001.

Lingat, R. 1989. *Royautés bouddhiques. Aśoka et la fonction royale à Ceylan.* Eds. G. Fussman and É. Meyer. Paris.

Lopez, D. S. 1998. *Prisoners of Shangri-La. Tibetan Buddhism and the West.* Chicago.

Manu: *Laws of Manu.* See Olivelle 2005.

McClish, M. and Olivelle, P. 2012. *The Arthaśāstra: Selections from the Classic Indian Work on Statecraft.* Indianapolis.

Meisig, K. 1988. *Das Sūtra von den vier Ständen. Das Aggañña-Sutta im Licht seiner chinesischen Parallelen.* Wiesbaden.

Mertens, A. 2000. "Beobachtungen zur Herrschaftslegitimation im Aṅkor-Reich: die buddhistisch orientierte Vat-Sithor-Inschrift von Jayavarman V." In C. Chojnacki, J.-U. Hartmann, and V. M. Tschannerl (eds.), *Vividharatnakaraṇḍaka. Festschrift für Adelheid Mette,* 395–411. Swisttal-Odendorf.

Nāgārjuna: *Letter to King Gautamīputra.* See Jamspal et al. 1978.

Nāgārjuna: *Ratnāvalī/Precious Garland.* See Hopkins 1998.

Nattier, J. 2003. *A Few Good Men: The Bodhisattva Path according to the Inquiry of Ugra (Ugraparipṛcchā). A Study and Translation.* Honolulu.

Olivelle, P. 1997. *Pañcatantra. The Book of India's Folk Wisdom.* New York and Oxford.

Olivelle, P. 2005. *Manu's Code of Law: A Critical Edition and Translation of the Mānava-Dharmaśāstra.* New York and Oxford.

Olivelle, P. 2006. *The Five Discourses on Worldly Wisdom by Viṣṇuśarman.* New York.

Olivelle, P. 2013. *King, Governance, and Law in Ancient India: Kauṭilya's Arthaśāstra. A New Annotated Translation.* New York and Oxford.

Parenti, M. 2007. "Friendly feudalism: the Tibet myth." www.michaelparenti.org/ Tibet.html#notes (accessed November 20, 2015).

Pingree, D. 1981. *Jyotiḥśāstra: Astral and Mathematical Literature.* Wiesbaden.

Plofker, K. 2007. "Mathematics in India." In V. Katz (ed.), *The Mathematics of Egypt, Mesopotamia, China, India, and Islam: A Sourcebook,* 385–514. Princeton.

Plofker, K. 2009. *Mathematics in India.* Princeton.

Renondeau, G., and Demiéville, P. 1957. *Histoire des moines guerriers du Japon,* by G. Renondeau; *Le bouddhisme et la guerre,* by Paul Demiéville. Paris.

Robinson, J. B. (trans.). 1979. *Buddha's Lions: The Lives of the Eighty-Four Siddhas. Caturaśīti-siddha-pravṛtti by Abhayadatta.* Berkeley.

Salomon, R. 2007. "Ancient India: peace within and war without." In K. A. Raaflaub (ed.), *War and Peace in the Ancient World,* 53–65. Malden and Oxford.

Samuel, G. 1993. *Civilized Shamans: Buddhism in Tibetan Society.* Washington DC.

Samuel, G. 2002. "Buddhism and the state in eighth-century Tibet." In H. Blazer (ed.), *Religion and Secular Culture in Tibet,* 1–19. Leiden.

Samuels, J. 1997. "The Bodhisattva ideal in Theravāda Buddhist theory and practice: a reevaluation of the bodhisattva-śrāvaka opposition." *Philosophy East and West* 47.3: 399–415.

Sanderson, A. 1988. "Śaivism and the tantric traditions." In S. Sutherland, L. Houlden, P. Clarke, and F. Hardy (eds.), *The World's Religions*, 660–704. London.

Sanderson, A. 1994. "Vajrayāna: origin and function." In *Buddhism into the Year 2000*, 87–102. Bangkok and Los Angeles.

Sanderson, A. 2005. "Religion and the state: Śaiva officiants in the territory of the king's brahmanical chaplain." *Indo-Iranian Journal* 47 (2004): 229–300.

Sanderson, A. 2007a. "Atharvavedins in tantric territory. The Āṅgirasakalpa texts of the Oriya Paippalādins and their connection with the Trika and the Kālīkula. With critical editions of the Parājapavidhi, the Parāmantravidhi, and the Bhadrakālīmantravidhipr akaraṇa." In A. Griffiths and A. Schmiedchen (eds.), *The Atharvaveda and its Paippalādaśākhā: Historical and Philological Papers on a Vedic Tradition*, 195–311. Aachen.

Sanderson, A. 2007b. "The Śaiva exegesis of Kashmir." In D. Goodall and A. Padoux (eds.), *Mélanges tantriques à la mémoire d'Hélène Brunner / Tantric Studies in Memory of Hélène Brunner*, 231–442. Pondichéry, Paris.

Scharfe, H. 1989. *The State in Indian Tradition*. Leiden.

Scharfe, H. 1993. *Investigations in Kauṭalya's Manual of Political Science*. 2nd rev. ed. of *Untersuchungen zur Staatsrechtslehre des Kauṭalya*. Wiesbaden.

Scherrer-Schaub, C. 2007. "Immortality extolled with reason: philosophy and politics in Nāgārjuna." In B. Kellner, H. Krasser, H. Lasic, et al. (eds.), *Pramāṇakīrtiḥ: Papers Dedicated to Ernst Steinkellner*, part 2: 757–93. Vienna.

Schmithausen, L. 1996. "Buddhismus und Glaubenskriege." In P. Hermann (ed.), *Glaubenskriege in Vergangenheit und Gegenwart*, 63–92. Göttingen.

Schmithausen, L. 1999. "Aspects of the Buddhist attitude towards war." In Houben and van Kooij 1999: 45–67.

Schmithausen, L. 2003. "Einige besondere Aspekte der 'Bodhisattva-Ethik' in Indien und ihre Hintergründe." *Hōrin* 10: 21–46.

Schmithausen, L. 2007. "Zur Frage, ob ein Bodhisattva unter bestimmten Voraussetzungen in einer neutralen Geisteshaltung (*avyākṛta-citta*) töten darf." In K. Klaus and J.-U. Hartmann (eds.), *Indica et Tibetica. Festschrift für Michael Hahn*, 423–40. Vienna.

Shen, W. 2004. "Magic power, sorcery and evil spirit: the image of Tibetan monks in Chinese literature during the Yuan dynasty." In C. Cüppers (ed.), *The Relationship Between Religion and State (chos srid zung 'brel) in Traditional Tibet*, 189–227. Lumbini.

Shih, H.-C. 1994. *The Sutra on Upāsaka Precepts. Translated from the Chinese of Dharmarakṣa*. Berkeley.

Skilling, P. 1997. *Mahāsūtras: Great Discourses of the Buddha*, II. 2 Parts. Oxford.

Skilling, P. 2005. "Cutting across categories: the ideology of relics in Buddhism." *Annual Report of the International Research Institute for Advanced Buddhology at Soka University for the Academic Year 2004*: 269–310. Tokyo.

Skilling, P. 2007. "Zombies and half-zombies: Mahāsūtras and other protective measures." *Journal of the Pali Text Society* 29: 313–30.

Skorupski, T. (ed., trans.). 1983. *The Sarvadurgatipariśodhana Tantra: Elimination of All Evil Destinies*. Delhi.

Snellgrove, D. L. 1987. *Indo-Tibetan Buddhism: Indian Buddhists and their Tibetan Successors*. London.

Strickmann, M. 1996. *Mantras et mandarins. Le Bouddhisme tantrique en Chine*. Paris.

Thapar, R. 1963. *Aśoka and the Decline of the Mauryas*. Delhi and Oxford.

Thapar, R. 2002. *The Penguin History of Early India, from the Origins to AD 1300*. London.

Trautmann, T. R. 1971. *Kauṭilya and the Arthaśāstra: A Statistical Investigation of the Authorship and Evolution of the Text*. Leiden.

Trimondi, V. and Trimondi, V. 1999. *Der Schatten des Dalai Lama. Sexualität, Magie und Politik im tibetischen Buddhismus*. Düsseldorf.

Tucci, G. 1963. "Oriental notes II: an image of a devi discovered in swat and some connected problems." *East and West* 14: 146–82.

Verardi, G. 2011. *Hardships and Downfall of Buddhism in India*. Singapore and Manohar.

Verhagen, P. C. 1999. "Expressions of violence in Buddhist tantric mantras." In Houben and van Kooij 1999: 275–85.

Walshe, M. 1987. *The Long Discourses of the Buddha: A Translation of the Dīgha Nikāya*. Boston.

Walters, J. S. 1997. "Stūpa, story and empire: constructions of the Buddha biography in early post-Aśokan India." In J. Schober (ed.), *Sacred Biography in the Buddhist Traditions of South and Southeast Asia*, 160–92. Honolulu.

Wangchuk, D. 2007. *The Resolve to Become a Buddha. A Study of the Bodhicitta Concept in Indo-Tibetan Buddhism*. Tokyo.

Warder, A. K. 1980. *Indian Buddhism*. 2nd rev. ed. Delhi.

White, D. G. 2005. Review of Davidson 2002. *Journal of the International Association of Tibetan Studies* 1: 1–11.

Yano, M. 1987. "The Hsiu-yao Ching and its sanskrit sources." In G. Swarup, A. K. Bag, and K. S. Shukla (eds.), *History of Oriental Astronomy*, 125–34. Cambridge.

4

Searching for Peace in the Warring States: Philosophical Debates and the Management of Violence in Early China

ROBIN D. S. YATES

One who takes pleasure in war will perish, and one who covets the spoils of victory will incur disgrace. War is not something to be enjoyed, and victory is not something to profit from.[1]

Sun Bin (mid-fourth century BCE)

Introduction

Yuri Pines has recently argued that all the thinkers of the Warring States period in China (circa 500–221 BCE), from Confucius (551–479) on, were unanimous in their advocacy of a unitary empire, what he calls "The Great Unity Paradigm,"[2] as a result of their disappointment with the collapse of the multi-state international order in the preceding Spring and Autumn period (mid-eighth to fifth centuries) of the Eastern Zhou dynasty.[3] The times in which they lived saw increasingly savage warfare waged between rival states, and philosophers and statesmen traveled from one state to another offering their services to the rulers, proposing different policies and recommendations both on how to unify the "All-under-Heaven" (the world as they

Peace in the Ancient World: Concepts and Theories, First Edition. Edited by Kurt A. Raaflaub.
© 2016 John Wiley & Sons, Inc. Published 2016 by John Wiley & Sons, Inc.

knew it) and how to survive physically in those turbulent times. The rulers themselves in turn sought to attract talented men to advise them on what policies to follow and to serve in their increasingly complex administrative organizations, just as they sought to attract peasants from other states who would plow their fields, providing them with tax revenue in the form of grain and textiles, and serve in their armies.[4]

Some states chose the path of aggression, others, in weaker strategic situations, chose to ally themselves with the stronger, hoping that they would not be eliminated. Over time, various coalitions were formed both for and against the rising menace on the western frontier, the state of Qin, and in the end only seven states were left to compete for the ultimate prize of unifying the subcontinent. The most prominent among them were Qin and Chu, the latter a vast country based in the central Yangzi River valley, modern Hubei Province, which had expanded in all directions.[5] In fact, although the accepted wisdom is that no empire was founded in China until the unification of the subcontinent by the infamous First Emperor of Qin (Qin Shihuangdi) in 221, both Qin and Chu were empires by approximately 300, whereas the other states were more local or regional polities.[6]

As for how rulers and their subjects were to survive physically in those turbulent times philosophers proposed a very wide range of answers, and much of the intellectual debate centered on such questions, as well as on how rulers were to gain and maintain the support of their people and attract and retain migrants into their territories. These debates led to profound analyses of human nature and its relation to the divine or the suprahuman realm, the nature of morality and ethics, appropriate courses of personal and political behavior, and many other topics. Recent archaeological discoveries of long-lost texts relating to views and traditions that contributed to these debates have deepened our understanding of the complex intellectual environment, but often have raised as many questions as they have answered.[7]

The first unified empire was created by the Qin, but it only lasted for barely more than a decade (221–206) before its collapse in a bitter civil war after the First Emperor's death.[8] Unity was eventually restored by Liu Bang, who founded the Han dynasty in 206. Known in history as Han Gaozu, Liu, a former low-ranking Qin official who served in the former territory controlled by Chu, spent most of his reign mopping up resistance to his rule and meeting military and political challenges to his supremacy not only from his rivals for the throne and the leader of the northern steppe peoples (the Xiongnu), but also from his former generals who sought, as warlords, to return to the multi-state system of the time before the imperial unification by the Qin. Although Han apologists sought to distinguish the Han from their Qin predecessors, new discoveries of legal texts dating from the early Han make it possible to see that there were very significant continuities in political, legal, and social institutions between the two regimes of imperial Qin and early Han.[9]

Pines quotes from one of these Han apologists, the early Han Confucian philosopher and statesman Jia Yi (circa 200–168) who criticized the Qin in a famous set of essays titled "Finding Fault with Qin" (*Guo Qin lun*) that the Han historian Sima Qian (circa 145–circa 86) preserved in his *Historical Records*:

> Now, after Qin faced south and ruled All under Heaven, this meant that there was a Son of Heaven above. The masses hoped that they would obtain peace and security and there was nobody who did not whole-heartedly look up in reverence. This was the moment to preserve authority and stabilize achievements, the foundations of lasting peace.[10]

The ideal of unity formulated by the Warring States thinkers dominated all later conceptions of the Chinese imperium, Pines argues, and still influences Chinese policy today. Thus, he ignores the many later centuries when the East Asian subcontinent was divided into competing polities and empires, so that different forms of accommodation and peaceful relations had to be worked out between essentially equal partners, and different philosophical and religious ideologies, such as Buddhism, played crucial, if not central roles. But Pines is not alone in assuming that little changed over the millennia between the Warring States and modern times. Yuan-kang Wang neatly sums up this strain of thinking when he states, "Rarely in human history can we find a case like China in which a single pacifist culture (that of Confucianism) dominated both the bureaucracy and the society for two thousand years."[11] Given that China was among the most inventive cultures in the arts of war and has a rich military history, this claim is far from the mark: China was never a "pacifist culture" and Confucianism was never a pacifist ideology, nor, indeed, was Confucianism uninterruptedly dominant for two thousand years.[12] Nevertheless, Wang, Wright, Standen, and Cui, among others, have documented the nature and structure of international relations in some of these later stages of Chinese history,[13] while Johnston has written an influential, although historically flawed, study of international relations in the Ming dynasty (1368–1644 CE).[14] The conceptions of peace and the means of achieving it in these later periods of Chinese history, and the influence of Confucian culture and philosophy on those practices, although fascinating, are not the subject of the present chapter, which concerns itself with the time prior to the establishment of the unified empire under the Qin in 221 BCE.[15]

Political Conditions in Early China

The three centuries of the Warring States (fifth to third centuries) were a period of intense and almost permanent warfare between rival states that could be viewed as a time of "chronic conflict" in the terms of Caplow and Hicks,[16] while at the same time it was a period of drastic social, political, intellectual, and economic change.

Earlier, in the Western Zhou period (mid-eleventh to mid-eighth centuries), the Zhou kings dominated and controlled their subordinates—polities that were centered on aristocratic lineages linked by blood or marriage to the Zhou Ji clan—through ritual rules (*li*), administrative techniques, and their own military might.[17] In this earlier period, Zhou power managed interstate rivalries as well as the expansion of those polities into unclaimed territory in the East Asian subcontinent, including the traditional territory of non-Zhou peoples, only some of whom were at a state level of organization. Central Zhou dominance was lost in the years just prior to 770, as a result of a succession dispute and an internal revolt. In the subsequent decades, the Zhou were forced from their original homeland in the Wei River valley in north-western China to move to a much smaller territory surrounding the city of Luoyang in the flood plain of the Yellow River in modern Henan province.[18] There, the Eastern Zhou rulers maintained their ritual authority until their line eventually died out in 256.[19]

The early Eastern Zhou is known as the Spring and Autumn period after an annalistic chronicle of the minor state of Lu supposedly edited by Confucius (died 479).[20] During this period, a series of hegemonic leaders (*ba*), whose military might was vastly superior to that of the Zhou, was able to maintain a balance of power between increasingly restless and expansionist states by acting in the name of the Zhou kings to enforce international agreements or treaties called covenants (*meng*).[21] These covenants initially had strong religious overtones: they were confirmed by oaths and blood sacrifice and guaranteed by the gods. Violation of the treaties was punished not only by the sworn partners themselves but also by the gods who would administer divine justice. But over a relatively short time these covenants lost their religious and legal authority to enforce peace between warring parties and their allies. Those involved, including the hegemons themselves, cynically manipulated the force of the covenants: they brought forbidden weapons and armor to the covenant site or swore the oath in full knowledge and expectation that they would violate the terms of the peace treaty in order to conduct their foreign policy in accordance with current and fleeting changes in international military power relations; in doing so, they completely ignored the higher authority and wishes of their nominal overlords, the Zhou kings, any commitment to principles of peace, or fear of divine retribution.[22]

In the sixth century, states that had expanded in the Spring and Autumn period at the expense of their smaller neighbors began to split apart internally as lineages headed by close relatives of the rulers started to assert their independence and vie for political and economic power. They established their own seats of government based on their own walled hometowns, and they began to build their own military organizations and administrative networks to exploit the resources in the surrounding countryside. The structured world of the Zhou polity seemed to be disintegrating and lineage fission worked its way down lower into the social hierarchy. It is striking that it was just at this period of seeming social disintegration that the beginnings of conscious intellectual ferment began.[23]

Both the rulers of the states whose authority was being challenged and the upstart heads of the lineages who were expanding their power at their nominal ruler's expense needed men to advise them on policy initiatives and to carry them out in practice. Thus the conditions of apparent social and political collapse in a period of increasing military strife actually opened the doors for the rise of a new type of individual: a man with talent and intelligence who could serve loyally and offer innovative solutions to the practical problems of governance. This type of man seems to have been found among the members of the lesser lineages whose connections to the ruling houses were more distant. They wanted employment and opportunities to exercise their talents. These men eventually developed into the so-called *shi* class and they sought out teachers who could provide them with an education, which they could then parlay into service for the leaders of the competing powers. The first of such teachers was Confucius, followed in short order by Mozi (Master Mo, otherwise known as Mo Di), among many others whose names mostly have not come down to us.

The Warring States

In his article on the Grand Unity Paradigm, Pines (2000) reviews the ideas of the leading proponents of this new intellectual activity—the Ru or Confucians, Mohists (the followers of Mozi), and Daoists—and argues that all of them believed strongly that the anarchy of the Warring States period succeeding that of the Spring and Autumn could only be solved by the elevation of a single ruler as Son of Heaven. Only the creation of a strong centralized monarchy could end the constant warfare among the competing independent states and their theoretically subordinate lineages. The rulers of these states paid no attention to the wishes of their erstwhile overlords, the Zhou kings, disrupted the lives of the people, and brought about general impoverishment of the population by their own personal extravagance and desires and their efforts to conquer their rivals by force of arms.

However, each of these traditions of thinkers (Confucians, Mohists, and Daoists) and others of the so-called Hundred Schools, proposed that this ideal single ruler should possess different moral qualities, act in different ways and conform in different ways to the cosmos, and initiate different policies to achieve unity of the All-under-Heaven.

Confucius and his immediate followers advocated a return to forms of government of the early Western Zhou kings; they emphasized the priority of ritual performance and urged that the ruler act as a moral exemplar and listen to advisors who cultivated themselves in the principles of humaneness or benevolence, right thinking (righteousness), trustworthiness, loyalty, filial piety, and wisdom. Their principal rivals were the Mohists—it was said that the founder of the school, Mozi, had initially been one of Confucius's disciples but had left his master as a result of profound philosophical disagreements. They deplored offensive warfare, saying that it was no more than robbery on a grand scale, and urged reduction of government and personal expenses and the establishment of a clear bureaucratic hierarchy in which the most worthy were placed in the higher positions and each lower rank accepted without question the dictates of the rank above them. All policies were to be subject to a test of their benefit to the people as a whole, a principle coupled with the imposition of the moral value of all-encompassing care (*jian'ai*),[24] whereby all were to treat everyone else with equal concern and without regard to their kin relationship. As Confucians modeled their moral system on the basis of kin relations, this was a direct challenge to Confucian ideas.

The Daoists, on the other hand, such as those represented in the "Inward Training" chapter of the compendium *Guanzi* ("Neiye"),[25] and later the *Laozi*,[26] emphasized that the ruler should engage in psychosomatic training through meditation, avoid actively engaging in governing, and let things in the world take their natural course. The ruler would rule by harmonizing himself with the Way, the origin of all things in the cosmos. When people's desires were reduced to the basic necessities (food, drink, and housing), there would no longer be destructive wars and peace would come of itself; those in one village would not even know the affairs of the next village, and everyone would live out their natural life-span without fear or strife.

All these traditions essentially argued that it was only through the methods of peace that war could be brought to an end. In fact, it was only the militarists, such as Wu Qi, and the "legalists," such as Lord Shang in Qin, Shen Buhai in Han, and Han Feizi, one of the two famous students of the Confucian philosopher Xunzi, who advocated the creation of unity by force of arms and developed a strategy of strengthening the military, legal, and economic resources of the state to overcome, by military might alone, all other competing states.[27]

Nevertheless, as far as I can determine at present,[28] each of the states in the Warring States period developed its own internal system of laws and legal procedures with little input from the policy suggestions of the philosophers. It was rather the numerous and now mostly unidentifiable administrators who issued legal statutes and ordinances in the name of the rulers of their respective states and developed the legal procedures that were directed towards ensuring internal peace and stability, the monopoly of force by state authorities, the definition and limitation of jurisdiction, and the preservation of the boundaries of the state against external enemies. Their efforts provoked tremendous resistance from the population. Abscondence (*wang*), in other words, migration and flight, became a major problem for all the states,[29] and great efforts had to be invested into forcing the population to stay put, so that the state functionaries could register them, tax them, and force them to perform corvée labor, and train and fight in the increasingly large armies.

All these administrative measures and other innovations were a necessary condition, in my opinion, for the development of more abstract notions concerning the form that an ideal peace might take, and of ideas about people's obligations and duties and even rights to life and property. For example, by the late Warring States period, rules of military combat had been worked out that aimed at preventing innocent civilians from suffering harm by an invading army and punishing violators of the army's regulations under military law, which was even harsher than civilian law.[30] The Confucian scholar Xunzi was highly impressed by the internal peace and order that existed within Qin boundaries when he went to pay a visit to King Zhaoxiang and the prime minister Fan Sui in the 260s.[31] All that was lacking in Qin, he averred, were Ru (Confucian) scholars.

In short, I believe that the increasing ability of the states to reduce and punish crimes and random as well as inter-lineage violence within their own boundaries made it possible for the philosophers and theoreticians not only to demand peace abstractly but to contemplate what an ideal peace might actually look like. "Strengthening the State" became a buzzword not only for "legalists," but even for a Confucian philosopher like Xunzi.[32] Thus, while there is much of value in Pines' interpretation with which I began,[33] I disagree with it in essential respects. I will now turn to examine more closely and within the context of changing political and military conditions some of the ideas current in Warring States China concerning the notion of "peace" in a time of almost perpetual war.

Peace in the Warring States

Before going further, it is worth noting that the early Chinese language lacked a precise word that denoted warfare as an abstract concept. The word that was most commonly used in the abstract was *bing*, which also meant "weapons." The word with the closest associated meaning was *zhan*, meaning "battle" or "fight." On the other hand, the Chinese had a word, indeed several words, that came close in meaning to the concept of peace, such as *an*—the modern equivalent is a binome, *anping* or *ping'an*, that links originally similar words, *an* (literally "safe") and *ping* (literally "level," "flat" or "even-handed") or, more commonly, *heping* (literally "harmony" and "peace").[34] In addition, they also used the word *ding* (literally to "settle" or "fix" [the people and the state]) in the context of peace, as well as other words meaning "quiet" (like *ning*). For all this it hardly matters whether we accept Caplow and Hicks' opinion that "(p)eace is best visualized as an interim condition between wars…; (p)ermanent peace, as distinct from an interim between wars, is normally established when two formerly warring groups come under a common authority and lose their independent war-making capacity," or subscribe to Müller's more nuanced definition: "Peace is a state between specific social and political collectives characterized by the absence of direct violence and in which the possible use of violence by one against another in the discourse between the collectives has no place."[35]

Needless to say, there are many other ways to define peace, and Müller's definition begs for a clarification of the scope and meaning of "violence."[36] But many early Chinese came to view peace not as an *absence*, as Müller would define it, but as a condition or state with positive characteristics among which the emanation of moral virtue by the ruler and his high officials was especially important. If only the ruler emanated virtue or charisma (*de*) and faced south in the ritually correct posture, then the world would acknowledge his authority, and peace and prosperity would ensue; all would rush to till his fields, travel on his roads, and live in his cities. As the common saying went, if someone by mistake dropped a precious object on the road, no one would pick it up and steal it. And, further, the cosmos itself would be in order: the triad Heaven, Earth, and Man would be in harmony and all would follow its natural course.[37]

However, in the period that we are considering in early China, to a large extent the philosophers and statesmen were concerned with *order* (*zhi*) and *disorder* (*luan*) rather than with the notion of peace, as were early thinkers in ancient Greece, as Raaflaub demonstrates in his chapter.[38] As Sato has recently argued, the philosophers at the court of the rulers of the coastal state of Qi (modern Shandong province) in the fourth and third centuries, for example, engaged in an intense debate on what constituted order and disorder, although, since virtually all of their writings are now lost to us, we cannot clearly discern their differences of opinion.[39] This concern with the suppression of disorder is found throughout Chinese history down to the present day; hence the suppression of student unrest at Tiananmen in 1989: protest of current economic and political conditions was deemed "disorder" by the authorities and thus the communications between the demonstrators and the government were suspended and the crowds of students and their sympathizers were dispersed by force of arms.

But let us return to the fourth and third centuries to consider the views of some of the philosophers whose works have come down to us. Mencius (Meng Ke), whose ideas formed part of the "Confucian-Mencian paradigm" deemed by some scholars to represent the dominant pacifist ideology of pre-modern China, lived at a time of major military conflict between the states on the north China plain. As Nivison has cogently pointed out, when the lord of Qi won a great victory over the state of Wei in the famous battle of Maling in 342, he claimed the title of king (*wang*), a title that previously was officially reserved only for a Zhou dynast.[40] In short order, rulers of other states made the same claims, and there was some mutual recognition of the title. But these claims were interpreted by rulers of other states as an implicit declaration that the ruler was seeking hegemony over all the other states: it was an implicit declaration of war. And warfare did indeed erupt as a result.

At the same time, philosophers and rulers began a vigorous discussion about the nature and appropriateness of hereditary succession as opposed to merit-based rulership. Some advocated that a ruler should be the one who was most qualified, not one who had merely inherited his position from his father, and that the ruler had the right to abdicate and dispose of the throne as he saw fit. One ruler even went so far as to put this into practice and tried to give his throne to his leading official. This act only resulted in a civil war. Some of these heated debates have been recovered from newly excavated and retrieved texts,[41] and Nivison claims that the discussions recorded in the text of the book of *Mencius* about the right of rulers in China's ancient past to give the empire to another was therefore a most pressing and pertinent issue.[42] Mencius argued that no one had the right to give the empire to another: only Heaven had that right; so implicitly the lords of his own day had no authority to claim to be kings on the basis of victory in warfare. In other words, Mencius was arguing from historical precedent about current military and political affairs. His description of what a "true ruler" would be like—a moral exemplar who took care of his people first and who ruled under the authority and approval of

Heaven, with no mention of military preparations—was not an indication that Mencius was necessarily a devoted pacifist who had no interest in military affairs, but a measured philosophical response to the particular military and political conditions of his day: the claim to be a "king" resulted in war and war resulted in the destruction of the people.[43]

While Mencius did not directly confront the issue of war and peace in his own time, Xunzi (Xun Qing or Xun Kuang), a later follower of the Confucian tradition in Warring States times, certainly did. On the one hand, he engaged in a direct debate on the principles of warfare with the Lord of Linwu, one of the practitioners of the method of warfare propagated by Sunzi (also known as Sun Wu).[44] On the other hand, he addressed the question of peace by detailing policies that a true king should enact and institutions that such a ruler should establish so that "Perfect Peace" could be achieved. True to his Confucian principles, Xunzi argued that a "true king" would have his army act on the basis of humanity or benevolence and justice, and that therefore he would not engage in "warfare," but only in "punitive expeditions" against those who failed to acknowledge his supremacy: only those who sought their own personal immediate and short-term profit engaged in "warfare." The army of a true king would be so well-ordered and disciplined that it would win in any combat, no matter what formation it deployed.[45] When he was questioned by his student, the future prime minister of the Qin Empire, Li Si, who pointed out that Qin had been victorious for four generations without following the principles dear to Xunzi, the latter replied that, although Qin had been successful, "it has been constantly seized with fear and apprehension lest the whole world unite together in concerted action to crush Qin with their collective power."[46] Of course, at the time Xunzi could not have known that Qin was eventually going to be successful in defeating its rivals; but, then again, given the fact that Qin fell so quickly after the First Emperor's death in 210, the argument could be construed that the principles of humanity and justice were more important for long-term success. Indeed, Xunzi may have lived long enough to have seen the unification happen, but we do not know his reaction to it.

However, probably in Xunzi's lifetime, under the direction of Lü Buwei, a rich former merchant, who was prime minister of the state of Qin, scholars in 239 compiled a blueprint for the ideology of the Qin state—a couple of decades before it succeeded in eliminating all its rivals and founding the empire. This work, called the *Spring and Autumn Annals of Master Lü* (*Lü shi chunqiu*), was presented to King Zheng who later became the famous First Emperor of China and whose mausoleum with its enormous numbers of terracotta warriors and horses is one of the world's most remarkable archaeological sites.[47]

In Book 7, chapters 2–5, the writers consider the history of warfare and the issues of war and peace.[48] First, they argue that warfare existed in high antiquity, even from the beginning of human existence, that no ruler ever discarded the use of weapons, and that fear of weapons derives from human nature (*xing*), which in turn derives from heaven or nature (*tian*). Indeed, "Fighting and conflict originated long ago, so they can be neither forbidden nor halted. Thus the sage-kings of antiquity held to the righteous use of weapons, and none thought of abolishing weapons."[49] In the light of humans' natural instinct to fight each other, a hierarchy of authority had to be established from the bottom up, from chieftains to lords, and culminating in a Son of Heaven, who took his position above everyone else.

The writers were here adopting an idea of the Mohists, who had been the first to argue that social order required the establishment of a rigid hierarchy; otherwise, it would be just one man against another, and one group against another, each defending their own interests first and considering that they were right (*yi*) in their actions.[50] The Mohists, however, had argued that it was the quasi-religious entity of Heaven who had set up the hierarchy from the top down, rather than that such a hierarchy arose naturally out of human nature from the bottom up, as the *Lü shi chunqiu* writers asserted. Thus, the latter were arguing for the necessity of a supreme figure of authority, and they did this at a time when the line of the Zhou kings had disappeared; there was no such highest authority in China at the time and, in Qin, King Zheng was still a minor. In addition, they argued (as just pointed out), it was as absurd to abolish all weapons just because someone lost his state as it would be to banish food because someone died from food poisoning; you could no more abolish them than you could abolish fire or water. What mattered was *how* you used the weapons. They had to be employed in a righteous cause and used in a skillful fashion. Thus, they rejected the ideas and practices of those who opposed warfare, "(l)earned men of the present age (who) condemn offensive warfare… while adopting the policy of defensive warfare."[51]

These "learned men" most likely were the later Mohists who had developed practical expertise in defending cities and towns from attack, adopting and developing the latest technology to achieve their ends.[52] We no longer have access to any arguments that the latter may have made in support of their military activities, apart from the earlier ideas mentioned above—that war was a waste of resources, even for the victors, caused untold damage, and was of no benefit for the people as a whole. Still, the writers of the *Lü shi chunqiu* accused them of defending those who were immoral or "lacked the Dao (Way)." It is not possible, in other words, to determine whether these later Mohists believed that by resisting attack they were paving the way for some ideal ruler to appear to institute an ideal peace, or accepted the political status quo of a multi-state world and were trying to create a balance of power that would make a form of interim peace possible.

Such activities seem also to have been the aim of a group of mercenary diplomats called the "strategists of the horizontal and vertical alliance" (*Zongheng jia*), who travelled from state to state seeking employment and advocating alliances for and against the state of Qin, depending on the political realities of the day. For certain, they strove to preserve the existence of all the political entities of the time; by playing off one ruler and one state against another, so that the entire political system was maintained in a state of uneasy equilibrium, they gained riches, status, and political power for themselves, even if only for the time being.[53] Such opportunities would have disappeared under a single monarch in a unified state, for their activities would have challenged the ultimate authority of a supreme ruler.

Finally, another group of philosophers, whose works have only recently been recovered after being lost for more than two thousand years, known as the followers of the Huang-Lao tradition,[54] advocated that the ruler rest in peace or engage in active warfare only to defeat his enemies according to the rhythms of the cosmos.[55] Only by carefully and minutely examining the actual social and political conditions of his own country and of that of his enemy, of himself and the enemy ruler, as well as the seasons, and the greater rhythms of the cosmos, the perpetual movement of Yin and Yang and the Dao (Way), and acting at the right time, would he be able to manifest his power and bring peace to the world. Only then would he be able to rule as a "true king" (the concept of the "ideal ruler" that was also elaborated by the Confucian philosopher, Mencius) and bring "Grand Peace," if he acted as part of a triad with Heaven and Earth, making his punitive attacks against the immoral inevitable, and ruling without any private bias and only in the interests of the entire land.[56]

Conclusion

In the conclusion of his introductory essay in this volume, Raaflaub posits that "three conditions determined a society's ability to develop concepts or theories of peace—exceptionally harsh war experiences, capacity of abstract and philosophical thinking, and independence of the thinkers." I do not think that it is possible in the present state of our knowledge to determine whether the increasing occurrence of warfare in the Spring and Autumn period, and its changing nature, necessarily *caused* the development of philosophical debate and abstract thinking in early China. The harshest forms of warfare occurred in the fourth and third centuries, at least a century and a half after the beginnings of philosophical reflection that started with Confucius. Further, in China, the independence of thinkers from the state apparatus never seems to have gone as far as it did in Greece and Rome: most Chinese thinkers wished to have their ideas implemented in the real world and therefore argued their views in the presence and for the benefit of contemporary rulers or high officials and statesmen.[57] With the establishment of the Qin and Han Empires, thinkers, like all the rest of the population, were definitely subordinated to the dictates of the central authorities and struggled mightily through the rest of imperial Chinese history to free themselves from ideological constraints imposed from above. And while there seems in early times to have been some kind of cult devoted to a god of war, Chiyou, it was not widely disseminated, nor did a cult of peace develop.[58]

Nevertheless, we have seen that in China philosophical debate about crucial political issues, including war and peace, did begin in the sixth century, at a time when rulers of larger states had begun the process of assimilating their smaller neighbors through warfare and their polities were growing so big that they began to fission internally. This process necessitated the development of administrative reorganization and centralization, which in turn required the development of a new type of expert who was trained to execute the policies of the rulers and to manage the integration of increasing numbers of ordinary commoners into the state structure. Confucius was the first teacher of this new breed of experts, and he considered it most essential that such individuals be trained in moral self-cultivation. Later, military specialists appeared, such as Sunzi (Sun Wu), but they concentrated on developing techniques to be deployed on the battlefield in order to be victorious in warfare. They were not interested in what peace might look like once victory had been achieved.

The Mohists articulated principles on which policies should be instituted and they gave preference to those that would benefit the people as a whole. At the same time, as they began the process of thinking how a state should be ordered internally and that Heaven provided the justification for social and political hierarchy and thus for a ruler's authority, they organized themselves along military lines and developed expertise in the techniques of military defense. Objecting to the Mohists' emphasis on benefit, the Confucians Mencius and Xunzi elaborated what they believed would bring peace to the world as they knew it. They posited the notion of a "true king" whose moral rule would almost effortlessly bring about the end of war so that "perfect peace" would be achieved.

As these philosophers and others, such as the Daoists, were debating how to solve the problems of incessant warfare and social dislocation, the competing states in the fourth and third centuries developed internal legal structures and claimed a monopoly on the use of force both internally and externally: Qin appears to have become the most advanced in this respect and the most successful. Finally, in a somewhat specious argument, the writers of the *Lü shi chunqiu* rejected the positions of earlier thinkers and strategists, and claimed that "people express their hatred for those who lack the Dao and behave immorally by punishing them, and they seek those who possess the Dao and behave morally by rewarding them."[59] Killing the unrighteous in a righteous cause was perfectly acceptable. This, they claimed, was logical and rational. All an army had to do was to proclaim that it was righteous, march in, declare the leaders of the enemy unrighteous, and carry out the appropriate punishments. In essence, those who had might were right: any resistance by those who wished to retain their independence was ipso facto deemed unrighteous. Peace, therefore, was to be created by the subordination of the weaker to the stronger, by military means if necessary, with only a thin veneer of morality or justification.[60]

It was indeed this group around the Qin Prime Minister Lü Buwei who ultimately came out on top and oversaw the elimination of all the competing states and the unification of China under the First Emperor in 221, even though many of them lost their own lives in the process—Lü himself was accused of a plot against the Qin ruler and was forced to commit suicide. First under the Qin dynasty, and then under the Han (206 BCE to 220 CE), internal unity and peace was achieved, but at great cost in lives and property. Yet even this internal peace generated a new challenge: the Xiongnu steppe peoples under their leader Maodun seized the opportunity to raid the northern borders and demand trade. For decades after, the early Han emperors were obliged to sign treaties with the Xiongnu, pay them off with enormous quantities of silks and other precious commodities, and to marry off Han princesses to the khans, to seal the peace through marriage relations.[61] A new type of peace was achieved, until Emperor Wu (r. 140–87) took the offensive once again. At immense cost of men and material, he pushed Han forces far to the West and opened up the Silk Road.[62] But his military exploits resulted in a stalemate with the Xiongnu and near bankruptcy of the imperial coffers.[63]

Yet, despite these political realities, Chinese philosophers endorsed the importance of the ruler ensuring peace and harmony with the cosmos. By maintaining affairs of state in good order internally, ensuring that taxes were fair, crimes punished, duties and responsibilities carried out in a timely fashion from top to bottom of the social hierarchy, and gender relations harmonious, then, as Xunzi believed or hoped, "Rival states submit without first having to be subjugated. All the people within the Four Seas are unified without waiting for a decree. This may indeed be described as Perfect Peace."[64]

But the rulers and statesmen themselves realized that peace could never be maintained for long without a strong army. They took to heart Sunzi's dictum: "War is a vital matter of state: it is the field on which life or death is determined and the road that leads to either survival or ruin, and must be examined with the greatest care."[65] Those who forgot this paid the penalty not only with their own lives but with the demise of their dynasty.

Thus, the ultimate solution for the early Chinese thinkers was that war and peace alternated as part of the rhythms of the cosmos: in spring and summer, as Yang rose in strength, all things grew and flourished. Rewards should be offered then to encourage success. In autumn and winter, the natural world withered and died in harmony with Yin's ascendance. That was the right time when punishments should be administered and war should take place. It was never, therefore, possible to have a perpetual peace. Indeed, a perpetual peace would have been unnatural, and probably dangerous.

Notes

1   Lau and Ames 1996: 129 ("An Audience with King Wei of Ch'i [Qi]").
2   Pines 2000, 2009. All dates are BCE, except when explicitly noted otherwise.
3   Hsu 1999.
4   This policy is said to have been recommended by Shang Yang, otherwise known as Gongsun Yang or Lord Shang, the so-called "Legalist" statesman and philosopher who reformed the laws of the state of Qin in the mid-fourth century under Lord Xiao (r. 361–338). See Duyvendak's (1963) translation of the *Book of Lord Shang*, ch. IV, par. 15 ("The Encouragement of Immigration"), 266–74, a text that was probably composed about a century after Lord Shang's death and was attributed to him by later followers. In the text, Lord Shang suggests giving immigrants tax breaks for three generations. It is quite possible that the policies being recommended in the text were being proposed in Qin in the mid-third century. The men would provide the grain and the women would provide the cloth.
5   The seven states were Qin, Wei, Zhao, Han, Qi, Yan, and Chu. Most notably, Chu conquered the region of the lower Yangzi River Valley, previously controlled by the states of Wu and Yue, both of which were known for their advanced knowledge of metal technology, especially that of casting bronze swords, and for developing iron casting, as well as for their famous conflict in which it is said that some of China's leading military theorists, such as Sunzi (Master Sun), Wuzi Xu, and Fan Li took part (Sawyer 1993; Wagner 1993; Milburn 2013). For an overview of the political history of the Warring States period, see Lewis (1999), who calls the period leading up to the unification the "century of alliances" and divides it into three stages. However, he only focuses on the struggles in north China, and the three stages are "(1) the last half of the fourth century, (2) the period of Qi, 301–284 B.C., and (3) the period of Zhao, 284–260 B.C." (Lewis 1999: 634).

6 Whether or not Qin and Chu should be categorized as empires prior to the unification under the First Emperor depends, of course, on the definition of "empire." For a discussion of the concept of "empire" in the early Chinese context in relation to the comparative study of empires, see Yates 2001. Needless to say, the bibliography on empires is vast and it is beyond the scope of this chapter to enter into a discussion of the problems of the application of the concept to political and economic conditions of Warring States China.

7 Most notably, such texts have been found in tombs both of the early Han period (Mawangdui, Changsha, Hunan) and of the state of Chu (Tomb no. 1, Guodian), from circa 300. In the Mawangdui tomb, texts were found that probably belong to the Huang-Lao and Yin-Yang traditions (Yates 1997), together with two early versions of the Daoist (Taoist) *Laozi* (Ames and Hall 2003; Yates 1997), medical texts (Harper 1998), and texts and charts belonging to various other esoteric traditions (Chen Songchang 2001). The term "Huang-Lao" refers to texts attributed to the Yellow Emperor and Laozi, one of the three traditions of ancient Daoism. The other two traditions were based on the text of the *Laozi* or *Daode jing*, and on the text of the mystical *Zhuangzi* (see Yates 1997). For discussions of war and peace according to the *Laozi*, see Ellen Y. Zhang 2012; for the question of order in the *Zhuangzi*, see Vervoorn 1981. In the Guodian tomb, texts related to the *Laozi* and Confucian traditions were retrieved (Henricks 2000; Middendorf 2008; Perkins 2009; Cook 2012). Other texts have been looted from tombs and sold on the antiques market in Hong Kong. The most important cache of looted philosophical texts was purchased by the Shanghai Museum. On the challenges and problems of using such looted texts, see Goldin 2013.

8 For a discussion of the military aspects of the Qin's successful campaigns against its rivals, see Yates 2007b and Zhang Weixing 2001; cf. Pines et al. 2013.

9 Barbieri-Low and Yates 2015; cf. Loewe 2006; Sanft 2014.

10 *Shi ji* 6.283. Pines 2000: 317 bases his translation on that of Watson (1993: 81). A more accurate translation appears in Nienhauser (1994: I. 168), where the last sentences read: "Since the multitude of people were longing to settle down to a peaceful life, everyone gave up his preoccupations to look up to the sovereign. Just at this time, the First Emperor could keep his prestige and secure his merit. The basis of stability or instability lay in this."

11 Wang Yuan-kang 2011: 5.

12 Among the outstanding military inventions of the Chinese must be counted the crossbow, the trebuchet, gunpowder and gunpowder weapons (such as cannons and anti-personnel mines), flags, and so on; see Needham, Yates, et al. 1994.

13 Wright 2005; Standen 2007. More generally, for a history of the relations between northern frontier or borderland peoples and polities and those based in what is now the Chinese heartland, see Cui 2005. For studies of Han-Xiongnu relations, see Duman 1981; Psarras 2003; Holotová Szinek 2005; Kroll 2010.

14 Johnston 1995.

15 For a discussion of the Buddhist influence on Chinese ideas during the Tang dynasty, see Chapter 3 (Bronkhorst) this volume, at n. 76; see also Jerryson and Juergensmeyer 2010. It should be noted that the appellation "Xiongnu" probably was a derogatory epithet applied to northern steppe peoples by the Qin and Han; it was not the only eponym they used for themselves, and by its generalized application it may hide what was a diversity of peoples on the steppe.

16 Caplow and Hicks 2002: 8–9.

17 Li Feng 2008.

18 Li Feng 2006.

19 There is much debate as to whether the Qin destroyed the Zhou (the traditional Chinese view) or whether the Zhou royal line simply died out and its people scattered before the Qin invasion; see Pines 2004 for the evidence.

20 See Schaberg 2001; Pines 2002; Wai-yee Li 2008.

21 Lewis 1990; Weld 1997; Liu 1998: 147–72; Yates 2007a; Williams 2012–13.

22 For a lengthy discussion of the fall of the Western Zhou, the formation of the hegemonic system, and the development of the multi-state system, see Hsu 1999 and his previous analysis of social mobility in this time period (Hsu 1965).

23 Nivison 1999: 747–48.

24 The standard translation of this Mohist concept is "universal love." Here, I follow the rendition proposed by Roberts 2012–2013: 436 in his review of Johnston 2010.

25 Rickett 1998; Roth 1999.

26 See Lau 1982. The earliest versions of the *Laozi* or *Daode jing*, dating from roughly the latter part of the fourth century, were recovered from Tomb no. 1, Guodian, in the Chu culture sphere. See note 7 above.

27 On Wu Qi, see Griffith 1973; on Lord Shang, Duyvendak 1963; on Shen Buhai, Creel 1974; on Han Feizi, Liao 1959; Wang and Chang 1986.

28 Ye Shan 2007.

29 Zhang Gong 2006.

30 Yates 2009.

31 Knoblock 1988–1994: II, ch. 16 ("On Strengthening the State"), 246.

32 See the same chapter of *Xunzi*. Knoblock, ibid. 235, believes that the concept of "strengthening the state" originated with Ru (Confucian) thinking in the state of Wei, as Marquis Wen had invited Confucius' disciple Zixia there, and military and legal experts such as Wu Qi followed. Li Kui became the prime minister of that state after studying under Zixia. This latter statesman is credited with writing a *Canon of Laws*, which, it was said, Lord Shang took with him into Qin before he changed the laws of that state. However, the story of Li Kui's writing such a text is most likely apocryphal, despite its continuing popularity among scholars studying the history of Chinese law. For a strong argument in favor of considering the *Canon of Laws* a later forgery, see Pokora 1959; see also Moriya Mitsuo 2010: 414–41.

33 See introductory section above.

34 The police in contemporary China are referred to by the term "public peace" (*gong'an*).

35 Caplow and Hicks 2002: 21; Müller 2005: 62.

36 For a discussion of the various forms of violence in late imperial and modern times in China, see the essays in Lipman and Harrell 1990, and Yates' critique of Harrell's introduction to the volume (Yates 1991).

37 Aihe Wang 2000.

38 Chapter 5 (Raaflaub) in this vol., e.g., at n. 55. Lloyd (2010) provides an enlightening analysis of the techniques of persuasion from the late Warring States through to the reign of Han Wudi by analyzing the topos of *luan* (disorder).

39 Sato 2003: 120–25.

40 Nivison 2002: 294–98: "Chinese history in Mengzi's times and its impact on Mengzi's thought." It was at this battle that the military expert Sun Bin defeated his rival Pang Juan. Portions of the text attributed to Sun Bin were recovered from Tomb no. 1 Yinqueshan, Linyi, Shandong, in 1972 (Lau and Ames 1996). A short military text in two chapters was also attributed to Pang Juan in ancient times: fragments of this text may be preserved in the *Heguanzi*, but this attribution is hotly debated; see Defoort 1997.

41 Pines 2005, 2005–2006; Allan 2009.

42 Nivison: see n. 40 above.

43 For an earlier discussion of Mencius's conception of a benevolent government and the implications of the historical precedents for rulers passing their throne to another, see Schwartz 1985: esp. 278–88 and, more recently, Chung-ying Cheng 2003: 447–48.

44 The Lord of Linwu is recorded as having been a general of the state of Zhao and also possibly employed by the state of Chu.

45 See Twiss and Chan 2012.

46 Knoblock 1988–94: II. 229.

47 Portal 2007.

48 See Knoblock and Riegel 2000 for a complete translation of this work.

49 Knoblock and Riegel 2000: 175–76.

50 Mei 1973: 71: "Identification with the Superior," Part 3.

51 Knoblock and Riegel 2000: 179.

52 Yates 1979.

53 See the "persuasions" contained in the *Zhanguo ce* translated by Crump 1970. Lewis 1999: 639 argues that it was the strategist Fan Sui (d. 255), who had fled from his home state of Wei to serve King Zhaoxiang of Qin, who first proposed the idea of abandoning the policy of shifting alliances and moving to one of continuous expansion for the state of Qin. Lewis does so on the basis of the quotation of a persuasion recorded by Sima Qian in the latter's biography of Fan Sui. For this biography, see Nienhauser 1994: VII. 232–46 (quotation: 239). While it is entirely possible that Fan Sui did advocate a policy shift in the state of Qin, the historical accuracy of this persuasion is open to question, given that Sima Qian relied for the

sources of his history not only on Qin archival material that is no longer extant and thus cannot be verified, but also on the often highly elaborated stories about the activities and persuasions of the various strategists that circulated in late Warring States and early Han times. These cannot be taken as historical fact.

54 See note 7 above. The dating of their texts is the subject of much speculation. Some scholars suggest that they may have originated as early as the fifth century, in the ideas of a military expert by the name of Fan Li, who participated in the wars between the states of Wu and Yue referred to above. Others argue for a date as late as the first few decades of the Han dynasty, just before the manuscripts were placed in the Mawangdui tomb, which was sealed around 168. See the discussion of the various theories about the date in Yates 1997: 197–202. The consensus at this point seems to be that the texts were produced at different times by different hands and probably are accretions from multiple sources; see Wei Qipeng 2004: 307–19.

55 Yates 1997; Sato 2003: 121–22.

56 See the text "The Great Distinctions" (Yates 1997: 69).

57 Even the radical Daoist Zhuangzi, who rejected personal involvement in political affairs, seems to have been a friend of the logician Hui Shi, who was a high official in the state of Liang (i.e., Wei). The *Laozi* or *Daode jing*, a text which seems to have evolved in the late fourth and third centuries, may well have been interpreted as a guide for rulers and high officials, since, in early versions of the text (recently excavated and retrieved) the two chapters into which the text is traditionally divided, the *Dao* and the *De* (the 'Way' and its 'Power'), are reversed to read *De* and *Dao*.

58 Lewis 1990: 137–63; Loewe 1990.

59 Knoblock and Riegel 2000: 180.

60 For a more extended discussion of "righteous warfare" in the context of third-century intellectual developments, see McNeal (2012), ch. 2 ("Righteous warfare: laying siege to an enemy in disorder"): 40–69.

61 Arminio 1996; Cui 2005; Kroll 2010.

62 The history of the Silk Road(s) has been the subject of a great deal of recent research and debate. See, among others, Beckwith 2009; Hansen 2012.

63 Yü Ying-shih 1967.

64 Knoblock 1988–1994: II. 78.

65 Ames 1993: 103.

References

Allan, S. 2009. "Not the *Lun Yu*: the Chu script bamboo slip manuscript, *Zigao*, and the nature of early Confucianism." *Bulletin of the School of Oriental & African Studies* 72.1: 115–51.

Ames, R. T. 1993. *Sun-Tzu, The Art of Warfare: The First English Translation Incorporating the Recently Discovered Yin-ch'üeh-shan Texts*. New York.

Ames, R. T. and Hall, D. L. 2003. *Daodejing "Making This Life Significant:" A Philosophical Translation*. New York.

Arminio, J. A. 1996. *Precedent for Peace: Ancient China's Strategy and a Plan for the Prevention of World War*. Montchanin DE.

Barbieri-Low, A. J. and Yates, R. D. S. 2015. *Law, State, and Society in Early Imperial China: Study and Translation of the Zhangjiashan Legal Texts*. Leiden.

Beckwith, C. I. 2009. *Empires of the Silk Road: A History of Central Eurasia from the Bronze Age to the Present*. Princeton.

Caplow, T. and Hicks, L. 2002. *Systems of War and Peace*. 2nd edition. Lanham MD.

Chen Songchang. 2001. *Mawangdui boshu* Xingde *yanjiu lungao*. Taibei.

Cheng, C.-Y. 2003. "Mencius." In A. S. Cua (ed.), *Encyclopedia of Chinese Philosophy*, 440–48. New York and London.

Cook, S. 2012. *The Bamboo Texts of Guodian: A Study and Complete Translation*. 2 vols. Ithaca NY.

Creel, H. G. 1974. *Shen Pu-hai: A Chinese Political Philosopher of the Fourth Century B.C.* Chicago.

Crump, J.I., Jr. 1970. *Chan-Kuo Ts'e*. Oxford.

Cui Mingde. 2005. *Zhongguo gudai heqin shi* (*The History of the Policy of Harmony through Marriage Relations in Ancient China*). Beijing.

Defoort, C. 1997. *The Pheasant Cap Master* (*He guan zi*): *A Rhetorical Reading*. Albany.

Di Cosmo, N. 2002. *Ancient China and Its Enemies: The Rise of Nomadic Power in East Asian History*. Cambridge.

Duman L. I. 1981. "Chinese relations with the Xiongnu in the first to third centuries A.D." In S. L. Tikhvinsky and L. S. Perelomov (eds.), *China and Her Neighbours, from Ancient Times to the Middle Ages*, 43–58. Moscow.

Duyvendak, J. J. L. 1963 (1928). *The Book of Lord Shang: A Classic of the Chinese School of Law*. Chicago.

Goldin, P. R. 2013. "*Heng Xian* and the problem of studying looted artifacts." *Dao* 12: 153–60.

Griffith, S. B. (trans.). 1973 (1963). *Sun Tzu: The Art of War*. Oxford.

Hansen, V. 2012. *The Silk Road: A New History*. Oxford.

Harper, D. J. 1998. *Early Chinese Medical Literature: The Mawangdui Medical Manuscripts*. London and New York.

Henricks, R. G. 2000. *Lao-tzu's Tao Te Ching: A Translation of the Startling New Documents Found at Guodian*. New York.

Holotová Szinek, J. 2005. "Les relations entre l'empire des Han et les Xiongnu: vestiges archéologiques et textes historiques." *Études chinoises* 24: 221–31.

Hsu, C.-Y. 1965. *Ancient China in Transition: An Analysis of Social Mobility, 722–222 B.C.* Stanford.

Hsu, C.-Y. 1999. "The Spring and Autumn Period." In Loewe and Shaughnessy 1999: 545–86.

Jerryson, M. and Juergensmeyer, M. (eds.). 2010. *Buddhist Warfare*. Oxford and New York.

Johnston, A. I. 1995. *Cultural Realism: Strategic Culture and Grand Strategy in Chinese History*. Princeton.

Johnston, I. (trans.). 2010. *The Mozi: A Complete Translation*. New York.

Knoblock, J. 1988–1994. *Xunzi: A Translation and Study of the Complete Works*. 3 vols. Stanford.

Knoblock, J. and Jeffrey Riegel. 2000. *The Annals of Lü Buwei: A Complete Translation and Study*. Stanford.

Kroll, J. L. 2010. "The Han-Xiongnu Heqin treaty (200–135 B.C.) in the light of Chinese political and diplomatic traditions." *Bulletin of the Museum of Far Eastern Antiquities* 78: 109–24.

Lau, D. C. (trans.). 1982 (1963). *Lao-tzu: Tao Te Ching*. Harmondsworth.

Lau, D. C. and Ames, R. T. 1996. *Sun Pin: The Art of Warfare. A Comprehensive Translation of the Fourth-century B.C. Chinese Military Philosopher and Strategist*. New York.

Lewis, M. E. 1990. *Sanctioned Violence in Early China*. Albany.

Lewis, M. E. 1999. "Warring States political history." In Loewe and Shaughnessy 1999: 587–650.

Li Feng. 2006. *Landscape and Power in Early China: The Crisis and Fall of the Western Zhou, 1045–771 BC*. Cambridge.

Li Feng. 2008. *Bureaucracy and the State in Early China: Governing the Western Zhou*. Cambridge.

Li, W.-Y. 2008. *The Readability of the Past in Early Chinese Historiography*. Cambridge MA.

Liao, W. K. (trans.). 1959 (vol. 1, 1939). *The Complete Works of Han Fei Tzu: A Classic of Chinese Legalism*. 2 vols. London.

Lipman, J. N. and Harrell, S. (eds.). 1990. *Violence in China: Essays in Culture and Counterculture*. Albany.

Liu, Y. 1998. *Origins of Chinese Law: Penal and Administrative Law in Its Early Development*. Hong Kong and Oxford.

Lloyd, G. 2010. "The techniques of persuasion and the rhetoric of disorder (*luan* 亂) in late Zhanguo and western Han texts." In M. Nylan and M. Loewe (eds.), *China's Early Empires: A Re-appraisal*, 451–60. Cambridge.

Loewe, M. 1990. "The Juedi games: a re-enactment of the battle between Chiyou and Xianyuan?" In W.L. Idema and E. Zürcher (eds.), *Thought and Law in Qin and Han China: Studies Dedicated to Anthony Hulsewé on the Occasion of His Eightieth Birthday*, 140–57. Leiden.

Loewe, M. 2006. *The Government of the Qin and Han Empires 221 BCE–220 CE*. Indianapolis.

Loewe, M. and Shaughnessy, E. L. (eds.). 1999. *The Cambridge History of Ancient China: From the Origins of Civilization to 221 B.C.* Cambridge.

McNeal, R. 2012. *Conquer and Govern: Early Chinese Military Texts from the Yizhou Shu*. Honolulu.

Mei, Y.-P. 1973. *The Political and Ethical Works of Motse*. Westport.

Middendorf, U. 2008. "Again on *qing*: with a translation of the Guodian *Xing zi ming chu*." *Oriens Extremus* 47: 97–159.

Milburn, O. 2013. *Cherishing Antiquity: The Cultural Construction of an Ancient Chinese Kingdom*. Cambridge MA.

Moriya, M. 2010. *Zhongguo gudai de jiazu yu guojia*. Translation into Chinese of *Chūgoku kodai no kazoku to kokka*, by Qian Hang and Yang Xiaofen. Shanghai.

Müller, H. 2005. "Theories of peace." In M. Evangelista (ed.), *Peace Studies: Critical Concepts in Political Science*, 53–87. London.

Needham, J., Yates, R. D. S. et al. 1994. *Science and Civilisation in China*, V pt. 6: *Military Technology: Missiles and Sieges*. Cambridge.

Nienhauser, W. H., Jr. (ed.). 1994. *Ssu-ma Chien: The Grand Scribe's Records*. 9 vols. Bloomington.

Nivison, D. S. 1999. "The classical philosophical writings." In Loewe and Shaughnessy 1999: 745–812.

Nivison, D. S. 2002. "Mengzi as a philosopher of history." In A.K.L. Chan (ed.), *Mencius: Contexts and Interpretations*, 282–304. Honolulu.

Perkins, F. 2009. "Motivation and the heart in the *Xing Zi Ming Chu*." *Dao: A Journal of Comparative Philosophy* 8.2: 117–31.

Pines, Y. 2000. "'The one that pervades the all' in ancient Chinese political thought: the origins of the 'great unity' paradigm." *T'oung Pao* 86: 280–324.

Pines, Y. 2002. *Foundation of Confucian Thought: Intellectual Life in the Chunqiu period, 722–453 B.C.E.* Honolulu.

Pines, Y. 2004. "The question of interpretation: Qin history in the light of new epigraphic sources." *Early China* 29: 1–44.

Pines, Y. 2005. "Disputers of abdication: Zhanguo egalitarianism and the sovereign's power." *T'oung Pao* 91.4-5: 243–300.

Pines, Y. 2005–2006. "Subversion unearthed: criticism of hereditary succession in the newly discovered manuscripts." *Oriens Extremus* 45: 159–78.

Pines, Y. 2009. *Envisioning Eternal Empire: Chinese Political Thought of the Warring States Era*. Honolulu.

Pines, Y., Shelach, G., von Falkenhausen, L., and Yates, R. D. S. (eds.). 2013. *Birth of an Empire: The State of Qin Revisited*. Berkeley.

Pokora, T. 1959. "The canon of laws by Li K'uei: a double falsification?" *Archiv Orientalnyi* 27: 96–117.

Portal, J. (ed.). 2007. *The First Emperor: China's Terracotta Army*. Cambridge MA.

Psarras, S.-K. 2003. "Han and Xiongnu: a reexamination of cultural and political relations." *Monumenta Serica* 51: 55–236.

Rickett, W. A. (trans.). 1998. *Guanzi: Political, Economic, and Philosophical Essays from Early China*, II. Princeton.

Roberts, M. 2012–2013. Review of Johnston 2010. *Early China* 35–36: 431–38.

Roth, H. D. 1999. *Original Tao: Inward Training and the Foundations of Taoist Mysticism*. New York.

Sanft, C. 2014. *Communication and Cooperation in Early Imperial China: Publicizing the Qin Dynasty*. Albany.

Sato, M. 2003. *The Confucian Quest for Order: The Origin and Formation of the Political Thought of Xun Zi*. Leiden.

Sawyer, R. D. (trans.) 1993. *The Seven Military Classics of Ancient China*. Boulder CO.

Schaberg, D. 2001. *A Patterned Past: Form and Thought in Early Chinese Historiography*. Cambridge MA.

Schwartz, B. I. 1985. *The World of Thought in Ancient China*. Cambridge MA.

Sima Qian. 1985. *Shi ji*. Beijing.

Standen, N. 2007. *Unbounded Loyalty: Frontier Crossings in Liao China*. Honolulu.

Twiss, S. B. and Chan, J. 2012. "The classical Confucian position on the legitimate use of military force." *Journal of Religious Ethics* 40.3: 447–72.

Vervoorn, A. A. T. 1981. "Taoism, legalism and the quest for order in warring states China." *Journal of Chinese Philosophy* 8.3: 303–24.

Wagner, D. B. 1993. *Iron and Steel in Ancient China*. Leiden.

Wang, A. 2000. *Cosmology and Political Culture in Early China*. Cambridge.

Wang, H.-P. and Chang, L. S. 1986. *The Philosophical Dimensions of Han Fei's Political Theory*. Honolulu.

Wang, Y.-K. 2011. *Harmony and War: Confucian Culture and Chinese Power Politics*. New York.

Watson, B. (trans.). 1993. *Records of the Grand Historian by Sima Qian*. Hong Kong.

Wei Qipeng. 2004. *Mawangdui Han mu boshu Huangdi shu jianzheng*. Beijing.

Weld, S. 1997. "The covenant texts from Houma and Wenxian." In E. L. Shaughnessy (ed.), *New Sources of Early Chinese History: An Introduction to the Reading of Inscriptions and Manuscripts*, 125–60. Berkeley.

Williams, C. 2012–2013. "Dating the Houma covenant texts: the significance of recent findings from the Wenxian covenant texts." *Early China* 35–36: 247–75.

Wright, D. C. 2005. *From War to Diplomatic Parity in Eleventh-century China: Sung's Foreign Relations with Kitan Liao*. Leiden.

Yates, R. D. S. 1979. "The Mohists on warfare: technology, technique and justification." *Journal of the American Academy of Religion*, Thematic Supplement 47.3S (*Studies in Classical Chinese Thought*): 549–603.

Yates, R. D. S. 1991. Review of Lipman and Harrell 1990. *Sino-Platonic Papers* 31: 1–5.

Yates, R. D. S. 1997. *Five Lost Classics: Tao, Huang-Lao and Yin-Yang in Han China*. New York.

Yates, R. D. S. 2001. "Cosmos, central authority, and communities in the early Chinese empire." In S. Alcock, T. D'Altroy, K. Morrison, and C. Sinopoli (eds.), *Empires: Perspectives from Archaeology and History*, 351–68, 441–44. Cambridge.

Yates, R. D. S. 2007a. "Making war and making peace in early China." In K. A. Raaflaub (ed.), *War and Peace in the Ancient World*, 34–52. Malden MA and Oxford.

Yates, R. D. S. 2007b. "The rise of Qin and the military conquest of the warring states." In Portal 2007: 30–57.

Yates, R. D. S. 2009. "Law and the military in early China." In Di Cosmo 2009: 23–44, 341–43.

Ye Shan (R. D. S. Yates). 2007. "Qin de falü yu shehui: Guanyu Zhangjiashan *Ernian lüling* deng xin chutu wenxian de sikao." *Rujia wenhua yanjiu: Xin chu Chu jian yanjiu zhuanhao* 1: 299–325.

Yü Ying-shih. 1967. *Trade and Expansion in Han China: A Study in the Structure of Sino-barbarian Economic Relations.* Berkeley.

Zhang, E. Y. 2012. "Weapons are nothing but ominous instruments: the *Daodejing*'s view on war and peace." *Journal of Religious Ethics* 40.3: 473–502.

Zhang Gong. 2006. *Qin Han taowang fanzui yanjiu.* Wuhan.

Zhang Weixing. 2001. *Qin zhanzheng shulüe.* Xi'an.

Greek Concepts and Theories of Peace[1]

Kurt A. Raaflaub

Introduction: Homer, Thucydides, Peace, and Just War

I begin with a case study that illustrates an abiding Greek concern with peace and just war. Despite centuries of intensive scholarly attention, there are still aspects of Homer's art and thinking that are often ignored, among them the poet's tendency to engage in political reflection. The famous proem of the *Iliad* offers a good starting point.

> Rage: Sing, Goddess, Achilles' rage,
> black and murderous, that cost the Greeks
> incalculable pain, pitched countless souls
> of heroes into Hades' dark,
> and left their bodies to rot as feasts
> for dogs and birds, as Zeus' will was done.
> Begin with the clash between Agamemnon—
> the Greek warlord—and godlike Achilles.
> (1.1–7; trans. Stanley Lombardo)

Peace in the Ancient World: Concepts and Theories, First Edition. Edited by Kurt A. Raaflaub.
© 2016 John Wiley & Sons, Inc. Published 2016 by John Wiley & Sons, Inc.

This proem does not, as we might expect, emphasize the glorious deeds of great heroes but their faults in causing the deaths of countless men. Despite his focus on the two leaders, the poet here assumes a communal perspective. From this beginning, the poet weaves into the epic's dramatic narrative a series of political considerations that center our attention not least on the leaders' responsibility for the community's well-being.[2] The quarrel between Agamemnon and Achilles that erupts in Book 1 and is finally resolved in Book 19, involves the overall leader and his strongest follower. The community (here the Greek army that in its fortified camp is represented as a temporary polis) is helpless.[3] It lacks laws, powerful public institutions, and a developed political culture that would enable it to control even its strongest members. The other leaders can only resort to persuasion, but where a leader's honor and status are at stake, persuasion is ineffective. In the absence of a superior agency, arbitration is no option.

All this concerns a community's internal sphere. But it illuminates a crucial problem in interstate relations, too, which explains the classical Greeks' difficulties in resolving conflicts by other means than war. Even if two states have agreed by treaty to submit their differences to arbitration, how is such arbitration going to work if there is no agency that has enough authority to be respected by both contestants, or enough power to impose its will, and if the prevailing political culture does not encourage peaceful rather than violent conflict resolution? I do not need to emphasize that this remains one of the greatest challenges even in our own time—and we have at our disposal a world organization created for this very purpose. In early Greece, when power was distributed more evenly, arbitration was possible.[4] It was not least Sparta's role as strongest military power without imperial ambitions that enabled it to serve in this function. Moreover, in the highly developed political culture of archaic Greece, there emerged a number of individuals who were able to serve as arbitrators and "straighteners" in conflicts within and among poleis. They represented a peaceful alternative to civil strife or tyranny, were closely connected with Apollo's oracle in Delphi (famous for advocating moderation), stood above the conflicting parties, thus represented a "third position," and as sages (*sophoi*) enjoyed far-reaching authority. As lawgivers, some of them enacted important reforms.[5] By the mid-fifth century, however, the Greek world was polarized between two power blocs, Sparta and Athens, each with its allies (a constellation often compared with that of the Cold War). Those trying to remain neutral were viewed with suspicion by both sides.[6]

This constellation made arbitration very difficult. The historian Thucydides exemplifies this in his analysis of the outbreak of the Peloponnesian War.

I give the pertinent sections of a speech he attributes to the Athenian statesman Pericles:

> It is laid down [by treaty] that differences between us should be settled by arbitration, and that, pending arbitration, each side should keep what it has. The Spartans have never once asked for arbitration, nor have they accepted our offers to submit to it. They prefer to settle their complaints by war rather than by peaceful negotiations, and now they come here not even making protests, but trying to give us orders… If you give in, you will immediately be confronted with some greater demand, since they will think that you only gave way on this point through fear… But if you take a firm stand you will make it clear to them that they have to treat you properly as equals… When one's equals, before resorting to arbitration, make claims on their neighbors and put those claims in the form of commands, it would be slavish to give in to them, however big or however small such claims may be. (1.140–42; trans. Rex Warner)

Athens thus insisted on arbitration, as provided by an existing treaty: this, Pericles said, was the only way to resolve conflicts among equal powers. Sparta refused. Arbitration could not even be initiated unless both parties were determined to take it seriously. But one of them was not, and even if it had been, the practical problems might have been unsurmountable.[7] In the ensuing war, however, Sparta suffered serious setbacks that prompted it to seek peace on the status quo. The Athenians, now hoping for victory rather than compromise and led by an intransigent demagogue, rejected the offer.[8] Ten years and an uneasy peace later, the war resumed. Thucydides writes:

> The Spartans considered that Athens had been the first to break the peace treaty. In the first war they thought that the fault had been more on their side, partly… because in spite of the provision in the previous treaty that there should be no recourse to arms if arbitration were offered, they themselves had not accepted the Athenian offer of arbitration. They therefore thought that there was some justice in the misfortunes they had suffered… But now, [the Athenians were the aggressors. Moreover,] whenever any dispute arose on doubtful points in the treaty, it was Sparta who had offered to submit to arbitration and Athens who had refused the offer. It was now Athens, the Spartans thought, who was in the wrong through having committed exactly the same faults as theirs had been before, and they went into the war with enthusiasm. (7.18)

Fighting for a just cause guaranteed divine support and justified hope for victory. In the play *Heraclidae*, performed around the time of the war's outbreak, the tragic poet Euripides dramatizes the same idea, emphasizing, as Pericles does in Thucydides, that it is incompatible with liberty to yield to foreign ultimatums.[9]

I return to the *Iliad* and an episode that illustrates precisely the importance of fighting for a just cause. The Trojan War was caused by the abduction of Helen, wife of Menelaus, king of Sparta, by Paris, a Trojan prince. In the poet's imagination, the Greeks first sent ambassadors to Troy who demanded restoration and compensation (and, no doubt, threatened war if their demand were refused). The Trojan assembly debated their request and sided with Paris. The Greeks thus resorted to war only when they failed to achieve a peaceful settlement of the conflict. Other stories confirm such diplomatic efforts to avoid war.[10]

The justice of the Greek cause in this epic war is thus never in question. Even so, the poet reiterates this fact within the epic action—that is, within the roughly six weeks of the tenth year of the war during which the *Iliad*'s "Anger of Achilles" episode plays out—by placing here an event that clearly belongs in the war's very beginning, thus emphasizing its crucial significance. Before the first battle in the epic, Paris offers to fight a duel with Menelaus, perpetrator with injured party, to decide upon possession of Helen. All the others, "having cut oaths of faith and friendship," will dwell peacefully in their respective countries. Both armies react with great joy, "hoping now to be rid of all the misery of warfare." The two leaders conclude a treaty, witnessed by both armies, with all the necessary prayers, oaths, and sacrifices, and spelling out the conditions of the agreement. The hopes of both armies that this will seal peace are captured in their prayers to Zeus. Moreover, the poet leaves no doubt about the Trojans' resentment of Paris for having caused the war: they "hated him like black death is hated."[11]

Yet the duel remains inconclusive. Paris, about to die, is whisked away by Aphrodite, his divine protectress, and dumped unceremoniously in Helen's bed: no victim, no proof of victory! An ally of the Trojans, expecting rich rewards, tries to kill Menelaus and wounds him with an arrow. He thus violates oaths and truce and causes the renewal of hostilities. The Greeks realize immediately that this places justice (and with it divine support) firmly on their side. And promptly they refuse further negotiations: "Now let no one accept the possessions of Paris or take back Helen; one who is very simple can see it, that by this time the terms of death hang over the Trojans."[12]

In other words, at this point even the Trojans' compliance with the Greeks' initial demands would no longer suffice to end the war. Trust in the justice of their cause and their ability to win, greed and pride propel the Greeks back into war. So too the Athenians, smelling victory after their early successes in the Peloponnesian War, and driven by greed for more (*pleonexia*), reject Spartan peace offers that earlier they would have accepted gladly.[13]

Overall, then, early Greek society as depicted in the *Iliad* had clearly developed procedures in ritual and diplomacy to avoid war and resolve conflicts peacefully, and it was acutely aware of the importance of fighting

for a just cause. The poet explains carefully, both politically and psychologi-
cally, why peace efforts tend to fail detrimentally. The soldiers' reactions
reveal a deep resentment of war and yearning for peace among the masses.
Juxtaposing on the famous shield of Achilles, crafted by the divine smith
Hephaestus, a city at war and a city at peace, the poet conceptualizes a contrast that is crucial for the society of his time.[14] The misery caused by war is
highlighted in Hector's sad description of the fate that awaits his wife
Andromache when she will become the slave of one of the enemy leaders,
deprived of liberty and forced by necessity. The *Iliad* even characterizes the
war god, Ares, in most negative terms, as a "maniac who knows nothing of
justice," as a coward and adulterer who has no decency or dignity and is
despised even by his father, Zeus.[15]

The epic invites identification by exemplifying elementary patterns in human
interaction on both the individual and communal levels. Not surprisingly,
therefore, similar patterns recur in Thucydides. Focusing on the Athenians'
detrimental enthusiasm for war, fueled by a powerful communal ideology and
self-serving, ambitious demagogues, he says less on their sentiments about
peace. But, like democracy, imperialism, and civil strife, the issue of war and
peace is most important to him.[16] He pursues it throughout his work, asking
questions like: why does war break out and cannot be avoided even if the
instruments to do so (diplomacy, arbitration) exist? What are the factors that
propel a community towards war, despite the hardships and losses it causes—
even if it knows these and has a choice? What are the ideological dimensions of
war, and how can we unmask them? Is propensity for war and desire for domination typical especially of democracy, and if so, why?

The case study I have presented documents an abiding concern with the
issue of peace that links Homer to Thucydides, early archaic to classical Greece:
epic and historical narrative illustrate an effort to deal with the same basic
problems revolving around the contrasting poles of peace and war. Nor were
Homer and Thucydides alone. In this chapter, I shall first discuss three examples that illustrate intense Greek efforts in the late fifth and fourth century to
achieve peace by containing endemic inter-communal war and overcoming
civil strife (*stasis*). I shall then show that we need to see such efforts in the
context of a long-standing dicourse on peace that we can trace from the early
epic poets through the tragic and comic poets and the historians of the fifth
century. This discourse greatly intensified from the last third of the fifth century and prompted attempts to deal with the problems of war and peace by
applying deeper political analysis and theoretical approaches. Finally, I shall try
to explain what conditions and factors made this development possible or
even necessary.

Containing External War and Ending Civil War: Three Examples

Large-scale inter-polis organizations to secure peace

After its defeat in the Peloponnesian War (in 404), Athens had to dissolve its empire and join Sparta's alliance system. Many Athenian allies, believing in Sparta's promise of liberty and protection, had defected from Athens much earlier. Yet in 412 Sparta formally accepted Persian sovereignty over the Greeks on the Anatolian coast in exchange for Persian financial support against Athens.[17] Others found the liberty they had hoped to gain quashed by Sparta's increasingly oppressive rule and were soon tormented by incessant wars about hegemony in Greece.[18] These wars prompted new efforts to achieve some measure of stability or perhaps even peace and resulted in a series of treaties establishing a "common peace" (*koinē eirēnē*). Ultimately, they all failed, but they reflect a new way of tackling the problem even if they grew out of earlier alliance systems—the only model for "organizing" the inter-polis sphere that existed in the Greek world.[19] A few decades earlier, though, an unsuccessful initiative had perhaps pointed in a new direction.

We have information about an Athenian proposal (unfortunately, of contested authenticity) that was launched around the mid-fifth century. It called for a Panhellenic Congress to discuss, among other issues, how the security of the seas and "the peace" could be kept. We do not know what peace Pericles, the initiator, had in mind: scholars think of peace agreements with Persia (around 450) or Sparta (446).[20] In any case, nothing came of it because Sparta balked, suspecting an Athenian attempt to expand her hegemony over all of Greece.[21] If this really was Pericles' intention both the plan and the cause of its failure anticipated the later "common peace" treaties. If not, the idea would have been remarkable: the congress would have tried to establish, outside of (and perhaps above) existing alliances that aimed at winning prospective wars, a system of inter-polis collaboration that would prevent wars, guarantee peace, and thus safeguard the status quo in Greece. Presumably, as was generally the case in such structures, a synod of delegates of all member states would have met to deliberate common issues and make common decisions that might result in common action. Such a synod, once established and gaining authority and trust through successful collaboration, could have served as an agent to arbitrate inter-polis conflicts, even between the superpowers—thus mending the deficiency (identified above) that essentially rendered arbitration clauses in treaties among superpowers futile.[22] Most likely, though, such an idea, effectively limiting imperial expansion, would not have been feasible even in Athens because it collided with the ambitions of the demos and all its leaders, including Pericles.

After the Peloponnesian War, Sparta's harsh rule soon caused a rebellion among its own leading allies and new wars. Eventually, in 386, Sparta's enemies were forced by the combined pressure of Persia and Sparta to accept a humiliating agreement, the King's Peace: it confirmed, with few exceptions, Persian sovereignty over the Greek poleis in Asia Minor and Cyprus, and established the principle of autonomy for all other Greek poleis, threatening those with war who did not accept these terms.[23]

This was the first peace achieved in Greece since 404, ominously dictated by Persia. All poleis involved eventually signed it, although some only under threat of an immediate Spartan attack. Sparta took further advantage of its power as "leader (or guarantor) of the peace" (*prostatēs tēs eirēnēs*) by settling old scores with neighbors and interfering in the domestic affairs or regional arrangements of other poleis.[24] The King's Peace, aptly named, thus was an instrument to keep Greek affairs under control and to prevent any action that might threaten Persian rule over the Anatolian Greeks. It was enforced by Sparta's leadership position and power and thus also served the purpose of cementing Spartan domination. Moreover, there was no institutionalized consultation and decision-making process based on independent and equal voting among all signees. All this combined to cause the eventual failure of the King's Peace, despite its purpose to establish peace on a broad base. Other efforts followed to stop feuding among Greeks by setting up similarly broad common peace arrangements, often explicitly referring to the King's Peace, always based on the condition of general autonomy, but sometimes complemented by other clauses. They all failed after a short time for the same reasons that had doomed the King's Peace. Still, as Van Wees emphasizes, "the key point is that peacekeeping and upholding the sovereignty of other Greek states, on a permanent basis, was now explicitly the task of the hegemonic power."[25]

By the late 380s Sparta's interventionist policies were widely hated. Athens presented itself as a leader of anti-Spartan resistance and in 378 created the nucleus of a new alliance system, based on the members' autonomy, Athenian hegemony, and a common council (*synedrion*) that met in Athens and represented each ally with equal vote.[26] According to the "charter" of the "Second Athenian League" (modern terms), advertised in early 377, only a defensive alliance was intended, and its purpose was clearly defined: "So that the Spartans shall allow the Greeks to be free and autonomous, and to live at peace occupying their own territory in security." Moreover, officially the purpose was to enforce the King's Peace—which implied that the treaty's guarantor, Sparta, had violated it. The specific measures that had enabled Athens in the fifth-century to rule over its allies were emphatically excluded; violations were to be handled by the councilors (*synedroi*).[27]

The *synedrion* is mentioned only in the context of this "charter;" neither its functions nor the powers of the *hēgemōn* are defined here, there is no mention of a "constitution" of the alliance, and the relationship between decisions by the Athenian assembly (*ekklēsia*) and those by the *synedrion* is not clarified. Given what had happened in Athens' earlier League, all this would have been essential and was perhaps formulated in a lost document.[28] Other evidence suggests, at any rate, that the *synedrion* was intended to be independent of Athenian political control, and final policy decisions had to be made by both the Athenian assembly and the *synedrion*. It would be important to know exactly how this was supposed to work. If the allies were indeed bound by a multilateral agreement, linked to one another as well as to Athens, the intention must have been to create a more integrated organization.[29]

The league seems to have functioned well for a few years, but changing conditions—Thebes' rise to dominance after its defeat of Sparta in 371, a peace (371) and alliance (369) between Athens and Sparta and their allies (which made the League's initial purpose obsolete), and Athens' renewed ambitions in the northern Aegean—led to tensions, dissatisfaction, and eventually a war with the allies (357–355), which Athens was unable to sustain.

In the end, the League was formally replaced by the "League of Corinth," another common peace treaty that was imposed on the Greeks in 337 by Philip II of Macedon after his victory at Chaeronea.[30] Its purpose was to pacify and unify the Greeks before the planned war against Persia (to which they were to contribute troops); its structure was probably influenced partly by that of the Athenian League. Philip established a common council (*synedrion*) and fixed the size of the forces each member had to supply, which in turn determined the number of representatives in the council. The oath bound the members to abide by the peace and treaty, not to wage war against those who did, to be loyal to the monarchy of Philip and his heirs, respect the members' constitutions, and support wars against transgressors as determined by the council and requested by the *hēgemōn*. All we know about the activities of the *synedrion* suggests that it was an instrument of empire in the service of the Macedonian kings. Still, by "linking a general peace with the obligation to recognize his leadership and with proportional representation… Philip created a procedure for efficient enforcement of the general peace, and at the same time gave his hegemony over the Greeks a form that was more acceptable to them."[31]

We thus have evidence for a sequence of organizations that comprised a large number of poleis with the purpose (among others) to establish and maintain peace in Greece. They were in part based on the structures of traditional alliance systems but drew consequences from features that had proved unsuccessful in the past, and experimented with institutions that provided stronger integration. At least the Second Athenian League seems to represent a conscious effort to make the League's governing council independent from and equal to the hegemon's decision-making body. With a couple of possible and partial exceptions, however, these organizations did not succeed in (and in most cases not even aim at) balancing the hegemon's power by an equally powerful or superior governing body. Although motivated by a widespread desire to control endemic warfare, and proclaiming the establishment of lasting peace as a primary goal, these leagues tended to remain (or soon to become again) tools serving the imperial goals of the hegemonic power—quite apart from Persian interests. In most cases, their failure was thus due to their inability to subordinate hegemonic ambition to alliance and integration: the dominant principle, provoking resistance rather than cooperation, remained rule through peace rather than alliance for peace.[32] These shortcomings, however, should not distract us from the fact that for decades international peace stood in the center of serious efforts at political experimentation.

Isocrates' thoughts on exterminating war

Isocrates (436–338 BCE), rhetorician, philosopher, and teacher of Plato, often ignored or underestimated, presents in one of his model speeches, *On the Peace*, an extraordinary idea.[33] At the time (355), the Athenians were involved in a war against their allies, trying to prevent them from abandoning their league (discussed above). Long ago, Isocrates observed, before and during the Persian Wars, the Athenians had been supporters of the oppressed and saviors of Greek liberty and thus enjoyed a very positive reputation. Later they built their empire and fought war after war to keep and enlarge it, bringing upon themselves the hatred of most Greeks and paying an enormous price in misery, lives, and resources for a dream (supremacy in Greece) they were incapable of realizing. And still they continued to chase this dream. Would it not be more sensible, Isocrates asked, to stop pursuing illusions and resume the good policies of the ancestors?

> Now it is the war [against the allies] which has robbed us of all the good things; for it has made us poorer; it has compelled many of us to endure perils; it has given us a bad name among the Hellenes; and it has in every way overwhelmed us with misfortune.

But if we make peace and present ourselves as our common covenants command us
to do, then we shall dwell in our city in great security, delivered from wars and perils
and the turmoil in which we are now involved amongst ourselves, and we shall advance
day by day in prosperity, relieved of paying war-taxes, of fitting out triremes, and of
discharging the other burdens which are imposed by war, without fear cultivating our
lands and sailing the seas and engaging in those other occupations which now, because
of the war, have entirely come to an end (8.19–20; trans. George Norlin).

Most importantly, Isocrates understood that to end not only one specific war
by concluding a peace agreement, but all wars and the misery they caused, one
needed to change deeply ingrained common attitudes:

No such thing can come to pass until you are persuaded that tranquillity is more
advantageous and more profitable than meddlesomeness (*polypragmosynē*), justice
than injustice, and attention to one's own affairs than covetousness of the possessions
of others (ibid. 26).

In other words, if the Athenians really wanted to secure lasting peace, happiness, and the admiration of all other Greeks, they must voluntarily abolish
imperialism and resume their earlier policies of generosity towards others.

This sounds naïve and idealistic. But there is more to it. In fact, Isocrates'
proposal is his response to an intense debate that had been going on for a
while. On the one hand, his allusion to Athens' earlier good reputation echoes
ideas that are familiar from Athenian suppliant plays and funeral orations and
were rooted in Athenian ideologies of power and freedom.[34] On the other
hand, a widespread view attributed to the Athenians a collective character that
was dominated by *polypragmosynē* (aggressive activism), a trait that continued
to edge them on in their quest of supreme power.[35] Thucydides uses this trait
as a recurrent theme in his historical interpretation. For example, in the assembly debate preceding the fateful Sicilian expedition in 415, one of the appointed
generals, Nicias, mature and experienced, knows well "that no speech of mine
could be powerful enough to alter your characters," but still warns his fellow
citizens that this time it is too dangerous to yield to their inclination always to
reach for more. By contrast, Alcibiades, his fellow general, young and extremely
ambitious, encourages the Athenians to act according to their nature: this has
led them to the peak of success and only by living up to it can they continue to
be successful: "a city which is active by nature will soon ruin itself if it changes
its nature and becomes idle."[36]

This attitude, visible in Athens' policies long before it caused the disastrous
intervention in Sicily, alarmed many contemporaries. A debate ensued about
whether and how an imperial power, used to war and conquest, could change

itself to pursue peace and moderation. Both Herodotus and Thucydides, perhaps echoing other thinkers, came to the conclusion that this was not only extremely difficult but also dangerous, given the subjects' hatred of the imperial ruler. Thucydides lets Pericles say this explicitly in his last assembly speech: "Your empire is now like a tyranny: it may have been wrong to take it; it is certainly dangerous to let it go!" Herodotus illustrates it with the example of Maiandrios (tyrant of the island of Samos and heir to the famous Polycrates) who tried to step down from tyranny but was forced by his fellow citizens' hostile reaction to hold on to it.[37] More than that: both historians realized that to change from aggressively imperialist to peaceful policies required a radical change of thinking, mental disposition, and habits. Thucydides lets Alcibiades say this explicitly in the Sicilian debate, advising the Athenians to stick with their success-proven disposition because they will not be able to change their policies suddenly without at the same time changing their entire character and way of life. Herodotus makes the same point, but through a "historical" anecdote, the advice the former Lydian king Croesus gives to his conqueror, the Persian king Cyrus, about how to suppress any rebellious instincts in the Lydians who are known to be a great warrior nation: to transform them by disarming them, inducing them to become a nation of shopkeepers and musicians, and thus in fact turning men into women! In Herodotus' historical fiction this worked—after all, the Lydians did not revolt again—but the absurd proposal is intended to signal the enormous difficulty of suddenly and profoundly changing one's way of life.[38]

It is against the background of such pessimistic realism that Isocrates took his provocative stand. He understood that lasting peace could be achieved only if one was able to change radically even the most deep-seated and long-standing patterns of thinking and behaving. This is precisely what he recommended to the Athenians. Unrealistic though it was, I suggest that his insight was profoundly correct: statesmen throughout history into our very own days would have done well to heed it.[39]

An end to civil strife in Athens

In 403 BCE the Athenians made an extraordinary decision to eradicate *stasis* from their community. The last phase of the Peloponnesian War and its immediate aftermath (411–403) had witnessed a roller coaster of constitutional conflict and change, civil strife and war. The democracies and oligarchies that succeeded each other had become ever more radical and oppressive. When the narrow oligarchy imposed on defeated Athens by Sparta in 404 (soon called the "Thirty Tyrants") was overthrown by exiled democrats in 403 and civil war broke out, the Spartan king Pausanias and ten Spartan mediators negotiated a settlement—and democracy was restored once more. The reconciliation decree the assembly passed was most remarkable.[40] It separated the fighting parties and assigned to the oligarchs and their supporters one township (Eleusis), which they would govern with complete autonomy, retaining their full Athenian citizenship and property rights in Attica. This arrangement was to be implemented under the protection of oaths and by a deadline, although changes were permitted thereafter. Most importantly, "they swore not to remember wrongs (*mē mnēsikakein*)," except of those who had held office under the Thirty, "and not even these if they successfully submitted to an examination." Those unwilling to do so were allowed to emigrate. The oligarchic haven in Eleusis soon proved unnecessary, and some forty years later Xenophon wrote: "and still today they live together as a community and the people abide by their oaths." The decision "not to remember wrongs" is perhaps most amazing. It made it difficult, though perhaps not impossible, later on to prosecute an opponent for wrongs committed under the Thirty, and thus truly built a foundation for lasting civic peace.[41] Essentially, it anticipated by two-and-a-half millennia one of the methods the "Truth Commission" in South Africa used in trying to overcome the fallout of Apartheid. Comparable reconciliation decrees are attested in two other poleis.[42]

Preliminary conclusions

We have examined three cases that all aimed at containing war or civil strife and establishing lasting peace: large-scale experiments in assigning responsibility for peace to hegemonic structures and intercity collaboration, a blueprint requiring profound changes in thinking and attitudes to overcome ingrained imperialist tendencies, and an effort to eradicate *stasis* from a polis by separating democrats and oligarchs. Vastly different though these efforts are, they all share important common traits: they were largely born from desperation about brutal and exhausting conflicts and wars; they transcended traditional ways of dealing with these problems; and they were based not only on common sense and political experience, but especially on specific political concepts and theoretical approaches. These in turn grew out of a long-standing political discourse on war and peace and a recently intensified and theoretically enriched debate about possibilities to overcome war and *stasis*. This again would not have been possible without the development of abstract thinking, philosophy, and, in particular, a type of thought and theory that focused specifically on politics and communal problems. In the next sections, we will look more closely at these developments.

Background: Peace in Political Thought, Discourse, and Conceptualization

As we saw in the opening section, Homer's *Iliad* reflects negative sentiments about war and an acute awareness of its destructive impact on communities and people, a widespread desire for peace, and the use of diplomacy and treaties to avoid war, preserve peace, or restore peace if war breaks out. Some of these issues connect Homer with Thucydides. Other authors engaged in such thinking too. Around 700, Hesiod, author of didactic epics, placed peace in the center of some of his efforts to conceptualize systematically the powers and forces that have an impact on human life and society.[43] Both he and the Athenian lawgiver Solon (around 600) emphasized the crucial importance of peace as a primary communal value. Moreover, in a pioneering theoretical insight Solon postulated that elite abuse of power was linked by a direct and inevitable chain of cause and effect to communal suffering that included civil strife and war; this causal connection affected all citizens and played out entirely on the social-political level, independent of divine intervention. Understanding and identifying the causes of civil strife thus made intervention, correction, and restoration of domestic peace and good order possible. The instruments to achieve this were provided by legislation and reform.[44] The scanty fragments that survive of the early philosophers' writings at least indicate that they did not ignore the problems of war and peace.[45]

In the fifth century, citizen crowds in the theater of Athens were confronted with tragic and comic plays that criticized the brutality and senselessness of war and, undercutting warmongering politicians and the Athenian ideology of war, emphasized the desirability of peace. In *Lysistrata*, for example, Aristophanes pointedly subverts the Athenian civic ideology, echoed in Thucydides' Funeral Oration, that demands that the citizen be a "lover (*erastēs*) of his city," subordinating his own interests to those of his beloved, the *polis*. The result, the poet claims, is a war-crazy city destroying itself. In the guise of a hilarious utopia, he raises crucial questions.[46]

At the same time, some of the sophists (itinerant philosophers and teachers) developed theories about peace and the possibility of controlling war. The political philosophers of the fourth century too dealt with the issue of war and peace.[47] So did the historians, Herodotus as much as Thucydides. Much suggests that Herodotus had little sympathy for war. He lets the Persian general Mardonius criticize the Greeks not only for fighting wars in the most stupid way (by fighting hoplite battles on level plains rather than taking advantage of their terrain) but also for fighting wars at all (instead of using diplomacy and other means to resolve their conflicts). Herodotus says categorically in his own voice: "the evil of internal strife is worse than united war in the same proportion as war itself is worse than peace."[48] His comment on the earthquake—the only one ever—that shook Delos after the passing of the Persian fleet on its way to Athens in 490 is revealing: "It may well be that the shock was an act of God to warn men of the troubles that were on the way; for indeed, during [the reigns of Darius, Xerxes, and Artaxerxes] Greece suffered more evils than in the twenty generations before Darius was born—partly from the Persian wars, partly from her own internal struggles for supremacy" (6.98.1).[49] Just so, the twenty ships the Athenians sent to support the Ionian Revolt against Persia in 499 "were the beginnings of evils for Greeks and barbarians" (5.97.3).

The list could be continued. The Greek discourse on peace, culminating in the late fifth and early fourth century, was intense, pervasive, and, most importantly, entirely public. Narrative and didactic epic, lyric poetry, tragedy, and comedy were performed in public, in front of various types of audiences that always represented important segments of a community's citizen body. Such performative art reacted to concerns that were relevant to these audiences whose interest in the performance was stimulated by their ability to identify with the issues and dilemmas presented to them. Sophists, physicians, historians of Herodotus's type, geographers, and other "knowledge experts" performed their wisdom in public presentations as well, competing with each other and depending for their success on the audience's positive reaction.[50] Here, too, the subject matter's relevance to the audience was crucial. What we read about war and peace in late-fifth-century authors thus echoes not only ideas of these authors (and thus of "intellectuals") but concerns of larger parts of the population. It is this *pervasiveness* and *public nature* of the discourse on war and peace that seems to me to distinguish the Greeks from other ancient societies and especially from early China—the only other ancient civilization of which we know that it thought intensely and even theoretically about peace.[51] Other intellectuals (such as Thucydides and the philosophers) primarily addressed readers or taught small groups of pupils. Even so, they interacted intensively with other intellectuals of all types. All this explains why echoes not only of political, geographical, or medical theories but also of an intensive discourse on peace pervade virtually all extant literature of the period and why this discourse was also enhanced by theoretical considerations (below).

Moreover, from the very beginning of Greek literature, we find efforts at conceptualizing war and peace and using them as contrasting principles. As mentioned before, on Achilles' shield, Homer juxtaposes a city at peace and one at war, defining a decisive organizing principle of human life.[52] War is prompted by greed and hate, and causes confusion and destructive death;

peace permits happiness, prosperity, procreation, and justice. In *Works and Days*, Hesiod too juxtaposes two cities, here characterized by justice and injustice. Zeus and Dikē (Justice) reward the just city—among other blessings—with peace, and punish the unjust city with war and destruction.[53] In *Theogony*, Eirēnē (Peace) is one of the Hōrai, goddesses of growth and prosperity, and daughters of Zeus himself. They represent the prime values of Zeus' new order. Recognizing the importance of peace for human and communal well-being, Hesiod thus ranks Eirēnē high up in the divine hierarchy. This suggests a normative perspective. In the Myth of the Ages, anticipating a theory of cultural evolution with antecedents in the Near East, the Golden Age is blessed by peace and abundance. War and violence emerge only in the Bronze Age and dominate in the present Iron Age. In an ideal world, then, there are no wars, only peace and abundance.[54]

Solon identifies both external and internal war as symptoms of a state of disorder (*dysnomia*), while *eunomia* (good order) is blessed by peace and prosperity.[55] Fragments surviving from early philosophical works and Orphic religious speculation make it clear that the contrast of war and peace continued to serve as an essential structuring principle.[56] Empedocles' ideas on these matters influenced later philosophers.[57]

Theories of Peace

Overcoming civil strife

With the emergence of the sophists in the mid-fifth century, the discourse on peace reached a new level. Unlike the earlier "natural" philosophers, the sophists focused in their thinking and teaching on social and political problems, developing critical and innovative ideas and theories, and thus becoming the first "political scientists."[58] Several of them dealt intensively with the concept of concord (*homonoia*) that emerged in the late-fifth century when many poleis were shaken by violent internal strife (*stasis*).[59] Such strife usually pitted democrats against oligarchs, although such labels often camouflaged power struggles among rivaling factions; in contemporaneous thinking, democracy and oligarchy represented mutually exclusive systems that aimed at controlling power in the polis by securing the rule of one part of the citizen body over the other. This tension was detrimentally enhanced by the outside support both factions could find among the superpowers that favored democracy (Athens) or oligarchy (Sparta).[60] Realizing the significance of this phenomenon for the Peloponnesian War's history, Thucydides described in detail an exceptionally heinous example of civil strife spiraling out of control on the island of Corcyra, and then offered a penetrating political analysis: his "pathology of civil war" is an exceptional piece of abstract and theoretical thinking.[61]

This intellectual tour de force was possible only because several other thinkers around that time wrote and lectured on *stasis* and stimulated an intense debate that we find reflected in scattered pieces of extant evidence. The philosopher Democritus emphasized that *stasis* knows only losers (because the victors too suffer egregious harm), that only concord makes it possible to muster the greatest strength in communal efforts (especially external wars), and that concord needs to be fostered by breaking traditional ways of thinking and behaving; thus, for example, generosity of the powerful toward the poor is a sure way to foster friendship, mutual aid, and concord.[62] Since we do not know the context of these statements, we cannot say how far Democritus developed these ideas and whether they included a fuller discussion or even theory of *stasis* and *homonoia*. But we do know that the Athenian sophist Antiphon, best known as leader of an oligarchic coup in 411, wrote an essay on *homonoia*. In this apparently brilliantly formulated piece, Antiphon declared anarchy the greatest evil and education a crucial need, and used fantasy peoples, living near the edges of the world, to illustrate the realization of some of his ideas.[63] Unfortunately, not enough survives to indicate how he dealt specifically with the issue of concord.

The type of treatise Antiphon and perhaps Thrasymachus (below) wrote is preserved in the *Anonymus Iamblichi*, a piece from an unknown classical sophist's essay that was inserted in a work by the late antique philosopher Iamblichus. This piece ends with an encomium of *eunomia* (good order) that highlights, among other blessings, the absence of war, the greatest bane of humankind, and condemns *anomia* (lack of order) that causes, among other disasters, frequent foreign war, internal strife, and tyranny. Although the author does not focus explicitly on concord, the emphasis he places on justice, good order, and obedience to law reflects an effort to conceptualize the conditions for communal stability and peace.[64]

In one of his "show-piece orations," the sophist Thrasymachus, best known as Socrates' interlocutor in the first book of Plato's *Republic*, proposed as a solution to civil strife the return to an "ancestral constitution."[65] The fragment breaks off with Thrasymachus's claim that it is possible to find out about this constitution (and presumably how it was structured and how well it worked) from those who had witnessed it, but before he offers any details. We know, however, that such a proposal was seriously considered in the constitutional crisis of 411/10.[66] The concept probably refers to a stage in constitutional development before democracy "turned radical" in the mid-fifth century: a moderate constitution between oligarchy and democracy and thus acceptable to both sides.

This brings us to constitutional theory. By the mid-fifth century, scholars were drafting ideal constitutions from scratch. In the following decades, the pros and cons of democracy and the question of *the* best constitution were discussed widely and intensely: reflections of this discussion are visible in formal "constitutional debates" inserted by Herodotus and Euripides into their works and in allusions scattered throughout every genre of contemporaneous literature. This discussion too contained important theoretical elements, for example about constitutional change.[67] Various constitutional models were considered in 411/10. The democracies that were restored in Athens in 410 and 403 established committees to write a revised law code that, for the first time, approximated the concept of a "constitution." Further reforms did much to control the power of the assembly and to stabilize democracy in a more moderate form.[68]

This is the intellectual and theoretical context in which Thrasymachus's proposal of an ancestral constitution needs to be placed. One step farther along the path toward constitutional theory, Thucydides praises the "Oligarchy of the Five Thousand" in 411/10 as a constitution that combined in a moderate balance democratic and oligarchic elements: it was the best constitution Athens had in his life time and decisive in helping Athens recover from its difficulties. Here lie the beginnings of the theory of the mixed constitution that was further developed by Plato, Aristotle, and Polybius.[69] Constitutional reform, based on experience and theory, was thus seen as a promising way to overcome *stasis* and restore domestic peace.

Like Thucydides, the tragic poet Euripides absorbed contemporary political ideas and debates and integrated them into his plays. His urgent appeal to strengthen the citizens' sense of communal responsibility and train the young carefully for their functions as citizens must have been attractive to his audiences: mythical figures who sacrificed themselves for the common good offered a model of civic selflessness that contrasted starkly with the self-centered ambition that populated the contemporaneous political and tragic stages.[70]

Another, more important, approach again drew upon theoretical debates on a crucial issue: given the polis' propensity for *stasis*, was there an element in the polis that was least vulnerable to it and could be trusted to maintain balance, order, and the common good? An answer was found in emphasizing equality and the middle—in the sense of the middle ground (long postulated as an ideal in political thought) and the middling element among the citizens (between rich and poor, democrats and oligarchs). Hence, Euripides repeatedly praises the independent farmer as the type of solid, down-to-earth citizen whose views are based on common sense. In *Phoenician Women* he involves Oedipus's sons, Eteocles and Polynices, and their mother Jocasta in a debate that contrasts the desire for absolute power with equality as a value that distributes power more widely and thus fosters communal stability and peace.[71]

Given such variety of approaches, it would not seem surprising if in such debates about how to overcome the violent ideological confrontation between democrats and oligarchs somebody had floated the idea that was realized in Athens in 403:[72] to separate the two factions by assigning within the same polis distinct towns to them in which they could govern themselves according to their political preferences. Such separation would diffuse civil strife, help emotions cool down, and eventually facilitate reconciliation and peace.

Ending endemic war among poleis

As mentioned above, Thucydides and others were painfully aware of the close link between domestic strife and external war.[73] The master rhetorician and sophist Gorgias reportedly focused explicitly on the desirability of external peace. In his *Funeral Oration*, he said: "Trophies against barbarians demand hymns of praise but those against Greeks lamentations." In his *Olympic Oration* of 408, he developed this idea, that wars among Greeks should be condemned, even more strongly—followed by Isocrates and, to some extent, Plato and Aristotle.[74] What they proposed to end wars among Greeks was a desperate means: to combine and deflect their warlike energies against an outside enemy, the Persians.[75]

Two later sources preserve a range of arguments in praise of peace that were probably developed by the sophists. One is a famous chapter on peace in Augustine's *City of God* that is likely to draw, via Roman and perhaps Hellenistic middlemen, on ideas originating in the late fifth century.[76] The other is a passage in which the historian Polybius criticizes his predecessor Timaeus for attributing "most foolish and childish" words concerning peace and its advantages to the Syracusan general Hermocrates. In a speech he gives to the same Hermocrates at a Peace Congress in 424, Thucydides too acknowledges that there was a large set of arguments one would normally expect to hear at such occasions.[77]

We thus know some popular arguments proclaiming the blessings of peace and the evils of war. Literary pieces on such topics were often embellished by all tricks of rhetoric and saturated with commonplaces. This displeased purists like Polybius, and may make us cringe, but it corresponded to the tastes of the time and impressed audiences. That such ideas "were in the air" at the time in turn explains their insertion in contemporary works (such as tragedies and histories) that drew on a pool of common ideas and theories.[78] For example, both

Herodotus and Polybius use the same specific argument to condemn war, and Herodotus lets the Persian general Mardonius criticize not only the "foolish" principles of Greek hoplite warfare but also the Greek propensity to fight wars among each other—a comment that does not fit the occasion and thus clearly reflects contemporaneous Greek debates.[79]

What we do not find in the extant evidence is a focused theoretical discussion of the causes of endemic inter-polis warfare—comparable to Thucydides' "pathology of civil war"—and of possibilities to overcome it. One might accept such lack of evidence as proof for the lack of discussion and explain it, for example, with Greek tendencies to consider character and emotions crucial in fostering attitudes favoring war and imperialism. The debate, reflected in the historians and Isocrates (summarized above), about the Athenian collective character, its impact on Athenian foreign policy, and the difficulties of changing it, attests to this; so do the emphasis various authors place on civic education and building a strong sense of communal responsibility in young citizens, and the attention Thucydides pays to the role mental dispositions such as greed (*pleonexia*) or enthusiasm (*erōs*) played in political decisions about war.[80]

Still, several reasons suggest that the problem of how to contain war was also intensely discussed and that abstract or theoretical proposals were part of this debate. First of all, the Greeks had for centuries used instruments to avoid war and preserve or restore peace. Homer already mentions the religious protection of heralds and envoys, negotiations, truces and treaties, and duels between one eminent fighter from each side to obviate a mass battle.[81] In the archaic period, the Greeks developed sophisticated tools in international relations: diplomacy and treaties, bilateral or multilateral alliances, and "amphictyonic" organizations in which neighboring communities collaborated for a specific shared purpose (often the administration and protection of an important sanctuary). These organizations did usually not exclude wars among members but reduced the likelihood of war, excessive abuses in war, or war on specific occasions (like the "Olympic truce").[82] Moreover, we saw, archaic Greeks made frequent use of arbitration and legislation to settle conflicts both within poleis and among poleis.[83] Undoubtedly, such institutions were subject to experimentation and change; as in other areas of political life, theoretical thinking must often have pointed the way.[84]

Second, the Greeks' long experience with various kinds of alliances and leagues is especially interesting. It eventually became clear that hegemonic leagues tended to develop into empires and that "peace leagues" forced upon the participants by a superior power and ultimately again serving the hegemon's interests did not work. Hence, it seems, the architects of the "Second

Athenian League" tried something new: a "bicameral" system in which the decision-making body of the alliance (the *synedrion*) was independent from and equal to that of the hegemon, the Athenian assembly.[85]

That theoretical approaches were possible and used in this sphere is perhaps suggested by the daring proposal Herodotus attributes to Thales, the sixth-century mathematician and philosopher from Miletus who was also a practical genius. When in the late 540s the East Greeks were threatened by Persian conquest, he recommended that they form a united state (a "super-polis") centered on the island of Teos. The other poleis would continue to exist but hold a position similar to that of villages or towns in the countryside of a polis.[86] Such unification would have made it possible to maximize the common resources under a central command and decision-making body. I suspect that Thales here adapted for the inter-polis sphere a model of structuring the polis such as that which Cleisthenes later realized in Athens: this model, aimed at improving the polis' integration, provided a representative central council that assisted the central decision-making body (the assembly). This council was composed of delegates from the villages, districts, and towns of Attica in proportion to their citizen numbers.[87] In Thales' case, the central council of delegates from the formerly independent poleis would presumably have served both in a deliberative and decision-making capacity. Other models for the merging of several poleis into one (synoecism or *sympoliteia*) had been around for a long time and became attractive again in the fourth century.[88] It thus seems entirely possible that solutions along those lines would have been discussed at least theoretically to help resolve the problem of endemic warfare.

Third, Thucydides and Isocrates reflect an ongoing debate about one of the conditions that might make it possible to end war: fundamental changes in attitudes toward war and empire.[89] Moreover, in analogy to his "pathology of civil war" Thucydides offers in the "Melian Dialogue" an analytical debate about the principles guiding imperialism and its incompatibility with liberty. This debate is clearly inspired by sophistic theories of power and justice that are based on the distinction between "natural law" (*physis*) and "convention" (*nomos*), best known to us from Plato's *Republic* and *Gorgias*.[90] The clash between imperialism and liberty is one of the leitmotifs in Thucydides' work, used to analyze comprehensively the reasons why polities (in this case particularly Athens) continually decide to go to war and squander opportunities to restore peace. Since, therefore, systematic analysis and theories were applied to explaining imperialism and war, we should expect that the same tools were used to understanding the problems of peace as well.[91]

Explanations and Conclusion

Near Eastern influences on Greek thinking on peace can be ruled out with confidence.[92] I have offered elsewhere explanations for the emergence, in archaic Greece, of a pervasive, intense, and public discourse on peace (summarized above).[93] Such explanations include the emergence and nature of the polis as a small citizen-state in a system of many such states that fiercely competed with each other but shared values and structures and were thus able to develop mechanisms of collaboration, that helped balance each other's power as well as war and peace. Such mechanisms included diplomacy, treaties, alliances, arbitration, and ethics of moderation supported by the authority of Apollo's Delphic Oracle. War was not endemic but intermittent, motivated by intercity rivalries and fought for booty and contested lands rather than subjection, imperial control, or survival; losses were usually limited, and the destruction of cities was rare.[94]

The Greek poleis developed beyond the control of great empires (before the Persians reached the Aegean in 546) and (unlike early republican Rome) were not exposed to other kinds of outside pressure. They therefore lacked incentives to develop militaristic attitudes or ideologies that emphasized conquest and imperial control;[95] nor was there a need for centralized, cohesive, and strong leadership.[96] Despite their ambitions, the emerging aristocracies rarely rose far above the large mass of land-owning farmers who, moreover, were indispensable in the polis army. Hence, the citizen communities had to work out their problems themselves, in communal deliberation, decision, and legislation. The archaic Greek polis was a citizen-state, based on a strong egalitarian foundation and characterized by a rich public culture and participation of large segments of the citizen population in public affairs. Hence, early on, issues of communal concern became part of political reflection and were embedded in the poetry performed at public festivals.[97]

Such issues included the resolution of civic conflicts and the maintenance of peace. Here lie the foundations for early attempts at conceptualizing war and peace (observed in the epics), for the first quasi-theoretical effort at defining the role of peace as a central condition for communal well-being (visible in Hesiod's systematization of communally important forces and values in *Theogony*), and for Solon's model of political causation that offered a theoretical base for political measures to restore and secure peace within the polis.[98] Programs of incisive communal reform (such as those of Solon and Cleisthenes in Athens) that aimed at overcoming civil strife and achieving peace and stability through communal integration were impossible without theoretical thinking.

These conditions changed dramatically in the fifth century, when the Greeks were confronted with Persian imperialism and subsequently new forms of imperial ambition and rule emerged in Greece itself. The power controlled by the largest poleis grew exponentially, the stakes in wars became huge, and war changed radically, becoming permanent, ubiquitous, brutal and total, while occurrences of violent civil strife and civil war (*stasis*) increased dramatically.[99] These developments, culminating during and after the Peloponnesian War, forced the Greeks to think in new ways about war and peace and to seek new solutions to overcome war and *stasis*. At the same time, the emergence of philosophy in the sixth century and of early forms of political science in the middle of the fifth offered new tools to tackle these burning issues. Like all "intellectuals" in the world of Greek poleis, political thinkers and philosophers did not serve powerful rulers, ideologies, or special interests; they were free and independent citizens—and often strongly critical of traditional views and those traditionally wielding power, or conversely of the masses and their shortcomings.

Some of the sophists developed new ideas and theories on community, society, and politics, and specialized in teaching communally useful skills. Poets and historians applied their ideas and theories in their works. Such theoretical analysis concerned, for instance, the causes and nature of *stasis*, the connection between external and internal war, and possibilities to overcome the rift between democracy and oligarchy and to secure internal peace.[100] The internal sphere of the polis could be controlled and regulated by the citizens themselves, and at least in some poleis they eventually improved their abilities and instruments to do so. Open debate in the assembly and freedom of speech of all citizens helped to focus public attention on these issues and keep them in peoples' minds, thus stimulating further thought and discussion.

Conversely, the inter-polis sphere was extremely difficult to control. No disinterested supra-local or supra-regional organizations existed. The great authority the Delphic Oracle had enjoyed in the archaic period and the safety of the seas guaranteed by the Athenian empire fell victim to the anarchic jungle of power struggles in the late fifth and fourth centuries.[101] Competitiveness and a fierce spirit of independence on the one side, imperial ambitions to be realized by war on the other, made every agreement and treaty temporary. Peace was observed until one power believed it could gain more by going to war. Attempts to propagate large-scale systems of inter-city collaboration and peace (such as the "common peace" treaties discussed above) went in the right direction but failed because they did not aim at peace *per se* but in most cases served the interests of the hegemonic power. In addition, lower classes often favored war because economically they depended on and profited from war—a fact that prompted critical authors to consider the connection between economy and war and to offer innovative proposals to improve the lower classes' circumstances.[102] Still, war between communities, the Greeks believed, was an unalterable condition of human society. No theory could change that. Only pragmatic solutions seemed available, including the desperate effort to secure peace among the Greeks by uniting them against non-Greek enemies.[103] This kind of peace was eventually achieved under Macedonian leadership—but only at the expense of the liberty of the Greek states.

Hence, at first sight it seems that no theories were developed to improve the chances for external peace. Yet our close examination has revealed some evidence, hints, and clues that penetrating analyses, discussions, and experiments were not lacking. They were based in part on long-standing experience, in part on new and even theoretical approaches. That they did not produce any tangible or lasting results is regrettable but understandable. Ultimately, again, peace was achieved only by the superior power and autocratic ruler of a conquering state.

I conclude with two brief observations, widening the perspective. One is that the Greek defeat at Chaeronea and the foundation of the Corinthian League in 338/37, which imposed peace and unity on the Greeks under Macedonian hegemony, ended an experiment, rare in world history, of independent collective "war and peace management" by an assemblage of free poleis. Despite its flaws and failures, it did not lack potential and creative possibilities. From now on, as in the Roman and Persian empires, in India and China, peace was sought and achieved through unification in an empire and ensuing imperial control.[104]

The second observation is that similar conditions—incessant and increasingly oppressive warfare among clustered city-states or kingdoms, culminating in the "Warring State Period"—prompted in early China as well the emergence of an intense discourse (including theoretical and philosophical debates) on peace, and this too was a society that had developed a rich literature and discourse on public issues. Although most of the thinkers and officials that dealt with such issues were employed at aristocratic and royal courts and aimed at realizing their ideas there, it seems relevant that some of the most influential philosophers and teachers (including Confucius and Mencius) remained independent and taught their pupils at their own schools.[105]

The three conditions for the emergence of concepts and theories of peace that I identified in my earlier chapter in this volume—an exceptionally dire experience of war, the development of abstract and philosophical thinking, and an economically and politically independent status of the thinkers involved—were thus met in both pre-Hellenistic Greece and (at least to some extent) in pre-imperial China—but apparently not elsewhere.[106]

Notes

1   Although the title is similar and it uses some of the same evidence, this chapter is not identical with Raaflaub 2009. Similarly, the first section is a condensed version of Raaflaub 2007a. I thank the responsible editors for permission to reuse these essays here.—All dates are BCE unless indicated otherwise.

2   For political thought in Homer, see, e.g., Raaflaub 2000, 2001b; Hammer 2002.

3   On the society reflected in the epics, see Ulf 1990; van Wees 1992; Raaflaub 1997a; Finkelberg 2011: 3. 810–13.

4   Arbitration: Tod 1913; Piccirilli 1973; Giovannini 2007: 177–84; Low 2007: 105–8.

5   Meier 1990a: 28–52 (third position); 2011: ch. 21; Faraguna 2001; Wallace 2009. Seven Sages: Martin 1993. Lawgivers: Hölkeskamp 1999.

6   Polarization preventing arbitration: Low (n. 4). Cold war parallels: Lebow and Strauss 1991. Suspicion towards neutrals is exemplified by Thucydides' Melian Dialogue (5.84–114); see also 3.82.8. On neutrality: Bauslaugh 1991. On Greek just war theories, see now Dewald 2013.

7   On various levels beneath that of the "superpowers" arbitration continued for centuries to be a useful tool for conflict resolution; see Ager 1996.

8   Thucydides 4.15ff., 41.

9   See esp. 243–46, 284–87. Euripides' agreement with Pericles is all the more remarkable as the poet is often critical of Athens' policies. On interpretations of this play: Zuntz 1955; Mendelsohn 2002: ch. 2. My own view: Raaflaub 1988: 342–44.

10   *Iliad* 3.205–24; 11.122–25, 138–42; see also *Odyssey* 21.11–21. For discussion, Raaflaub 1997b: 3–8.

11   All this is in book 3 of the *Iliad*. Resentment of Paris: 3.451–54; cf. 38–57; 6.523–25; 7.390. Trans. Richmond Lattimore. On the truce, see Elmer 2012.

12   *Iliad* 7.400–2. The reported events are in books 4 and 7.

13   See n. 8 above.

14   See below at n. 52.

15   Andromache: *Iliad* 6.450–58. Ares: 5.761, 831, 890–91; see Burkert 1985: 169–70; Schachter 2002.

16   Cobet 1986; Luginbill 1999; Raaflaub 2006.

17   Thucydides 8.18, 58; Lewis 1977; Raaflaub 2004: 199–201.

18   Hamilton 1979; Strauss 1986; Cartledge 1987, and relevant chs. in *CAH* VI.

19   Busolt and Swoboda 1926: 1320–60.

20   Bengtson 1975: nos. 152, 156; Fornara 1983: no. 95; Thucydides 1.113–115.1; *CAH* V: 121–27, 133–38.

21   Plutarch, *Pericles* 17; Stadter 1989: 201–9; Podlecki 1998: 70.

22   See above at nn. 4–7.

23   Xenophon, *Hellenica* 5.1.31; complete sources in Bengtson 1975: no. 242; Crawford and Whitehead 1983: no. 263; see further Ryder 1965, ch. 2; Urban 1991; Jehne 1994: 31–47; Victor Alonso, in *W&P* 206–25; Low 2012; Wilker 2012b (both with further bibliog.).

24   Xenophon, *Hellenica* 5.1.32–35.

25   Van Wees, Chapter 6 below, at n. 37. For the other treaties, see Bengtson 1975: nos. 265, 269, 270, 292 with sources. See Ryder 1965; Jehne 1994 for details and discussion.

26   Diodorus 15.28.2–5.

27   Bengtson 1975: no. 257; Rhodes and Osborne 2003: no. 22; Crawford and Whitehead 1983: no. 269; see Ryder 1965, ch. 3; Cargill 1981; Schmitz 1988, esp. 256ff.; Dreher 1995.

28   *CAH* VI: 171–72; Rhodes and Osborne 2003: p.100.

29   Sealey 1976: 410. The "bicameral" system itself was not entirely new; in the Peloponnesian League, for example, the assembly of the allies and the Spartan assembly deliberated and decided separately (Thucydides 1.67–88, 118–25), although there was no formally established *synedrion*.

30   Rhodes and Osborne 2003: no. 76; Crawford and Whitehead 1983: no. 350; Ryder 1965: ch. 7 and app. 10; Jehne 1994: pt. 3.

31   Rhodes 2003.

32   For a detailed discussion of the Greek failure in creating integrative "supra-polis" structures, see Raaflaub forthcoming.

33   Isocr. *Or.* 8. 3–7, 12, 16, 18–20. See further 29–32, 63–65, 95, 133–44. On Isocrates, see briefly Cawkwell 1996; Weissenberger 2005; on his political ideas, Bringmann 1965; Dobesch 1968.

34   Suppliant plays (tragedies in which, according to myth, persecuted people supplicate the Athenians or suitable "alter-Athenians" for help and are rescued by them: Aeschylus, *Suppliant Women;* Euripides, *Children of Heracles* and *Suppliants*); funeral orations (or similar pieces): see esp. Lysias, *Or.* 2; Demosthenes, *Or.* 60; Hyperides, *Or.* 6; Isocrates, *Or.* 4 (*Panegyric*), 12 (*Panathenaic*); Plato, *Menexenus;* see Loraux 1986. Athenian ideologies: Raaflaub 2004: chs. 5.1–2.

35   Thucydides 1.70; for parallels (esp. in Euripides' *Suppliants,* and interpretation), see Raaflaub 1994.

36   Thucydides 6.9, 18.

37   Thucydides 2.63; Herodotus 3.142–43.

38   Thucydides 6.18; Herodotus 1.154–56. Herodotus' fiction probably consists mainly of turning chronological sequence into cause and effect: the Lydians had been warlike in Croesus's time but were peaceful and known for their music and crafts in Herodotus' time. Carolyn Dewald points out to me that Croesus' advice to Cyrus may also have the purpose of characterizing his personality and ineffective thinking as it is reflected in his failed attempts to save not only his country but also his son, his rule, and his benefactor Cyrus (1.34–45, 53–56, 71–81, 84–86, 204–14).

39   See additional comments by Van Wees in Chapter 6 below (at n. 42) and his discussion of more pragmatic and realistic proposals by Xenophon (at n. 43).

40   Aristotle, *Constitution of the Athenians* (henceforth *CA*) 39; Xenophon, *Hellenica* 2.4.24–43; Loening 1987. On the "Thirty:" Krentz 1982. On the preceding

"constitutional roller coaster," see Ostwald 1986: pt. 3; Bleckmann 1998; Munn 2000: pt. 2; Shear 2001.

41 Aristotle, 39.7 (trans. Peter Rhodes); Xenophon, 2.4.43 (trans. Peter Krentz). Even if tensions and conflicts continued (Strauss 1986: 86–120), remarkably democracy lasted without interruption until it was overthrown by outside interference late in the fourth century. The best example of how the decree could be circumvented is the trial of Socrates that was almost certainly motivated politically; for discussion: Hansen 1995; Parker 1996: 199–217; Scholz 2000.

42 Cyrene (401 BCE, also mentioning *mē mnēsikakein;* Diodorus Siculus 14.34.6) and Dikaia, a colony of Eretria in the Chalcidice (first half fourth century; Voutiras and Sismanidis 2007).

43 See below at nn. 53–54.

44 See Solon's poem no. 4 in West 1992 (trans. in West 1994); Raaflaub 2001b: 89–99 with bibliog.

45 See below at n. 56. Generally on peace in Greek literature: Zampaglione 1973: pt. 1; Arnould 1981; Spiegel 1990; see also Graeber 1992; relevant chs. in Sordi 1985; Binder and Effe 1989.

46 Euripides' war plays: esp. *Hecuba, Andromache, Trojan Women, Suppliant Women;* Aristophanes' peace plays: *Acharnians, Peace, Lysistrata.* See, generally, Zampaglione 1973: 71–90; Lawrence Tritle, David Konstan, in *W&P* 172–90, 191–205. On the role of war in classical Athens: Meier 1990b; Tritle 2013. On the Athenian ideology of war: Raaflaub 2001a. Civic ideology: Thuc. 2.43.1; Connor 1971: ch. 3; Meier 1990a: ch. 6. On *Lysistrata:* Henderson 1980; Raaflaub, 329–34.

47 Sophists: below at n. 58. Since I am mostly interested in the origins of such ideas, I omit here Plato and Aristotle, whose comments would repay careful examination: see Nestle 1938: 28–31; Zampaglione 54–64; Spiegel 1990: 190–210, and esp. Ostwald 1996; also Chapter 6 (Van Wees) at n. 33.

48 Herodotus, *Histories* 7.9; 8.3.1; see also 1.87 (trans. de Sélincourt and Marincola). On Herodotus and war, see Cobet 1986; Raaflaub 2011.

49 Thucydides (2.8.3) famously claims the same unique earthquake on Delos for the time shortly before the Peloponnesian War: one of the clearest intertextual references to his predecessor (on which see Hornblower 1996: 122–45).

50 Thomas 1993, 2000.

51 See Robin Yates' chs. in *W&P* (34–52) and in this volume (ch. 4 with bibliog.); for a broader comparison with other ancient societies, see ch. 1 (Raaflaub) above.

52 *Iliad* 18.490–508 (city at peace) and 509–40 (city at war). See Bernd Effe's ch. in Binder and Effe 1989: 9–26.

53 Hesiod, *Works and Days* 225–47 (cf. *Iliad* 16.384–92; *Odyssey* 19.109–14).

54 *Theogony* 901–3: the Hōrai (Eunomia, Dikē, Eirēnē [Good Order, Justice, Peace]) as daughters of Zeus and Themis. *Works and Days* 110–201: Myth of the Ages. Near Eastern precedents: West 1997: 312–19.

55 Solon, fr. 4 West (see n. 44 above).

56 Heraclitus, DK 22 B67 (see Kirk et al. 1983: ch. 6): "God is day-night, winter-summer, war-peace, satiety-famine." B80: "One should know that war is universal (common) and jurisdiction is strife, and everything comes about by way of strife and necessity." B53: "War is both king of all and father of all, and it has revealed some as gods, others as men; some it has made slaves, others free" (trans. Freeman 1948). On the Orphics and Pythagoreans: Ellinger 1992; Kirk et al. 1983: chs. 1.4 and 7.

57 Empedocles, DK 31 B16ff.; 112ff., esp. 128, 130, 135–139; see Kirk et al. 1983: ch. 10 and, generally, Nestle 1938: 9–10.

58 On the sophists, see Guthrie 1971; Kerferd 1981; de Romilly 1992.

59 On *stasis*, the origins of *homonoia*, and the cult of Homonoia, see Chapter 1 (Raaflaub) above at nn. 44–46.

60 Democracy: Hansen 1999; Raaflaub et al. 2007; oligarchy: Whibley 1896; Ostwald 2000; on the conflict between both: Ruschenbusch 1978: 24–66; Raaflaub 2004: 208–21; Shear 2011.

61 *Stasis* in Thucydides (3.69-85, esp. 82–84 [political analysis]; 8.45–98): Price 2001. Thucydides as a political theoretician: Ober 2001, 2006.

62 Democritus, DK 68 B249, 250, 255. This idea also underlies Isocrates' theory (at n. 33 above) and Aeneas Tacticus' advice about how to establish civic unity against external threats (14.1; Whitehead 1990: 60). See also Chapter 6 (Van Wees) at nn. 49–53.

63 On Antiphon, see Thuc. 8.68. *On Concord*: Gagarin 2002: 93–99; fragments: DK 87 B44a, 60, 61; Pendrick 2002: 49–46 and frr. 45–71; characterization: Philostratus, *Lives of the Sophists* 1.15 (end). Fantasy peoples: Nestle 1938: 14–15; an example of this method is in Herodotus 4.23.

64 DK 89; trans. in Gagarin and Woodruff 1995: 290–95. Encomium of *eunomia*: ch. 17; on *eunomia* as a concept, see Ostwald 1969: 62–95.

65 DK 85 B1. On "ancestral constitution" (*patrios politeia*), see Fuks 1953; Finley 1975; Ostwald 1986: ch. 7.

66 Aristotle, *CA* 29.3.

67 Formal constitutional debates: Herodotus 3.80–82; Euripides, *Suppliants* 419–55; see also Thucydides 6.38–39 (refuting oligarchic criticism of democracy). Ideal constitutions: Aristotle, *Politics* 2.8.1267b30–37 (Hippodamus of Miletus); 2.7.1266a37–b5 (Phaleas of Chalcedon). Ongoing debates about constitutions: Raaflaub 1989. Criticism of democracy: Roberts 1994; Ober 1998; theory of constitutional change: Ryffel 1949.

68 411/10: Aristotle, *CA* 30. On the Athenian law code of the early fourth century, Hansen 1999: ch. 7.

69 Thuc. 8.97.2; on Thucydides and constitutional thought: Leppin 1999; Raaflaub 2006. Mixed constitution: von Fritz 1954; Aalders 1968; Nippel 1980.

70 Euripides on overcoming *stasis*: Gregory 1991; Raaflaub 2001b: 99–117; also Mendelsohn 2002: 123–26.

71 Middle element: *Suppliants* 238–45. Farmer: e.g., *Orestes* 917–30. Debate: *Phoenician Women* 261–637; Raaflaub 2001b: 106–7.

72 See above at nn. 40–42.

73 Thucydides 3.82.1–2.

74 *Funeral Oration:* DK 82 B5b; cf. Philostratus, *Lives of the Sophists* 1.9 (where the *Olympic Oration* is mentioned); Isocrates, *Panegyric* 3, 115–16, 172–77; *To Philip* 7–9, 15–16 (see n. 33 above). On Plato and Aristotle: Ostwald 1996.

75 Similarly, Roman poets in the civil war period urged their leaders, if they had to fight, to fight distant enemies rather than shedding Roman blood.

76 Augustine, *City of God* 19.12. On the origins of his ideas, see Chapter 1 (Raaflaub) above, at nn. 21–22.

77 Polybius 12.25k–26. Arguments for peace: 12.26.1–8. Hermocrates' speech in Thucydides: 4.59–64; see Hammond 1973. Allusions to commonplaces on peace: Thuc. 4.59.2, 62.2; see also 61.1–2. Nestle 1938: 17–18; Walbank 1967: 400–1 argue for sophistic origin of Timaeus' arguments.

78 Thomas 2000.

79 Herodotus 1.87; Polybius 12.26.7. Criticism of Greek war: Herodotus 7.9b (see above at n. 48).

80 Education, civic responsibility: examples are Euripides' *Suppliants* (esp. 857–917) and *Phoenician Women* (991–1018); mental dispositions: e.g., Thucydides 4.21, 41; 6.24. Athenian collective character: at n. 35 above.

81 Diplomacy: Adcock and Mosley 1975; Wéry 1979; Piccirilli 2002. Duels: Giovannini 2007: 175–77. See further Raaflaub 1997b and above at nn. 11–12.

82 Alliance systems, amphictyonies: Tausend 1992; Baltrusch 1994; Giovannini 2007. Limitations on war: Kiechle 1958. The Olympic Truce: Finley and Pleket 1976: 98–100; Decker 1995: 116–18.

83 See above at n. 4.

84 Although this again concerns the domestic sphere, the complex and sophisticated reforms that Cleisthenes enacted in late sixth-century Athens (not least to eliminate civic strife) were unthinkable without a blueprint based on abstract and theoretical thinking; on these reforms, see Ostwald 1988; Meier 1990b: ch. 4; Anderson 2003.

85 See nn. 26ff. above.

86 Herodotus 1.170 (who also mentions a similarly daring proposal by Bias of Priene). Thales' practical solutions, based on "applied science:" 1.74–75. Quite possibly, Herodotus (or his source) here attributes to Thales an idea that was discussed later in the fifth century: see Raaflaub forthcoming.

87 See n. 84 above.

88 See, e.g., Xenophon, *Hellenica* 5.2.12; Giovannini 1971; 2007: 244–45, and, generally, Low 2007. See also Beck and Funke 2015.

89 See above at n. 33.

90 Melian Dialogue: Thuc. 5.84–112. On the *nomos – physis* debate, see Guthrie 1971: ch. 4; Kerferd 1981: ch. 10.

91 Thucydides: Raaflaub 2006. The contrast between imperialism and liberty plays a similarly important role in Herodotus: see, e.g., von Fritz 1965. Van Wees (Chapter 6 below, at nn. 42ff.) adds important arguments from Thucydides, Isocrates, and Xenophon supporting this suggestion.

92   Raaflaub 2009: 236–38. For this section, see esp. Van Wees 2001.
93   See Raaflaub 2009: 238–41.
94   On the latter, see Ducrey 1968; on archaic warfare, Raaflaub 1997c; 1999: 129–41; van Wees 2004. On the importance of polis clusters: Raaflaub 1990.
95   Sparta's early expansionist tendencies were soon counterbalanced by the difficulties of controlling, with a small and shrinking citizen body, a large population of slaves and dependent communities; see, e.g., Cartledge 1987, 2002.
96   Early and mid-Republican Rome offers a good counterexample: Raaflaub 1996a.
97   Polis as a citizen-state: Hansen 1993. Farmers as "semi-aristocrats": Starr 1977: ch. 6. Egalitarian element: Raaflaub 1996b; Morris 1996; 2000: chs. 4–5; Raaflaub and Wallace, in Raaflaub et al. 2007: 22–48. Working out problems themselves: Meier 2011. Public and political function of poetry: ibid. and Raaflaub 2000.
98   Above, at nn. 43–45.
99   Raaflaub 1999: 141–48; Hanson 2001; Tritle 2013. *Stasis:* at n. 59 above.
100 See also Spiegel 1990.
101 Anarchy in interstate relations: Eckstein 2006; Low 2007, esp. ch. 3.
102 See Chapter 6 (Van Wees) at nn. 44–53.
103 See Gorgias' and Isocrates' proposals mentioned at nn. 73ff. above.
104 See briefly Chapter 1 (Raaflaub) above, at nn. 67ff. On the Greek experiment, see Raaflaub forthcoming.
105 See Lun 1998; Robin Yates' chapter in *W&P* (34–52), and especially his chapter (4) in this volume.
106 Van Wees (Chapter 6, final section) adds important observations and additional factors.

Abbreviations

BNP   *Brill's New Pauly*
CAH   *Cambridge Ancient History*, 2nd edn.
DK   Diels and Kranz 1961–1964
W&P   Raaflaub 2007b

References

Aalders, G.J.D. 1968. *Die Theorie der gemischten Verfassung im Altertum*. Amsterdam.
Adcock, F. and Mosley, D.J. 1975. *Diplomacy in Ancient Greece*. London.
Ager, S.L. 1996. *Interstate Arbitrations in the Greek World, 337–90 B.C.* Berkeley.
Anderson, G. 2003. *The Athenian Experiment: Building an Imagined Political Community in Ancient Attica, 508–490 BC*. Ann Arbor.
Arnould, D. 1981. *Guerre et paix dans la poésie grecque de Callinos à Pindare*. New York.
Baltrusch, E. 1994. *Symmachie und Spondai. Untersuchungen zum griechischen Völkerrecht der archaischen und klassischen Zeit (8.–5. Jahrhundert v. Chr.)*. Berlin.

Bauslaugh, R.A. 1991. *The Concept of Neutrality in Classical Greece*. Berkeley.

Beck, H. and Funke, P. (eds.). 2015. *Federalism in Greek Antiquity*. Cambridge.

Bengtson, H. (ed.). 1975. *Die Staatsverträge des Altertums*, II. 2nd ed. Munich.

Binder, G., and Effe, B. (eds.). 1989. *Krieg und Frieden im Altertum*. Trier.

Bleckmann, B. 1998. *Athens Weg in die Niederlage. Die letzten Jahre des Peloponnesischen Krieges*. Stuttgart.

Bolmarcich, S. 2012. "Thucydides' theory of negotiation." In Wilker 2012a: 78–91.

Bringmann, K. 1965. *Studien zu den politischen Ideen des Isokrates*. Göttingen.

Burkert, W. 1985. *Greek Religion*. Cambridge MA.

Busolt, G., and Swoboda, H. 1926. *Griechische Staatskunde*, II. Munich.

Cargill, J. 1981. *The Second Athenian League: Empire or Free Alliance?* Berkeley.

Cartledge, P. 1987. *Agesilaos and the Crisis of Sparta*. London.

Cartledge, P. 2002. *Sparta and Lakonia: A Regional History 1300 to 362 BC*. 2nd edn. London.

Cawkwell, G.L. 1996. "Isocrates." *Oxford Classical Dictionary*, 769–71. 3rd edn. Oxford.

Cobet, J. 1986. "Herodotus and Thucydides on war." In I. Moxon, J.D. Smart, and A.J. Woodman (eds.), *Past Perspectives: Studies in Greek and Roman Historical Writing*, 1–18. Cambridge.

Connor, W.R. 1971. *The New Politicians of Fifth-Century Athens*. Princeton.

Crawford, M. and Whitehead, D. (eds.). 1983. *Archaic and Classical Greece: A Selection of Ancient Sources in Translation*. Cambridge.

Decker, W. 1995. *Sport in der griechischen Antike*. Munich.

Dewald, C. 2013. "Justice and justifications: war theory among the ancient Greeks." In J. Neusner, B. Chilton, and R. Tully (eds.), *Just War in Religion and Politics*, 27–50. Lanham MD.

Diels, H. and Kranz, W. (eds.). 1961–1964. *Die Fragmente der Vorsokratiker*, I. 10th edn. Berlin 1961. II. 11th edn. 1964.

Dobesch, G. 1968. *Der panhellenische Gedanke im 4. Jh. und der Philippos des Isokrates*. Vienna.

Dreher, M. 1995. *Hegemon und Symmachoi. Untersuchungen zum Zweiten Athenischen Seebund*. Berlin.

Ducrey, P. 1968. *Le traitement des prisonniers de guerre dans la Grèce antique des origines à la conquête romaine*. Paris.

Eckstein, A.M. 2006. *Mediterranean Anarchy, Interstate War and the Rise of Rome*. Berkeley.

Ellinger, P. 1992. "Guerre et sacrifice dans le mysticisme grec: Orphisme et Pythagorisme." In M.-M. Mactoux and E. Geny (eds.), *Mélanges Pierre Lévêque*, VI: *Religion*, 73–87. Paris.

Elmer, D.F. 2012. "Building community across the battle-lines: the truce in *Iliad* 3 and 4." In Wilker 2012a: 25–48.

Faraguna, M. 2001. "La figura dell'aisymnetes tra realtà storica e teoria politica." In R.W. Wallace and M. Gagarin (eds.), *Symposion 2001: Papers on Greek and Hellenistic Legal History*, 321–38. Vienna.

Finkelberg, M. (ed.). 2011. *Homer Encyclopedia*. 3 vols. Malden MA and Oxford.

Finley, M.I. 1975. "The ancestral constitution." In Finley, *The Use and Abuse of History*, 34–59. London.

Finley, M.I. and Pleket, H.W. 1976. *The Olympic Games*. New York.

Fornara, C.W. 1983. *Archaic Times to the End of the Peloponnesian War*. Translated Documents of Greece & Rome 1. Cambridge.

Freeman, K. 1948. *Ancilla to the Pre-socratic Philosophers*. Cambridge MA.

Fritz, K. von. 1954. *The Theory of the Mixed Constitution in Antiquity*. New York. Repr. 1975.

Fritz, K. von. 1965. "Die griechische *eleutheria* bei Herodot." *Wiener Studien* 78: 5–31.

Fuks, A. 1953. *The Ancestral Constitution*. London.

Gagarin, M. 2002. *Antiphon the Athenian*. Austin.

Gagarin, M. and Woodruff, P. (eds.). 1995. *Early Greek Political Thought from Homer to the Sophists*. Cambridge.

Giovannini, A. 1971. *Untersuchungen über die Natur und die Anfänge der bundesstaatlichen Sympolitie in Griechenland*. Göttingen.

Giovannini, A. 2007. *Les relations entre Etats dans la Grèce antique du temps d'Homère à l'intervention romaine*. Stuttgart.

Graeber, A. 1992. "Friedensvorstellung und Friedensbegriff bei den Griechen bis zum Peloponnesischen Krieg." *Zeitschrift für Rechtsgeschichte* 109: 116–63.

Gregory, J. 1991. *Euripides and the Instruction of the Athenians*. Ann Arbor.

Guthrie, W.K.C. 1971. *The Sophists*. Cambridge. First published as *A History of Greek Philosophy*, III.1. 1969.

Hamilton, C.D. 1979. *Sparta's Bitter Victories: Politics and Diplomacy in the Corinthian War*. Ithaca NY.

Hammer, D. 2002. *The* Iliad *as Politics: The Performance of Political Thought*. Norman OK.

Hammond, N.G.L. 1973. "The particular and the universal in the speeches of Thucydides with special reference to that of Hermocrates at Gela." In Stadter 1973: 49–59.

Hansen, M.H. 1993. "The *polis* as a citizen state." In Hansen (ed.), *The Ancient Greek City-State*, 7–29. Copenhagen.

Hansen, M.H. 1995. *The Trial of Sokrates—from the Athenian Point of View*. Copenhagen.

Hansen, M.H. 1999. *The Athenian Democracy in the Age of Demosthenes*. Norman OK.

Hanson, V.D. 2001. "Democratic warfare, ancient and modern." In McCann and Strauss 2001: 3–33.

Henderson, J. 1980. "*Lysistrate:* the play and its themes." *Yale Classical Studies* 26: 153–218.

Hölkeskamp, K.-J. 1999. *Schiedsrichter, Gesetzgeber und Gesetzgebung im archaischen Griechenland*. Stuttgart.

Hornblower, S. 1996. *A Commentary on Thucydides*, II. Oxford.

Jehne, M. 1994. *Koine Eirene*. Stuttgart.

Kerferd, W.G. 1981. *The Sophistic Movement*. Cambridge.

Kiechle, F. 1958. "Zur Humanität in der Kriegführung der griechischen Staaten." *Historia* 7: 129–56.

Kirk, G.S., Raven, J.E., and Schofield, M. 1983. *The Presocratic Philosophers*. 2nd edn. Cambridge.

Krentz, P. 1982. *The Thirty at Athens*. Ithaca NY.

Lebow, R.N. and Strauss, B.S. (eds.). 1991. *Hegemonic Rivalry: From Thucydides to the Nuclear Age*. Boulder.

Leppin, H. 1999. *Thukydides und die Verfassung der Polis. Ein Beitrag zur politischen Ideengeschichte des 5. Jahrhunderts v. Chr*. Berlin.

Lewis, D.M. 1977. *Sparta and Persia*. Leiden.

Loening, T.C. 1987. *The Reconciliation Agreement of 404–403 BC in Athens*. Stuttgart.

Loraux, N. 1986. *The Invention of Athens: The Funeral Oration in the Classical City*. Trans. Alan Sheridan. Cambridge MA.

Low, P. 2007. *Interstate Relations in Classical Greece*. Cambridge.

Low, P. 2012. "Peace, common peace, and war in mid-fourth-century Greece." In Wilker 2012a: 118–34.

Luginbill, R.D. 1999. *Thucydides on War and National Character*. Boulder.

Lun, T.W. 1998. "Subverting hatred: peace and nonviolence in Confucianism and Daoism." In D.L. Smith-Christopher (ed.), *Subverting Hatred: The Challenge of Nonviolence in Religious Traditions*, 49–66. Maryknoll.

Martin, R. 1993. "The seven sages as performers of wisdom." In L. Kurke and C. Dougherty (eds.), *Cultural Poetics in Archaic Greece: Cult, Performance, Politics*, 108–28. Cambridge.

McCann, D. and Strauss, B.S. (eds.). 2001. *War and Democracy: A Comparative Study of the Korean War and the Peloponnesian War*. Armonk NY and London.

Meier, C. 1990a. *The Greek Discovery of Politics*. Trans. David McLintock. Cambridge MA.

Meier, C. 1990b. "Die Rolle des Krieges im klassischen Athen." *Historische Zeitschrift* 251: 555–605.

Meier, C. 2011. *A Culture of Freedom: Ancient Greece and the Origins of Europe*. Oxford.

Mendelsohn, D. 2002. *Gender and the City in Euripides' Political Plays*. Oxford.

Morris, I. 1996. "The strong principle of equality and the archaic origins of Greek democracy." In Ober and Hedrick 1996: 19–48.

Morris, I. 2000. *Archaeology as Cultural History*. Malden MA and Oxford.

Munn, M. 2000. *The School of History: Athens in the Age of Socrates*. Berkeley.

Nardin, T. (ed.). 1996. *The Ethics of War and Peace: Religious and Secular Perspectives*. Princeton.

Nestle, W. 1938. *Der Friedensgedanke in der antiken Welt*. Göttingen.

Nippel, W. 1980. *Mischverfassungstheorie und Verfassungsrealität in Antike und früher Neuzeit*. Stuttgart.

Ober, J. 1998. *Political Dissent in Democratic Athens: Intellectual Critics of Popular Rule*. Princeton.

Ober, J. 2001. "Thucydides Theoretikos/Thucydides Histor: realist theory and the challenge of history." In McCann and Strauss 2001: 273–306.

Ober, J. 2006. "Thucydides and the invention of political science." In Rengakos and Tsakmakis 2006: 131–59.

Ober, J. and Hedrick, C. (eds.). 1996. *Dēmokratia: A Conversation on Democracies, Ancient and Modern.* Princeton.

Ostwald, M. 1969. *Nomos and the Beginnings of the Athenian Democracy.* Oxford.

Ostwald, M. 1986. *From Popular Sovereignty to the Sovereignty of Law.* Berkeley.

Ostwald, M. 1988. "The reform of the Athenian state by Cleisthenes." *CAH* IV: 303–46.

Ostwald, M. 1996. "Peace and war in Plato and Aristotle." *Scripta Classica Israelica* 15: 102–18.

Ostwald, M. 2000. *Oligarchia: The Development of a Constitutional Form in Ancient Greece.* Stuttgart.

Parker, R. 1996. *Athenian Religion: A History.* Oxford.

Pendrick, G.J. 2002. *Antiphon the Sophist: The Fragments.* Cambridge.

Piccirilli, L. 1973. *Gli arbitrati interstatali greci.* Florence.

Piccirilli, L. 2002. *L'invenzione della diplomazia nella Grecia antica.* Rome.

Podlecki, A. 1998. *Perikles and His Circle.* London.

Price, J. 2001. *Thucydides and Internal War.* Cambridge.

Raaflaub, K. 1988. "Politisches Denken im Zeitalter Athens." In I. Fetscher and H. Münkler (eds.), *Pipers Handbuch der politischen Ideen,* I: 273–368. Munich.

Raaflaub, K. 1989. "Contemporary Perceptions of Democracy in Fifth-Century Athens." *Classica & Mediaevalia* 40: 33–70.

Raaflaub, K. 1990. "Expansion und Machtbildung in frühen Polis-Systemen." In W. Eder (ed.), *Staat und Staatlichkeit in der frühen römischen Republik,* 511–45. Stuttgart.

Raaflaub, K. 1994. "Democracy, power, and imperialism in fifth-century Athens." In J.P. Euben, J.R. Wallach, and J. Ober (eds.), *Athenian Political Thought and the Reconstruction of American Democracy,* 103–46. Ithaca NY.

Raaflaub, K. 1996a. "Born to be wolves? Origins of Roman imperialism." In R.W. Wallace and E.M. Harris (eds.), *Transitions to Empire: Essays in Greco-Roman History, 360–146 B.C. in Honor of E. Badian,* 273–314. Norman OK.

Raaflaub, K. 1996b. "Equalities and inequalities in Athenian democracy." In Ober and Hedrick 1996: 139–74.

Raaflaub, K. 1997a. "Homeric society." In I. Morris and B. Powell (eds.), *A New Companion to Homer,* 624-48. Leiden.

Raaflaub, K. 1997b. "Politics and interstate relations in the world of early Greek *poleis:* Homer and beyond." *Antichthon* 31: 1–27.

Raaflaub, K. 1997c. "Soldiers, citizens, and the evolution of the early Greek *polis.*" In L. Mitchell and P.J. Rhodes (eds.), *The Development of the* Polis *in Archaic Greece,* 49–59. London.

Raaflaub, K. 1999. "Archaic and classical Greece." In Raaflaub and N. Rosenstein (eds.), *War and Society in the Ancient and Medieval Worlds,* 129–61. Washington DC.

Raaflaub, K. 2000. "Poets, lawgivers, and the beginnings of political reflection in archaic Greece." In C. Rowe and M. Schofield (eds.), *The Cambridge History of Greek and Roman Political Thought*, 23–59. Cambridge.

Raaflaub, K. 2001a. "Father of all, destroyer of all: war in late fifth-century Athenian discourse and ideology." In McCann and Strauss 2001: 307–56.

Raaflaub, K. 2001b. "Political thought, civic responsibility, and the Greek polis." In J. Arnason and P. Murphy (eds.), *Agon, Logos, Polis: The Greek Achievement and Its Aftermath*, 72–117. Stuttgart.

Raaflaub, K. 2004. *The Discovery of Freedom in Ancient Greece*. First Engl. ed., revised and updated from the German. Chicago.

Raaflaub, K. 2006. "Thucydides on democracy and oligarchy." In Rengakos and Tsakmakis 2006: 189–222.

Raaflaub, K. 2007a. "Homer and Thucydides on peace and just war." In M. Cosmopoulos (ed.), *Experiencing War: Trauma and Society in Ancient Greece and Today*, 81–94. Chicago.

Raaflaub, K. (ed.). 2007b. *War and Peace in the Ancient World*. Malden MA and Oxford.

Raaflaub, K. 2009. "Conceptualizing and theorizing peace in ancient Greece." *Transactions of the American Philological Association* 139: 225–50.

Raaflaub, K. 2011. "Persian army and warfare in the mirror of Herodotus' interpretation." In R. Rollinger, B. Truschnegg, and R. Bichler (eds.), *Herodotus and the Persian Empire*, 5–37. Wiesbaden.

Raaflaub, K. Forthcoming. "'Archē', 'Reich' oder 'athenischer Groß-Staat'? Zum Scheitern integrativer Staatsmodelle in der griechischen Poliswelt des 5. und 4. Jahrhunderts v.Chr." In E. Baltrusch, H. Kopp, and C. Wendt (eds.), *Seemacht und Seeherrschaft in der Antike*. Stuttgart.

Raaflaub, K., Ober, J., and Wallace, R.W. 2007. *Origins of Democracy in Ancient Greece*. With chs. by P. Cartledge and C. Farrar. Berkeley.

Rengakos, A. and Tsakmakis, A. (eds.). 2006. *Brill's Companion to Thucydides*. Leiden.

Rhodes, P.J. 2003. "Corinthian league." *BNP* 3: 791–92.

Rhodes, P.J. and Osborne, R. (eds.). 2003. *Greek Historical Inscriptions 404–323 BC*. Oxford.

Roberts, J.T. 1994. *Athens on Trial: The Anti-democratic Tradition in Western Thought*. Princeton.

Romilly, J. de. 1992. *The Great Sophists in Periclean Athens*. Trans. Janet Lloyd. Oxford.

Ruschenbusch, E. 1978. *Untersuchungen zu Staat und Politik in Griechenland vom 7.–4. Jh.v.Chr.* Bamberg.

Ryder, T.T.B. 1965. *Koine Eirene: General Peace and Local Independence in Ancient Greece*. Oxford.

Ryffel, H. 1949. *Metabolē politeiōn. Der Wandel der Staatsverfassungen*. Bern. Repr. New York 1973.

Schachter, A. 2002. "Ares." *BNP* 1: 1047–51.

Schmitz, W. 1988. *Wirtschaftliche Prosperität, soziale Integration und die Seebundpolitik Athens*. Munich.

Scholz, P. 2000. "Der Prozess gegen Sokrates. Ein 'Sündenfall' der athenischen Demokratie?" In L. Burckhardt and J. von Ungern-Sternberg (eds.), *Grosse Prozesse im antiken Athen*, 157–73. Munich.

Sealey, R. 1976. *A History of the Greek City-States, 700–338 B.C.* Berkeley.

Shear, J.L. 2011. *Polis and Revolution: Responding to Oligarchy in Classical Athens.* Cambridge.

Sordi, M (ed.). 1985. *La pace nel mondo antico.* Milan.

Spiegel, N. 1990. *War and Peace in Classical Greek Literature.* Jerusalem.

Stadter, P.A. 1989. *A Commentary on Plutarch's Pericles.* Chapel Hill.

Starr, C.G. 1977. *The Economic and Social Growth of Early Greece, 800–500 B.C.* New York.

Strauss, B.S. 1986. *Athens after the Peloponnesian War.* Ithaca NY.

Tausend, K. 1992. *Amphiktyonie und Symmachie.* Stuttgart.

Thomas, R. 1993. "Performance and written publication in Herodotus and the Sophistic generation." In W. Kullmann and J. Althoff (eds.), *Vermittlung und Tradierung von Wissen in der griechischen Kultur*, 225–44. Tübingen.

Thomas, R. 2000. *Herodotus in Context: Ethnography, Science and the Art of Persuasion.* Cambridge.

Tod, M.N. 1913. *International Arbitration amongst the Greeks.* Oxford.

Tritle, L. 2013. "Democracy at war." In J. Arnason, K. Raaflaub, and P. Wagner (eds.), *The Greek Polis and the Invention of Democracy*, 298–320. Malden MA and Oxford.

Ulf, C. 1990. *Die homerische Gesellschaft.* Munich.

Urban, R. 1991. *Der Königsfrieden von 387/86.* Stuttgart.

Voutiras, E. and Sismanidis, K. 2007. "*Dikaiopolitōn synnallagai. Mia nea epigraphē apo tē Dikaia apoikia tēs Eretrias.*" In *Ancient Macedonia: Seventh International Symposium*, 253–74. Thessaloniki.

Walbank, F.W. 1967. *A Historical Commentary on Polybius*, II. Oxford.

Wallace, R.W. 2009. "Charismatic leaders." In K. Raaflaub and H. van Wees (eds.), *A Companion to Archaic Greece*, 411–26. Malden MA and Oxford.

Wees, H. van. 1992. *Status Warriors.* Amsterdam.

Wees, H. van. 2001. "War and peace in ancient Greece." In A. Hartmann and B. Heuser (eds.), *War, Peace, and World Orders in European History*, 33–47. London.

Wees, H. van. 2004. *Greek Warfare: Myth and Realities.* London.

Weissenberger, M. 2005. "Isocrates." *BNP* 6: 979–83.

Wéry, L.-M. 1979. "Die Arbeitsweise der Diplomatie in Homerischer Zeit." In E. Olshausen (ed.), *Antike Diplomatie*, 13–53. Darmstadt.

West, M.L. (ed.). 1992. *Iambi et Elegi Graeci ante Alexandrum Cantati.* 2nd edn. Oxford.

West, M.L. (trans.). 1994. *Greek Lyric Poetry.* Oxford.

West, M.L. 1997. *The East Face of Helicon: West Asiatic Elements in Greek Poetry and Myth.* Oxford.

Whibley, L. 1896. *Greek Oligarchies: Their Character and Organization.* London. Repr. Chicago 1975.

Whitehead, D. 1990. *Aineias the Tactician. How to Survive under Siege*. Oxford.

Wilker, J. (ed.). 2012a. *Maintaining Peace and Interstate Stability in Archaic and Classical Greece*. Mainz.

Wilker, J. 2012b. "War and peace at the beginning of the fourth century: the emergence of the *Koine Eirene*." In Wilker 2012a: 91–117.

Zampaglione, G. 1973. *The Idea of Peace in Antiquity*. Trans. R. Dunn. Notre Dame.

Zuntz, G. 1955. *The Political Plays of Euripides*. Manchester.

6

Broadening the Scope: Thinking about Peace in the Pre-Modern World

HANS VAN WEES

> It is not peace which was natural and primitive and old, but rather war. War appears
> to be as old as mankind, but peace is a modern invention... Not only is war to be seen
> everywhere [in antiquity], but it is war more atrocious than we, with our ideas, can
> easily conceive.[1]

Sir Henry Maine did not explain what he meant by "modern" in this context, but Michael Howard, taking his cue from this passage, ventured to date "the invention of peace" to 1795, the year of the publication of Immanuel Kant's treatise on *Perpetual Peace* (*Zum ewigen Frieden*). Kant, in Howard's view, was the first to conceive of a world in which sovereign states could coexist without ever resorting to war.[2] The details of this particular vision of "peace" may well be peculiarly modern, but the chapters in this volume show that other forms of peace were very much on people's minds in the ancient world, too. Moreover, I will suggest that in Greece in the fourth century BCE something quite close to modern visions of peace was formulated.

At first glance, the chapters on Egypt, China, and India in this volume may seem to suggest that ancient thinkers had little interest in peace: in all three cultures the legitimacy of war was almost universally accepted. But all three cultures, and many of their contemporaries, looked beyond self-aggrandisement or survival

Peace in the Ancient World: Concepts and Theories, First Edition. Edited by Kurt A. Raaflaub.
© 2016 John Wiley & Sons, Inc. Published 2016 by John Wiley & Sons, Inc.

to the establishment of lasting peace as the ultimate goal of war, and indeed aimed to attain universal harmony rather than just an absence of war. The student of modern international relations may well be inclined to dismiss such ideals as "a mere pious aspiration," adopted by "visionaries throughout history," but not a viable objective in political practice.[3] However, if we are discussing *concepts* and *theories* of peace, religious and philosophical ideals are no less relevant than pragmatic political or legal notions, and from about 500 BCE onwards the former were often based on complex theories about the causes of war and conflict and the means by which personal or political "peace" might be attained.

"Universal Peace" in Ancient Empires

The picture of Egyptian attitudes to peace presented by Susanne Bickel is probably typical of Bronze Age and Iron Age empires. The king was seen as the sole legitimate authority in the world, charged by the gods with upholding order among his subjects and harmonious relations between the human and divine worlds. From time to time, this world order was threatened by outsiders or rebels, and the king resorted to devastating violence to restore it. In Egypt, the order of the universe was called *maat*, and "peace" was an important feature, both in the form of tranquillity, a lack of disturbance (*hrw/heru*), and in the form of positive feelings of contentment (*htp/hotep*) such as might be created by "food, flowers and music." Bickel cites an inscription celebrating a victory of Merneptah to illustrate how a pharaoh brings "peace" to "all countries" by defeating them in war, and it is worth stressing that elsewhere in this same text the psychological and economic blessings of peace are vividly imagined:

> Sit down and chatter happily, or walk out on your way: there is no fear in people's hearts. Fortresses are left to themselves, wells are open for the messengers' use. The battlements of the walls are becalmed, only sunlight wakes the watchmen. … People sing as they come and go; they do not lament or mourn. The towns are settled once again. He who tends his crop will eat it.[4]

Much the same was true of the Assyrian Empire, whose kings claimed to rule the four corners of the world on behalf of their god, and to guarantee order, justice, peace (*salimu*) and prosperity for all their subjects.[5] The coronation hymn of Ashurbanipal (668 BCE) stressed two features of peace to which we shall return: general material prosperity and concord between upper and lower classes. It prays that the people of Ashur may be able to buy large quantities of grain, oil, and wool for the trivial sum of "one shekel of silver" (lines 9–11), and that "the lesser" and "the greater" will "listen" to one another so that "concord and peace may be established in Assyria" (lines 12–14).[6] The kings of Achaemenid Persia similarly claimed to rule the world and to wage war with a mission to uphold the state of "happiness," *šiyati*—a concept denoting "prosperity, blissful tranquillity, serenity"—which the supreme god Auramazda had ordained for mankind.[7] In China, as Robin Yates notes, the Zhou kings claimed to uphold lasting peace (*an*) and order (*zhi*) in the world by a "Mandate of Heaven."

The striking imagery of peace in the Old Testament offers a twist on such concepts. For the inhabitants of, and exiles from, a small kingdom dominated by much greater powers, peace was not brought by the rulers of Egypt or Mesopotamia, but would be established in future, when god would overthrow all secular powers and establish his own kingdom on earth. Under a "Prince of Peace," not only would all wars between nations end as they "beat their swords into plowshares and their spears into pruning-hooks," but all forms of threat and danger would disappear from the world.[8] "They shall sit every man under his vine and under his fig tree; and none shall make them afraid;" "the wolf shall dwell with the lamb, and the leopard shall lie down with the kid… and the lion shall eat straw like the ox;"[9] snakes will not bite and there will even be "a covenant with the stones of the field."[10] This certainly counts as "visionary," but at its root is the common idea that the task of legitimate government is to unite the world in a divinely ordained universal peace.[11]

Not all ancient cultures believed that peace was the default state of the universe, which needed to be upheld against recurrent threats, but even those that saw conflict as the dominant relation between individuals and communities could develop an ideal of world peace imposed by war. The Romans, as discussed by Raaflaub in his opening chapter, saw threats everywhere, their policies dominated by "fear of the enemy" (*metus hostilis*) and their rituals designed to create a *pax deorum* by "pacifying" the gods themselves. Between the age of their legendary king Numa and the victory of Augustus in 30 BCE, they had only once formally recognised a state of peace, lasting for less than a year, by closing the doors of the Temple of Janus in 241. The Romans long regarded peace as a danger because it would "enervate" their men, and because it gave the common people an opportunity to assert themselves against the ruling elite.[12] Nevertheless, even they eventually began to justify their empire as a bringer of peace across the world. Cicero put this in plain pragmatic terms in a *Letter to Quintus*, his brother, governor of Asia:

> Asia ought to consider this, too: it would never be without the calamity of foreign war and domestic discord if it were not controlled by this imperial government. Since there is no way to maintain that *imperium* without revenues, let Asia be content to buy for itself, with some part of its produce, permanent peace and leisure (1.1.34).[13]

More elevated aspirations were proclaimed in Augustan poetry, which declared that the special skill of the Romans was "to rule nations with your power and to impose civilization upon peace" (*pacique imponere mores*; Virgil, *Aeneid* 6.851–2), and such ideas eventually inspired a vision of a future in which Roman world domination would make armies redundant.[14]

There was a significant difference between those who believed that peace was part of a primordial god-given order and those who believed, with the Romans and more recent imperialists, that peace had to be created by imposing a new order on the world (with divine help), but they had a fundamental idea in common: that the maintenance of peace required a resort to force, and that the desire for peace thus legitimated coercive power.

"Inner Peace" and Non-violence in the Axial Age

A radically different conception of peace emerged with the philosophical and religious schools of thought associated with the so-called Axial Age. Without necessarily endorsing any of the definitions and explanations offered for the phenomenon, it remains striking that around 500 BCE China, India, and Greece saw the emergence of ideas that to various degrees rejected the use of force and coercion, and advocated the cultivation of inner serenity as the best hope of peace for oneself and ultimately also for the community and the world. The idea of "inner peace" was not in itself new but attested for example, as Bickel points out, in Egypt as a quality to be cultivated by officials and scribes; here, however, it seems to amount to little more than restraint in showing anger and aggression, whereas some "Axial" thought went much further in rejecting violence and all selfish desires.

In China, as Robin Yates shows, after the Zhou kings had been reduced to ritual figureheads, for several centuries during the Spring and Autumn period, many thinkers began to advocate a return to a unified kingdom under a single ruler in order to put an end to warfare. This was eventually achieved by the First Emperor of Qin in 221 BCE, and then by the Han Dynasty, who were given legitimation in more or less traditional ways by "militarist" and "legalist" thinkers. But from Confucius onwards, several schools of thought offered quite different perspectives on how unification and the restoration of universal peace and order were to be achieved. Confucians urged kings and officials to maintain their authority by cultivating virtue and adherence to traditional moral obligations and the principle "do not unto others what you would not have done to you," rather than by coercion. Mohists advocated reform of governmental structures, policies aimed at the common interest, and an ethos of "universal love" (*jian'ai*) as the path towards order. Daoists, most radically, urged everyone to desire no more than the basic necessities, which would result in an end to "fear or strife" and in the establishment of peace. One thing all these philosophies seem to me to have in common is an implicit assumption that war was caused, not by "evil" outside forces attacking a harmonious world order, but by a structural internal problem: that kings, officials, and humanity at large pursued selfish desires, and often did so violently.

Similar developments took place in India at the same time. Johannes Bronkhorst's chapter is understandably concerned to downplay the modern (post-Gandhi) stereotype of Indian culture as non-violent, and accordingly stresses the prominence and legitimacy of war in a great deal of Vedic literature, as well as the limited application of religious ideals to practical politics. It does seem as if the gap between ideal and practice was even greater in India than in China, but that was perhaps not least because intellectual developments were even more radical. The pursuit of inner peace, *śānti*, and inner non-violence, *ahiṃsā*, in the Hinduism of the *Upanishads*, in Buddhism, and in Jainism (the latter briefly noted by Raaflaub) required to varying but high degrees the transcendence of sensual pleasures and self-interest, and abstention from violence even against animals. In their most extreme forms, as in Daoism, such principles could entail a withdrawal into an ascetic lifestyle, a pursuit of private peace without regard to social harmony, a personal connection to the cosmic order that bypassed disorder in the secular world. Bronkhorst concludes that 'Indian antiquity has produced no credible ideas about political peace.' Richard Salomon likewise summed up ancient India in the phrase "peace within and war without:" "it was taken for granted that the world is by its very nature a place of strife and war, and it was apparently assumed that to try to change this would be a waste of time."[15]

In terms of intellectual principles, however, these philosophies are highly significant: as in China, the fundamental assumptions are that the cause of war and violence lies in the selfish desires of individuals, that peace can only be achieved by overcoming these, and that desire cannot be conquered by coercion but only by emotional detachment and "enlightenment." One can see that such principles are unlikely to help end any particular war or conflict, but equally one can see how they might reduce the likelihood of war and violence in general if they were widely adopted. In the same way, one will agree with Bronkhorst that Buddhist kings would have had to wait a long time before a Treasure Wheel descended from heaven and conquered the world for them, but that does not diminish the importance of the principle expressed in such stories, namely that a "universal ruler" (*rājā cakkavattī*) should derive his position from virtue rather than force, have the world submit willingly to his authority, and use his power to create a peaceful order ("Do not take life. Do not take what is not given," and so forth). And although it is surely right to stress that Ašoka, the nearest thing to a universal ruler to establish himself in the subcontinent, relied on extreme force to achieve his conquests, it remains remarkable that, once in power, he tried to live up to the ideal by imposing on all his subjects the cultivation of Buddhist principles.

In Greece, Confucius and Buddha had a contemporary in Pythagoras, whose teachings inspired a long-lived school of Pythagoreanism, which is best attested in much later centuries when it had no doubt absorbed a range of other influences as well, but which appears to have advocated from the start a culture of abstinence, silence, harmony, and restricted violence against animals, along with a belief in reincarnation. We may infer that selfish desires and appetites were again held responsible for war and conflict; it was indeed a common Greek perception that "wanting more" (*pleonexia*) caused wars, and Plato, for instance, argued that a community need never wage war if it were prepared to live like "pigs" and be content with no more than basic necessities.[16] Pythagoras' early followers, we are told, belonged to the ruling classes of the Greek cities of Southern Italy and applied his precepts to bring "great concord and peace" to their states.[17]

Other philosophies which developed subsequently aimed at similar goals by different means: the Stoics sought "passionlessness" (*apatheia*) by reaching a "rational" understanding of the natural order; Epicureans aimed at "untroubledness" (*ataraxia*) by cultivating non-sensual pleasure rather than worldly success; Cynics found happiness (*eudaimonia*) in the rejection of all worldly goods and conventional values.[18] The latter thus had something in common with early Christianity, which added a notable emphasis on avoiding all conflict and not resisting oppression or retaliating for violence.[19]

These "Axial" philosophies in China, India, and the Greek world were thus all concerned with overcoming selfish desire—to various degrees, ranging from mere moderation to complete ascetic transcendence—in order to achieve inner peace. Only in the most radical schools of thought did inner peace entail pacifism, a rejection of violence against all living beings, and such ideals had little impact on public and political life. But their intellectual contribution was highly significant insofar as they provided a new understanding of the causes of war—internal to human psychology, not external to cosmic order—and the means to achieve peace, namely through self-control and consent rather than coercion.

"Common Peace" Inside and Outside Sovereign States

A third approach to peace—alongside regarding it either as something to be maintained by a central authority with coercive force or as something to be attained by the elimination of human appetites and emotions that cause conflict—is to conceive of it as something to be negotiated between individuals, groups, and communities pursuing their conflicting self-interests. This is of course the dominant approach to peace in modern thought, and accordingly the main subject of Raaflaub's introductory survey (Chapter 1) and chapter on Greece (5).

The essence of this way of thinking about peace was clearly formulated in Thomas Hobbes' *Leviathan* (1651), which explicitly rejected a search for inner peace: "there is no such thing as perpetuall Tranquillity of mind, while we live here; because Life it selfe is but Motion, and can never be without Desire, nor without Feare, no more than without Sense." Peace will be achieved, not by detachment from desire and worldly goods, but by creating conditions under which all equally can pursue key matters of self-interest: staying alive and making money. "The Passions that encline men to Peace" are "Feare of Death; Desire of such things as are necessary to commodious living; and a Hope by their industry to obtain them," and these objectives entail "the first, and Fundamentall Law of Nature, which is, *to seek Peace, and follow it.*" Only if it proves impossible to achieve peace should one resort to "the Right of Nature; which is, *By all means we can, to defend our selves.*" The self-interested pursuit of peace led to a "Covenant of every man with every man," whereby all agreed to be governed by a central authority for their common benefit.[20]

Writing during the English Civil War, Hobbes was concerned only with peace within the state, and took for granted that wars between states would continue: "in all times, Kings, and Persons of Soveraigne authority, because of their Independency, are in continuall jealousies, and in the state and posture of Gladiators; having their weapons pointing, and their eyes fixed on one another."[21]

In his day, those who did consider the question of international peace in Europe, in the wake of the Treaty of Westphalia (1648), were moving away from the ideal of a universal ruler who guaranteed peace and beginning to think instead in terms of a "balance of power" between states: "neutralizing conflicting interests and the rivalry of powers" was expected to create "a community of interests and a partnership of convenience" and thereby to increase the likelihood of peace.[22] Fundamentally, the model of behaviour which underlies this theory is the same as that of Hobbes: it envisages independent individuals and states with competing interests, and assumes that peace can be attained by balancing these interests.

From Kant onwards, so-called "Liberal" peace theory went further along these lines, arguing that the replacement of monarchies with republics as well as the development of Free Trade would bring about international peace, aided by the establishment of international organizations. The central idea was again that the interests of the majority of people are best served by peace, and that republics and democracies will allow this majority to pursue their peaceful self-interests in international relations—whereas kings, dictators, and oligarchs will resort to war to further their personal interests at the expense of their subjects. The growth of international trade in particular was thought to create such close intertwining of interests between nations that war would no longer be viable, because it "obstructs commerce, uproots industry, annihilates capital and labour," as the Liberal Richard Cobden said at a Universal Peace Congress in 1849. On the same occasion, Victor Hugo predicted that "a day will come when the only battlefield will be the market open to commerce."[23] Since World War One, similar claims have been made for the impact of the spread of democracy and the process of globalization on war and peace.[24]

Building on Raaflaub's rich surveys of the ancient evidence, I venture to suggest that Greek thinking developed on much the same lines as modern European thought on war and peace. In the earliest poetry, peace still seems largely ordained by the gods, beyond human control; from around 600 BCE, formal peace treaties and international arbitration imply a perception of peace as achieved by negotiation between competing interests; from the fifth century onwards, this perception was theoretically elaborated and peace was increasingly seen as vital to economic prosperity; in the fourth century, pragmatic proposals and attempts were made to create a permanent "zone of peace" across the Greek world.

The thoughts on war and peace of the poet Hesiod, circa 700 BCE, are particularly striking.[25] "In the beginning was vacant space (*chaos*), and then Earth," he said (*Theogony* 116–17). Earth went on to generate the rest of the natural and divine world, including "Order, Justice and flourishing Peace, who guard the works of mortal men," daughters of Zeus and Themis, "Law" (901–3). By contrast, *chaos* itself produced Night (123), and Night bore the evils that beset the lives of men, such as blame, resentment, old age, death, and above all "rivalry" (*eris*, 211–25). Rivalry in turn gave birth to all forms of conflict ("battles, fights, killings, homicides, quarrels, lies, words, disputes, disorder, and disaster, which live side by side with one another" and false oaths) as well as toil, neglect, famine, and pain (226–32). Bridging the gap between divine order and primordial disorder were the "lords" (*basileis*), "who judge law cases with straight justice" and "put an end even to a great quarrel" by persuasive eloquence (80–92). In outline, this seems similar to the ideas about divine peace, order, and kingship in Egypt, the Near East, and China, but there are vital differences: the forces of disorder are not outsiders or rebels but an integral part of all human life; internal peace and order are upheld not by a monarch but by a ruling elite, and not by coercive power but by arbitration.

At the start of his *Works and Days*, Hesiod makes an important modification to the conflict-model of human life adopted in *Theogony*. He observes that there are *two* kinds of rivalry rather than just one. One, "wretched rivalry," is again blamed for causing "war and conflict" (14–16), but the other is said to be an elder daughter of Night and declared "good for mortals," sanctioned by Zeus. This second form of rivalry represents the kind of competition that encourages farmers and craftsmen, as well as poets and even beggars, to outdo their peers by working hard for a living (11–26). Underlying the mythological language is a sophisticated model of society, in which competing self-interest is a universal phenomenon and not only the cause of internal conflict, in the manner of Hobbes, but also a cause of increased material prosperity, so that it should not be stopped, either by coercion or by transcending selfish desire, but channelled into legitimate forms of competition.

As for external peace, *Works and Days* reveals that it is not achieved by divinely sanctioned warfare but granted by Zeus as a reward for communities in which the lords uphold justice on his behalf (248–73). Zeus will give "Peace throughout the land" and will "never assign war to them" (225–9), whereas defeat in war is his punishment for an unjust city (245–7). The same sense that peace and war are out of mortal hands emerges from Homer's epics. In the *Iliad*, we are told emphatically that Greeks and Trojans want to make peace and swear a solemn oath to that effect (3.111–12, 275–323, 449–54), yet the gods intervene for reasons of their own and make sure that hostilities continue (4.1–85).[26] At the end of the *Odyssey* a civil war is about to escalate, but Zeus intervenes directly to put a stop to this, dictating "a forgetting of the murder of sons and brothers:" "let them live in friendship with one another as before, and have wealth and peace aplenty" (24.484–6). This is not to say that mortals make no efforts to preserve peace, since their first resort in Homer is to negotiation and diplomatic resolution of conflicts, as Raaflaub shows, but at a conceptual level these early poets seem to see peace as something only the gods can ultimately provide.

Yet the idea of directing competition into non-violent channels and settling disputes by arbitration could in principle be applied to international relations as well, and by 600 BCE we find signs that this conceptual leap had been made. Around that time the Athenians not only appointed Solon "mediator" (*diallaktēs*) to put a stop to escalating civil (internal) conflict, but also arbitrators in their external disputes: a Spartan committee was invited to settle their dispute with Megara over Salamis, and the dictator (*tyrannos*) of Corinth to arbitrate between them and Mytilene over occupied territory in the Troad.[27] Later in the sixth century, the text of a treaty inscribed at Zeus's sanctuary at Olympia reads: "The Sybarites and their allies and the Serdaioi united in friendship, faithful and without deceit, forever. Guarantors: Zeus, Apollo, and the other gods, and the city Poseidonia."[28] Alongside the gods, who did still play a role in securing not just peace but eternal friendship, there was now a formal and permanent role for a major secular power to act as neutral arbitrator for the alliance.

One of the features that made classical Greek historiography so different from Egyptian, Near Eastern, and other chronicles is this perception of war and peace as determined by competing legitimate interests, rather than by a divine mission to restore world peace by force: this way of looking at the matter invited an assessment of the rival interests at play. In Herodotus' *Histories*, divine will and intervention still play a role in the story, alongside a close analysis of human motivation, but in his account of the Peloponnesian War Thucydides analyses the causes of war and peace entirely in secular terms, and his investigation of motives aspires to look below the surface of stated aims to the "real" interests at stake. Time and again, he reports the ethical arguments for war and peace offered by politicians and diplomats, but indicates that in his view the underlying motivation was a self-interested calculation of profit and risk—bearing in mind that "profit" need not be material but could also take the form of enhanced "honour."[29]

Thucydides' version of the Sicilian peace conference of 424 BCE, after three years of widespread warfare between two coalitions of cities, as mentioned by Raaflaub, illustrates this concisely. Thucydides implies that on such occasions lengthy sermons on the horrors of war and blessings of peace would typically be delivered, but chooses to present a speech which offers a more calculating perspective: war breaks out when "what happens is that one side regards the profits as greater than the risks, while the other side is prepared to face danger rather than incur loss immediately. But if the two sides happen to act in this way at the wrong time, exhortations to seek reconciliation (*synallagē*) are beneficial."[30] In the same vein, Thucydides offers several pages of explanation of the reasons for the conclusion of the Peace of Nicias in 421, showing that both the Spartans and Athenians collectively, and their leading statesmen (king Pleistoanax and the general Nicias) individually, had more to gain by making peace than by prolonging war.[31] Elsewhere, in famous set pieces, Thucydides has public speakers argue that justice might require violent punishment of disloyal allies, but Athens should choose to treat them with moderation because in the long run this would be the more cost-effective way to maintain their hegemony, while weaker states should set aside a sense of "shame" and submit to Athens without a fight because resistance would be too costly.[32]

This school of thought, known in the modern study of international relations as Realism, is also reflected by an interlocutor in Plato's dialogue *Laws*, who declares—anticipating by 2,000 years Hobbes' notion that the natural state of mankind is a war of all against all[33]—that "what most people call 'peace' is nothing but a word, and in fact every city-state is at all times, by nature, in a state of undeclared state of war with every other city-state" (626a). Indeed, Plato goes one better than Hobbes and argues that "within each of us there is a war against ourselves," and that the first and most important victory must be that of our better over our worse nature (626d), reflecting the sort of Axial Age thinking outlined in the previous section. Whereas the speaker concludes from this premise that the goal of social organization must be maximum effectiveness in war (625c–626c), Plato himself argues, like Hobbes, that the goal of a state must be "reconciliation" between its rival elements, and that its ultimate goal must be peace: "one must legislate in military matters for the sake of peace rather than legislate in peace for the sake of war" (627a–628e).

The sentiment that peace is, after all, not just a temporary compromise between conflicting interests but a permanent condition to which a state ought to aspire must also lie behind treaties such as that between the Sybarites and their allies, which were explicitly meant to last "forever."[34] Even a time-limited peace treaty such as that of Nicias, concluded for a term of 50 years, was evidently meant to endure throughout the rest of the lives of every adult and last beyond the deaths of the leading men involved, regardless of inevitable changes in the individual and public self-interests which it supposedly served.[35]

A further step in this direction was taken by the "Common Peace" treaties of the fourth century, starting with the "King's Peace" of 386 BCE, which made it a formal principle that every Greek city-state, "big and small" (with a few stipulated exceptions), was entitled to autonomy and that any infringement of this rule would be punished by the concerted action of the other states, led by the Persian king.[36] From the king's point of view, the arrangement may well have been a simple extension of the divinely sanctioned imperial peace it was his duty to uphold, and Sparta, the leading Greek state at the time, used the terms of the treaty to justify the exercise of hegemonic power, but the key point is that peacekeeping and upholding the sovereignty of other Greek states, on a permanent basis, was now explicitly the task of the hegemonic power. Sparta derived new prestige from its role as "champion of the peace" (*prostatēs tēs eirēnēs*), and when the Athenians began to share this role at the renewal of the treaty in 375, they made a point of advertising their mission as peacekeepers by establishing an annual festival for the goddess Eirēnē/Peace.[37] At this point, the Greek world met, in principle, the essential conditions for Kant's "perpetual peace:" all, or nearly all, states were republican; they formed a "federation of free states;" and they recognized "the condition of universal hospitality," that is, everyone had the right to visit any other state.[38]

The idea that permanent peace in itself was beneficial to all individuals and communities, whatever their specific interests at any given time, received some theoretical elaboration beyond the obvious notion that an absence of death and destruction was a good thing. Although Thucydides has his Sicilian statesman reject preaching about generic blessings of peace in favour of a specific cost-benefit calculation, he ends up attributing to this speaker the argument that peace had to be concluded because it provided greater stability: "Why should we not amongst ourselves make peace, which is agreed by everyone to be the best thing? Or do you not imagine that for both sides tranquillity (*hēsychia*) rather than war will preserve what is good and put an end to the opposite, and that peace (*eirēnē*) holds less precarious honours and distinctions?" (4.62.2).

Moreover, Thucydides' reconstruction of early Greek history in the so-called "Archaeology" (1.2–19) relied heavily on the notion that violence inhibits prosperity while peace encourages the accumulation of resources. The earliest Greeks, Thucydides imagined, were constantly "forced to leave their territory by whoever outnumbered them, for there was no trade and they did not have safe contact with one another by land or sea" (1.2.1–2). The first step towards development was the building of a fleet by king Minos who conquered and colonized the Cyclades "and, we may assume, put down sea-raiding as much as he could, so that he would receive greater revenues" (1.4; cf. 8.2). The removal of this threat meant "people who lived by the sea engaged more in the acquisition of property and settled more stably, and some even built fortification walls now that they were wealthier." Powerful cities used their "surplus" to subject smaller cities, while the latter put up with such "slavery" because they hoped to "profit" from it (1.8.3). In the aftermath of the Trojan War, however, there was much instability "so that they did not maintain tranquillity and grow" (1.12.1). Only when Greece eventually did reach "stable tranquillity" (1.12.4), did it become "more powerful and engaged even more than previously in the acquisition of property": cities were governed by powerful "tyrants" who raised greater revenues and built navies (1.13.1); such new navies were again used to "put down sea-raiding" and increase revenues from trade (1.13.5). Tyrants were only interested in the "growth of their own households," so they fought few wars and "governed their cities as much as possible in safety" (1.17), but after the tyrants were deposed cities used their resources in war to achieve greater power than ever.[39]

Thucydides' historical model is thus that "tranquillity" (*hēsychia*) leads to "growth" (*auxēsis*) as trade expands and provides larger private and public revenues, and this economic growth allows cities to build up military resources, especially fortifications and navies, enabling them to wage more ambitious wars which will result in international power—which ought to be used to create greater tranquillity and growth. It is in line with this model that Athens apparently claimed to have used its naval power in the fifth century to get rid of sea-raiders from Scyros[40] and to have proposed a congress of all Greek city-states—blocked by Sparta—with a view to discussing, amongst other things, "how everyone might sail safely and keep the peace (*eirēnē*) at sea."[41]

When the Common Peace treaties of the fourth century were concluded, such ideas about the links between peace, war, trade, and prosperity gained additional momentum. Raaflaub discusses in detail Isocrates' speech *On the Peace*, written at the end of a war between Athens and its allies, which Athens lost in 355 BCE.[42] Not only did Isocrates urge the Athenians to extend their negotiations and make peace "with all mankind" (16), abandon imperialist ambitions (64–65), wage only defensive war (136–44), and seek international leadership on the basis of a good reputation and consent rather than by force (21, 135), but he stressed the economic benefits of doing so: "every day we shall add to our prosperity" (*euporia*, 20), and "we shall see the city receive twice as many revenues as it does now, and it will be filled with traders and foreigners and metics although it now stands deserted by them" (21).

Less often noticed are the remarkable proposals made by Xenophon in his pamphlet *Ways and Means* (*Poroi*), written at the same time and for the same reason. Like Isocrates, he argued that Athens should stop its imperialist use of force, but he went further in offering specific proposals for raising public revenue by non-violent means: first, a whole series of modern-sounding measures designed to encourage trade by providing better infrastructure, streamlining commercial legal procedures, offering incentives, and lifting disincentives for traders and ship owners (Chapters 2–3); then, a very unmodern plan to hire out public slaves for labour in the silver mines (Chapter 4). Towards the end of his pamphlet, he spelled out the implications of his plan for international relations: "it seems clear that peace must prevail in order for all revenues to come in" (5.1); "if anyone believes that in terms of money war is more profitable for the city than peace," history has proven him wrong (5.11–12); Athens' standing in the world will remain high without warfare because it will be "needed" by many people, "starting with ship-owners and traders" (5.2–4). The city should spend some of its revenue on training and maintaining its militia (4.52), but wage war only in self-defence (5.13). Its goal should be to achieve a position of leadership without using force (5.5–7), by putting itself forward as a peace-keeper and mediator in disputes between other cities (5.8–10), guided by a new board of magistrates, the Guardians of Peace (*eirēnophylakes*, 5.1).[43]

With Xenophon, we are far beyond "pious aspirations" and even beyond the broad principles of Kant, into something much like nineteenth-century Liberal theories about peace. His is a carefully worked out program for peaceful international relations, which is designed to be economically viable for Athens and indeed to improve the city's economic condition. Whereas modern Liberal thinking posited that free trade should be allowed because it would bring peace, Xenophon (and Isocrates) argued that peace should be maintained for the sake of trade, but the essential nexus between peace and trade was perceived as a major obstacle to war in fourth-century Greece as it was in modern Europe.

In one respect, however, Xenophon and other Greek thinkers differed notably from their modern successors. Kant saw a major force for peace in the self-interest of ordinary citizens, who would want to avoid bearing the human and material costs of war, while a major threat to peace was the selfishness of kings and aristo-crats who stood to lose nothing in war, which they regarded as "some kind of entertainment" (*eine art Lustparthie*) and waged for trivial reasons, justified in retrospect by their "ever ready" diplomats.[44] Greek intellectuals held precisely the opposite view: the elite bore the financial costs of war and sought to avoid it, while the masses benefited materially from military service and were eager to wage war.

In 390 BCE, an Athenian comedy put it bluntly: "Ships must be launched: the poor man is in favour, the rich men and the farmers are against."[45] In 323, we are told, the men of property in Athens wanted peace with Macedon but the great majority of citizens were men "who chose war and were used to drawing a livelihood from paid service;" king Philip II of Macedon had once described these Athenian lower classes as people for whom "there was war in peace and peace in war."[46] Less sharply, Thucydides distinguished between, on the one hand, the imperial ambitions of "the great mass and the common soldier," who expected to get paid and to fund future payments from conquered territory, and, on the other hand, the motives of the elite, whose main concern was that military expeditions should be low-risk, and who, insofar as they were of military age, looked forward to "the sight and spectacle of distant lands."[47] Hence Isocrates complained in *On the Peace*: "we treat with hostility those who desire peace as being oligarchically-minded, but we decide to be friendly towards those who make war as supporters of democracy" (8.51). Here, then, we have the exact reverse of modern peace theory: an argument, propounded by members of the elite, that democracies are liable to make war while more oligarchic regimes are a force for peace.[48]

The reason for such democratic belligerence, according to both Isocrates and Xenophon, was that the majority of people were poor and depended for survival on pay for military service and other public payments and doles, funded from imperial revenue.[49] Neither author addressed the causes of this wide-spread poverty, but both looked to non-violent acquisition of additional public resources to solve the problem and help maintain peace. Isocrates rather optimistically imagined that a peaceful disposition on Athens' part might encourage foreign kings to grant territory to Athenian settlers, so that "we will be able to carve out for ourselves such a large territory in Thrace that we will have not only an abundance for ourselves but can also provide a sufficient liveli-hood for those Greeks who are in need and wander on account of poverty."[50]

Xenophon, more pragmatically, proposed in his *Ways and Means* fundraising measures in order "to generate for all Athenians a sufficient subsistence from communal funds" (4.33; cf. 6.1): the new public revenue to be was to be spent on a dole of 3 obols a day for every citizen (3.9–10; 4.14–15, 23), a sum amounting to the subsistence minimum for a family. The introduction of a universal welfare payment may seem a radical idea, but it is mentioned by oth-ers, too, [51] and from the point of view of a wealthy landowner a public dole for the poor—raised at the expense of foreign residents, visiting merchants, and thousands of slaves—was preferable to more revolutionary measures such as the general redistribution of land and cancellation of debt, which were demanded by popular movements in other cities.[52]

Xenophon's and Isocrates' acknowledgement that the common people were not merely greedily bellicose but genuinely economically dependent on war-fare, and that economic measures were therefore necessary to prevent war, show a major development in Greek thinking about peace. Rather than assume that peace would be attained by eliminating evil outsiders, or suppressing self-ish human desire, or reconciling the rival interests of communities, fourth-cen-tury Greeks accepted that peace would require the elimination of a structural social and economic problem *within* each of their communities. The Assyrians regarded concord between social classes as a key ingredient of peace achieved through war, as we saw, while the Romans identified conflict between mass and elite as a persistent problem and drew the conclusion that it was vital to keep waging war in order to keep the plebs in its place. But Greek political thought concentrated on eliminating or balancing competing class interests within a city-state, ideally without the need to resort to external war and conquest. Plato believed the "better" and "righteous" elite ought to rule and "defeat" the "worse" and "unjust" masses[53] and Isocrates' *On the Peace* in effect presented emigration of the poor as the answer, but Aristotle's *Politics* dis-cussed constitutional ways of balancing the interests of the Few and the Many and Xenophon formulated an economic solution that involved taxation and slave labour but no war. One way or another, all these thinkers saw that a state needed to accommodate not only the private interests of competing individuals but also the collective interests of competing social classes, in order to maintain both internal concord and external peace.

Xenophon's proposals were not implemented, so far as we can tell, and within a couple of years of their publication, Athens engaged in one of its most brutal imperialistic campaigns ever, capturing the important city of Sestos in 353 BC, executing all its adult men, selling the rest of the population into slavery, and shortly afterwards sending colonists to occupy the town and all but one of the ten other cities of the Gallipoli Peninsula.[54] Perhaps the story would have been different if the recommendations of *Ways and Means* had been followed, but even if not, this is hardly the only example in history of plans for peace failing to prevent savage wars, and it is no reflection on the sophistication, seriousness, and pragmatism of the ideas being formulated.

Conclusion: Explaining Ideas about Peace

Concepts of peace have taken many different forms in history, as this volume shows, and an explanation of how and why these concepts developed must take into account the contexts in which they were formulated. It seems likely, as Raaflaub argues, that the experience of exceptionally destructive warfare is often a stimulus for reflection on peace; it is certainly no coincidence that Xenophon and Isocrates published their proposals for lasting peace in the immediate aftermath of a war in which Athens had suffered great losses. Raaflaub is surely right, too, to suggest that ideas about peace will acquire significant theoretical elaboration only in a culture that encourages and enables the formulation of general and abstract principles by "intellectuals" or "sages" of some sort.[55] I would suggest that two further structural factors will typically stimulate thinking about peace.

One factor is the need to legitimate certain forms of power. The ideal of peace commonly served in the ancient world to justify imperial control, and one might posit as a rule that peace becomes particularly highly valued when empires—ancient or modern—consolidate their position and seek to achieve stability rather than further expansion. Thus, in the case of Rome, the developing discourse of peace under Augustus may owe even more to the consolidation of empire than to the trauma of civil war. And this legitimating function of the ideal of peace is not limited to empires. Kant's claim that republics rarely wage war, like the modern theory that democracies rarely fight one another, is not a neutral "fact" but serves to legitimate these forms of government as preferable to others. Conversely, ancient claims that democracies were particularly warlike indirectly served as intellectual justification of a preference for a limited franchise or outright oligarchy. The ability to preserve peace seems to be a special virtue of whatever form of government one happens to support.

The other factor is the need for an intellectual response to the development of increasingly centralized states, which compete with one another within a shared cultural zone. All three elements—the process of state-formation, the multiplicity of states, and the perception of a shared culture—are vital to thinking about peace. The point is adumbrated by Yates, who stresses that the institutionalization and centralization of government in China were a precondition for the development of the various philosophical schools of thought about peace.[56] Similar processes took place in India and Greece and provide the context for both the Axial Age quest for "inner peace" and classical Greek efforts to achieve "common peace."

In China, during the Spring and Autumn period (771–476 BCE), hundreds of city-states fought one another while remaining notionally subject to the overall ritual authority of the kings of the Zhou dynasty. They gradually coalesced into "hegemonies" and then into the seven "Warring States" of the next period (476–221).[57] India and Greece, too, saw the rise of city-states from circa 700 BCE onwards, with a shared culture but without an overarching political authority: the sixteen major principalities (*Mahajanapadas*) and dozens of smaller states of India, and the hundreds of small *poleis* that made up the Greek world. In all three regions, urbanization and state-formation—measured amongst other things by the first appearance of coinage—accelerated in the late sixth century, precisely the age of Confucius, Buddha, and Pythagoras.[58] The growing power of the state over its subjects and the increasing demands of warfare against its rivals may have led to an intellectual reaction against what was seen as excessive use of coercion, both internally and externally. Hence the articulation of either an ideal of cultivating inner peace by detachment or even complete withdrawal from the violence of public life, or else an ideal of achieving a balance of interests within the state and between states, which removed the need for extremes of coercion and warfare.

If fourth-century Greeks went furthest in their intellectual and political efforts, creating a remarkably "modern" set of ideas about a zone of peace, it may be because the Greek city-states were—more than the states of China or India—united by a sense of ethnic and cultural identity as well as economically interdependent. Classical Greeks felt strongly that as "Hellenes" they differed from the "barbarians" who made up the rest of mankind, and that they ought not to fight their "kinsmen" (as Raaflaub notes).[59] This sense of identity was reinforced by the fact that most Greeks lived on the periphery of a great "barbarian" empire with which they were in frequent conflict. Moreover, most Greek states were situated near the coast and relied quite heavily on maritime trade, which entailed the growth of a level of mutual dependence that was probably not reached among the mostly land-bound states of China and India. Increasing state-formation, economic interdependence and a sense of "European" identity[60] were features of early modern European history, too, and if ancient Greeks produced modern-sounding ideas it may have been because they were responding to developments quite similar to those undergone by the nation-states of Europe.

These impressionistic ideas about correlations between intellectual developments in conceptions of peace and social developments in identity, economy, and structures of government are not (yet) based on a great deal of evidence. Further research could test our hypotheses. It might falsify them by finding historical societies with a low level of economic interdependence or disparate ethnic identities, which nevertheless developed ambitious programs for "common" peace, or cultures that encouraged withdrawal from the world and the cultivation of "inner" peace despite low levels of state-formation and coercion, or empires that did not claim to uphold "universal" peace. Alternatively, it may be possible to refine our hypotheses by establishing more precisely at what stage in the growth in state-formation or economic interdependence or imperial consolidation a paradigm shift in thinking about peace is likely to occur. In any case, the story of "peace" is not one of autonomous intellectual progress from ancient simplicity to modern sophistication, but of ever-changing notions of "peace" being articulated and applied in ever-changing societies. In order to understand these dynamics we need to look beyond a narrow "history of ideas" and engage in a broad "intellectual history" that places ideas in their contemporary context. Moreover, we need to engage in the kind of comparative research offered in this volume to help us determine whether "peace" was really invented by Kant in 1795 and a product of the unique conditions of modernity, or whether social, economic, and political conditions in some other periods of history were similar enough to have produced similar ideas.

Notes

1   Maine 1888: 8.
2   Howard 2000: 1–2 (peace, defined as "an international order in which war plays no part," was "invented by thinkers of the Enlightenment"), 29–31 ("if anyone could be said to have invented peace … it was Kant," 31).
3   Howard 2000: 2, 31.
4   Translation adapted from the versions in Lichtheim 1976: 77 and Liverani 2001: 85.
5   Oded 1992: esp. 101–20, 163–76; Kuhrt 1995: 505–19.

6 *State Archives of Assyria* on-line: SAA 03.011.
7 Kuhrt 2007: 304 n. 3. See also Josef Wiesehöfer's chapter in Raaflaub 2007.
8 Isaiah 9.6 (*šar shalom*); Isaiah 2.4; Micah 4.3; cf. Joel 3.10 (swords into plowshares). Translations follow the King James Version.
9 Micah 4.4; Isaiah 11.6–7; cf. 65.25.
10 Stones: Job 5.23; snakes: Isaiah 11.8; 65.25. See also Hosea 2.18 ("In that day will I make a covenant for them with the beasts of the field... and I will break the bow and the sword and the battle out of the earth, and I will make them to lie down safely"); Ezekiel 34.25; Isaiah 55.12; 60.18.
11 See further Krüger 2007; however, his view that the references in Isaiah 2.4 and Micah 4.3 to God "judging between many peoples" and "rebuking distant nations" are "amazingly modern" and "unique in the Hebrew Bible as well as in the Ancient Near East" (162–63, 170), apparently assumes that the concept here is (divine) arbitration between sovereign states to prevent war, whereas the parallels cited above rather suggest that all these peoples and nations are thought of as part of the ruler's world dominion, so that his peace is of the "imperial" kind widely attested in the Near East and elsewhere.
12 Temple of Janus: e.g., Varro, *On the Latin Language* 5.165, and Livy 1.19.1–4, the latter explaining that fear of the gods was essential to prevent the "extravagance and idleness" that would otherwise ensue when there was no human enemy to fear; see also, e.g., Tacitus, *Agricola* 11.4; Valerius Maximus 7.2.1, 3; Velleius Paterculus 2.1.1–2, with Barton 2007: 246–7. Social tensions: Polybius 6.18.3; Sallust, *Jugurthine War* 41; Plutarch, *Cato the Elder* 27.1–3.
13 On the connection between imperial control and peace on the frontiers, see also Cicero's speech, *On the Command of Gnaeus Pompey.*
14 As predicted by the emperor Probus (r. 276–282 CE), according to the *Scriptores Historiae Augustae* (*Writers of Augustan History*), *Life of Probus* 20; Eutropius, *Breviarium* (*Brief History*) 9.17; Aurelius Victor, *On the Caesars* 37. See also DeBrohun 2007 on Augustan "peace"; Woolf 1993; Sidebottom 1993; Zampaglione 1973: 135–84.
15 Salomon 2007: 53, 63.
16 Plato, *Republic* 372d–373e; see Van Wees 2004: 34–36; 2007: 281–90.
17 Dio Chrysostom, *Orations* 49.6; see further Zhmud 2012; Riedweg 2002.
18 See, e.g., Sharples 1996; Inwood 2003; Erskine 2011; on Cynics: Desmond 2008.
19 See esp. Matthew 5.21–48.
20 Hobbes 1651. The quotes are, in sequence, from pp. 29–30, 63, 64, 87.
21 Ibid. 63.
22 Strohmeyer 2009 (quotation: 69); see also Duchhardt 2001; Howard 2000: 15–16, 23–25.
23 Niedhart 2009: 87.
24 See Niedhart 2009 for a survey of liberal and democratic peace theory. On liberal views, see also Howard 2000: esp. 43–45.
25 Translations from Greek authors are my own.

26 See the detailed discussion in Chapter 5 (Raaflaub) above, at nn. 10ff.

27 Solon: [Aristotle], *Athenian Constitution* 5.2; arbitrations: Herodotus 5.95; Plutarch, *Solon* 10. For later Greek interstate arbitration, see Adcock and Mosley 1975: 210–14; Ager 1996.

28 See Bauslaugh 1991: 57; Fornara 1983: no. 29 (ML no. 10).

29 So too Hobbes: the three causes of conflict and war are to gain property, to defend one's property, and to win "Glory," "Reputation," over "trifles, as a word, a smile, a different opinion, and any other signe of undervalue" (1651: 62). On Thucydides' analysis of historical causation and motivation, see, e.g. Lendon 2010, 86–105; Crane 1998, 36–71; Rhodes 1987.

30 Thucydides 4.59.2–3, 62.2.

31 Thuc. 5.14–17.

32 Thuc. 3.36–49; 5.85–113.

33 Hobbes 1651: 62–63.

34 See above at n. 28.

35 For arguments against the misapprehension that time-limited peace treaties imply that Greeks regarded war as the norm and peace as the exception, see Van Wees 2001; 2004: 3–18; 2009. Many treaties take the form of a "truce," and I would stress the extreme length of such truces, as well as the commonness of permanent alliances, among Greeks.

36 Xenophon, *Hellenica* 5.1.31. For a more detailed discussion of these "Common Peace" treaties, see Chapter 5 (Raaflaub) at nn. 17–32.

37 As noted by Raaflaub: see Nepos, *Timotheus* 2.2; Isocrates 15.109. Plutarch, *Cimon* 13, dates this cult much earlier but also links it with an important peace treaty.

38 Kant 1795: 20–46.

39 See also Herodotus 5.66.1, 78. For a detailed discussion of this strand of thought in Thucydides' work, see Kallet 1993, 2001; van Wees, forthcoming.

40 Plutarch, *Cimon* 8.

41 Plutarch, *Pericles* 17.1. For more detailed discussion, see Chapter 5 (Raaflaub) at nn. 20–22. Even if these claims were unhistorical, as some scholars think (e.g., de Souza 1999: 26–30), they are significant for our purposes as evidence for what fourth-century Athenians thought their predecessors *should* have done: see de Souza, 38–41, for fourth-century measures.

42 See Chapter 5 (Raaflaub) at nn. 33–38.

43 See further Schorn 2012; Jansen 2012; Dillery 1993; Gauthier 1984.

44 Kant 1795: 23–24.

45 Aristophanes, *Assemblywomen* 197–98.

46 Diodorus 18.10.1.

47 Thuc. 6.24.3.

48 See Pritchard 2010 for a discussion of "the symbiosis between democracy and war"; also Robinson 2010 for the applicability of "democratic peace" theory to antiquity.

49 Isocrates, *On the Peace* 8.46, 128–31; Xenophon, *Ways and Means* 1.1.

50 Isocrates, *Or.* 8.22–24.
51 A similar dole was unsuccessfully proposed by Demosthenes a few years later (3.34–35): he saw it as an indirect means to fund citizen armies rather than establish peace.
52 See Lintott 1982; Gehrke 1985; note the suggestions of Aeneas Tacticus (ch. 14) for feeding the poor and (partial) cancellation of debt in order to maintain unity in war.
53 *Laws* 627ab.
54 Diodorus 16.34.3–4; resources of the peninsula: Xenophon, *Hellenica* 3.2.10; significance of Sestos to Athens as its "bread bin," i.e., centre of grain supply: Aristotle, *Rhetoric* 1411a14.
55 See the end of Chapters 1 and 5 (Raaflaub).
56 See the concluding section of Chapter 4 (Yates).
57 Yates 2007.
58 See Lewis 2000 (China); Chakrabarti 2000 (India); van Wees 2013 (Greece).
59 See Chapter 5 (Raaflaub) at n. 73.
60 See Duchhardt 2001: 194, on the idea of "Europe" replacing "Christendom" after 1700 CE.

Abbreviation

ML   Meiggs and Lewis 1988.

References

Adcock, F. and Mosley, D. J. 1975. *Diplomacy in Ancient Greece.* London.
Ager, S. 1996. *Interstate Arbitrations in the Greek World, 337–90 BC.* Berkeley.
Barton, C. A. 2007. "The price of peace in ancient Rome." In Raaflaub 2007: 245–55.
Bauslaugh, R. 1991. *The Concept of Neutrality in Classical Greece.* Berkeley.
Chakrabarti, D. K., "Mahajanapada states of early historic India." In Hansen 2000: 375–91.
Crane, G. 1998. *Thucydides and the Ancient Simplicity: The Limits of Political Realism.* Berkeley.
De Souza, P. 1999. *Piracy in the Graeco-Roman World.* Cambridge.
DeBrohun, J. B. 2007. "The gates of war (and peace): Roman literary perspectives." In Raaflaub 2007: 256–78.
Desmond, W. 2008. *Cynics.* Stocksfield.
Dillery, J. 1993. "Xenophon's *Poroi* and Athenian imperialism." *Historia* 42: 1–11.
Duchhardt, H. 2001. "Interstate war and peace in early modern Europe." In Hartmann and Heuser 2001: 185–95.
Dülffer, J. and Frank, R. (eds.). 2009. *Peace, War and Gender from Antiquity to the Present. Cross-cultural Perspectives.* Essen.

Erskine, A. 2011. *The Hellenistic Stoa: Political Thought and Action.* Bristol.

Fornara, C. W. 1983. *Translated Documents of Greece and Rome 1: Archaic Times to the End of the Peloponnesian War.* 2nd ed. Cambridge.

Gauthier, P. 1984. « Le programme de Xénophon dans les 'Poroi', » *Revue de Philologie* 58: 181–99.

Gehrke, H.-J. 1985. *Stasis. Untersuchungen zu den inneren Kriegen in den griechischen Staaten des 5. und 4. Jahrhunderts v. Chr.* Munich.

Hansen, M. H. (ed.). 2000. *A Comparative Study of Thirty City-state Cultures: An Investigation.* Copenhagen.

Hartmann, A. V. and Heuser, B. (eds.). 2001. *War, Peace and World Orders in European History.* London.

Hobbes, T. 1651. *Leviathan, or the Matter, Forme, & Power of a Common-Wealth Ecclesiasticall and Civill.* London (cited here with original pagination, from the Penguin edition edited by C.B. Macpherson, 1968).

Hobden, F. and Tuplin, C. (eds.). 2012. *Xenophon: Ethical Principles and Historical Enquiry.* Leiden.

Howard, M. 2000. *The Invention of Peace. Reflections on War and International Order.* London.

Inwood, B. (ed.). 2003. *The Cambridge Companion to the Stoics.* Cambridge.

Jansen, J. 2012. "Strangers incorporated: outsiders in Xenophon's *Poroi.*" In Hobden and Tuplin 2012: 725–60.

Kallet, L. 1993. *Money, Expense, and Naval Power in Thucydides' History 1–5.24.* Berkeley.

Kallet, L. 2001. *Money and the Corrosion of Power in Thucydides: The Sicilian Expedition and Its Aftermath.* Berkeley.

Kant, I. 1795. *Zum ewigen Frieden. Ein philosophischer Entwurf.* Königsberg.

Krüger, T. 2007. "'They shall beat their swords into plowshares': a vision of peace through justice and its background in the Hebrew Bible." In Raaflaub 2007: 161–71.

Kuhrt, A. 1995. *The Ancient Near East, c. 3000–330 BC.* London and New York.

Kuhrt, A. 2007. *The Persian Empire. A Corpus of Sources from the Achaemenid Period.* Abingdon and New York.

Lendon, J. E. 2010. *Song of Wrath: The Peloponnesian War Begins.* New York.

Lewis, M. E. 2000. "The city-state in spring-and-autumn China." In Hansen 2000: 359–74.

Lichtheim, M. 1976. *Ancient Egyptian Literature*, II: *The New Kingdom.* Berkeley.

Lintott, A. 1982. *Violence, Civil Strife and Revolution in the Classical City.* London.

Liverani, M. 2001. *International Relations in the Ancient Near East, 1600–1100 BC.* Basingstoke.

Maine, Sir H. J. S. 1888. *International Law: A Series of Lectures Delivered before the University of Cambridge.* Cambridge.

Meiggs, R. and Lewis, D. 1988. *A Selection of Greek Historical Inscriptions to the End of the Fifth Century.* Revised ed. Oxford.

Niedhart, G. 2009. "Liberal and democratic peace as a concept in nineteenth- and twentieth-century international relations." In Dülffer and Frank 2009: 81–95.

Oded, B. 1992. *War, Peace and Empire: Justifications for War in Assyrian Royal Inscriptions.* Wiesbaden.

Pritchard, D. M. 2010. "The symbiosis of democracy and war: the case of classical Athens." In Pritchard (ed.), *War, Democracy and Culture in Classical Athens,* 1–61. Cambridge.

Raaflaub, K. A. (ed.). 2007. *War and Peace in the Ancient World.* Malden MA and Oxford.

Rhodes, P. J. 1987. "Thucydides on the causes of the Peloponnesian war." *Hermes* 115: 154–65.

Rich, J. and Shipley, G. (eds.). 1993. *War and Society in the Roman World.* London.

Riedweg, C. 2002. *Pythagoras: Leben, Lehre, Nachwirkung.* Munich (English trans. S. Randall, Ithaca NY, 2005).

Robinson, E. W. 2010. "Greek democracies and the debate over democratic peace." In M. H. Hansen (ed.), *Démocratie athénienne—démocratie moderne: Tradition et influences,* 277–306. Geneva.

Salomon, R. 2007. "Ancient India: peace within and war without." In Raaflaub 2007: 53–65.

Schorn, S. 2012. "The philosophical background of Xenophon's *Poroi.*" In Hobden and Tuplin 2012: 689–723.

Sharples, R. W. 1996. *Stoics, Epicureans and Sceptics: An Introduction to Hellenistic Philosophy.* London.

Sidebottom, H. 1993. "Philosophers' attitudes to warfare under the principate." In Rich and Shipley 1993: 195–212.

Strohmeyer, A. 2009. "Ideas of peace in early modern models of international order: universal monarchy and balance of power in comparison." In Dülffer and Frank 2009: 65–80.

Van Wees, Hans. 2001. "War and peace in ancient Greece." In Hartmann and Heuser 2001: 33–47.

Van Wees, Hans. 2004. *Greek Warfare: Myths and Realities.* London.

Van Wees, Hans. 2007. "War and society." In P. Sabin, H. Van Wees, and M. Whitby (eds.), *The Cambridge History of Greek and Roman Warfare,* I: 273–99. Cambridge.

Van Wees, Hans. 2009. "Peace and the society of states in antiquity." In Dülffer and Frank 2009: 25–43.

Van Wees, Hans. 2013. *Ships and Silver, Taxes and Tribute: A Fiscal History of Archaic Athens.* London.

Van Wees, Hans. Forthcoming. "Thucydides and early Greek history." In R. Balot, S. Forsdyke, and E. Foster (eds.), *The Oxford Handbook of Thucydides.* Oxford.

Woolf, G. 1993. "Roman peace." In Rich and Shipley 1993: 171–94.

Yates, R. D. S. 2007. "Making war and making peace in early China." In Raaflaub 2007: 34–52.

Zampaglione, G. 1973. *The Idea of Peace in Antiquity.* Notre Dame.

Zhmud, L. 2012. *Pythagoras and the Early Pythagoreans.* Oxford.

Index

Peace in the Ancient World: Concepts and Theories, First Edition. Edited by Kurt A. Raaflaub.
© 2016 John Wiley & Sons, Inc. Published 2016 by John Wiley & Sons, Inc.